Cathy is expecting little Alice to be brought to her at any moment, when the phone rings. It is the social worker, anxiously telling her that Alice has been snatched by her mother, and the police are out looking for them. Cathy is very worried. Alice's mother is drug-dependent, mentally ill, and clearly desperate to keep her child. Cathy prays she won't do anything silly.

When Alice is finally found and brought to Cathy late one night she is asleep. Swaddled in a blanket in the social worker's arms with only her little face showing, she immediately wins a place in the heart of Cathy and her family. But the following day, when Alice begins talking about the nights she was missing, Cathy is horrified by what she tells her.

About the author

Bestselling author Cathy Glass, who writes under
a pseudonym, has been a foster carer for more
than twenty-five years. She has three children.
To find out more about Cathy and her story,
visit www.cathyglass.co.uk

Cathy Glass

I Miss Mummy

The true story of a frightened young girl
who's desperate to go home

HarperElement
An imprint of HarperCollins*Publishers*
77–85 Fulham Palace Road,
Hammersmith, London W6 8JB

www.harpercollins.co.uk

and HarperElement are trademarks of
HarperCollins*Publishers* Ltd

First published by HarperElement 2010

11

MIX
Paper from
responsible sources
FSC® C007454

FSC™ is a non-profit international organisation established to promote
the responsible management of the world's forests. Products carrying the
FSC label are independently certified to assure consumers that they come
from forests that are managed to meet the social, economic and
ecological needs of present and future generations,
and other controlled sources.

Find out more about HarperCollins and the environment at
www.harpercollins.co.uk/green

Certain details, including names, places, and dates, have been changed to protect the child.

Chapter One

Desperate

'Mum has snatched her! The police are looking for them now. Goodness knows where they could have gone! They're not at home.'

I could hear the anxiety and panic in the social worker's voice on the other end of the phone, and I appreciated why. From the little I knew of the child's mother, I knew she was very unstable, with ongoing mental health problems, compounded by drug addiction. I also knew she was fiercely opposed to having her daughter taken into care and had been fighting the social services for three months to stop it. But while no one wants to see a child forcibly removed from home, sometimes there is no alternative if the child is to be kept from harm.

'When did this happen?' I asked, equally concerned.

'Two hours ago. They can't have got far. The police have circulated a description of them, and the ports and airports have been alerted. No one could have foreseen this happening – otherwise we'd have taken Alice sooner.'

Alice was the little four-year-old I'd been expecting all afternoon. I'd been told the day before that the social services were going to court in the morning to ask the judge to grant an ICO (Interim Care Order) so that Alice could be brought into foster care. I knew from the referral (the print-out that gives the child's basic details) that both her parents were drug users, and because neither of them could look after Alice she'd been staying with her maternal grandparents. I also remembered reading that Alice attended nursery from 9.00 a.m. to 3.15 p.m. every day.

'Was Alice snatched from her nursery?' I asked, puzzled, aware of the high security that now surrounds schools.

There was a slight hesitation. 'No. The head teacher phoned the social services first thing this morning to say Alice wasn't in nursery. When we went to the grandparents' home after court this morning, to collect Alice, she wasn't there.'

Now, I don't think I've got incredible insight but if I'd been a social worker I think I might have heard alarm bells ringing if the child I was about to bring into care was suddenly absent from nursery on the morning of the court case.

'We think the grandparents may have colluded in their granddaughter's abduction,' the social worker added. 'They're being interviewed by the police now, and I'm going to see them soon. I'll phone you again later.'

'All right. Thanks for letting me know. I do hope you find Alice soon.'

'So do I,' the social worker said. 'And that she's found safe.'

I replaced the receiver and returned to the kitchen, where I had been preparing dinner. It was 5.30 p.m. and I'd been expecting Alice at 1.00. The apprehension and nervousness which I'd been feeling all afternoon, and indeed which I always felt when waiting for a new child to arrive, now developed into full anxiety. Although I'd never met Alice, and had only the briefest of details, I knew enough to be very worried. Her mother, mentally unstable and possibly under the influence of drugs, had snatched her daughter in a desperate bid to keep her, and was now on the run. Who knew what was going through that mother's mind or what she might do in desperation? News headlines flashed across my anxious thoughts: Mum leaps off bridge with daughter, Mum and daughter found dead. My morbid speculations were far fetched, but such things do happen, particularly when a parent is desperate or under the influence of drugs.

Ten minutes later the phone rang and I snatched it up, hoping it was news that Alice had been found safe and well. But it was Jill, my link worker from the agency I fostered for. In her voice I could hear the anxiety that I'd heard in the social worker's, and which I now felt.

'Did the social worker phone you?' Jill asked. 'I told her to contact you directly as soon as she heard anything. I've been in a meeting all afternoon.'

'She phoned a short while ago, but they haven't found Alice yet, although the police are out looking.'

'Poor child,' Jill said with a heartfelt sigh. 'Poor mum.'

'I know. But her mother must realize she can't get away with it. They'll be found eventually, and snatching her daughter is hardly going to count in her favour.'

'Mum won't have thought it through,' Jill said. 'With her level of problems she'll have acted on impulse and won't be thinking rationally.' Which did nothing to ease my fear for mother's and daughter's safety. 'Martha, the social worker, asked me if it was all right if they bring Alice straight to you when she's found, assuming she doesn't need hospital treatment, even if it's out of office hours. I said I thought it would be.'

'Yes, of course, bring her straight to me,' I confirmed; then, unable to resist a dig: 'I don't really work to office hours, Jill.'

'No, I know, but you know what I mean.'

'Yes. Hopefully the police will find her soon.'

'I hope so,' Jill said. 'The poor child will be upset enough already at having to come into care without all this.'

Deep in thought, I returned to the kitchen and the dinner I was preparing, which was now running late.

Adrian appeared, his stomach growling. 'When's dinner ready, Mum?'

At fourteen, my son was continuously hungry, and growing upwards at an quite a rate. He was already four inches taller than me, and he was going to be six foot, like his father – who unfortunately no longer lived with us.

'About half an hour till dinner,' I said. 'Have an apple if you're hungry.'

He nodded, and took an apple and banana from the fruit bowl, and a packet of crisps from the cupboard.

'I hope that's not going to spoil your appetite,' I called after him, envious. I couldn't have eaten all that and dinner without putting on weight. There was no answer, but I knew the snack wouldn't spoil his appetite. Adrian never left his food, unlike Lucy, my twelve-year-old foster daughter who picked at her food.

Presently Paula, my ten-year-old daughter, came into the kitchen and began foraging for food.

'No, leave the biscuits,' I said. 'Dinner will only be fifteen minutes.'

'Adrian's got crisps,' she said accusingly.

'I know, and you can have a packet after dinner, if you're still hungry. Although fruit would be better.'

She pulled a face but left the biscuit tin untouched in the cupboard. 'Isn't that little girl coming?' she asked, suddenly remembering that I'd said Alice would be with us for dinner.

'Hopefully later,' I said. 'She's been delayed.'

Paula looked at me questioningly and, while I didn't want to burden her with my anxiety about Alice's safety, I knew I had to give her some explanation. 'Alice is with her mother,' I said, 'and the social worker isn't sure where they are.'

Paula pulled another face, unimpressed. 'How can they be lost?'

'They're not lost, just temporarily misplaced,' I said lightly, and changed the subject. Paula can be a real worrier when it comes to little children, even worse than me. 'Could you pop up to Lucy's room and tell her dinner is ready? If she says she's not hungry, tell her I'd like her to come down and join us anyway. Thanks, love.'

Lucy had been with us for nearly a year and, having lived with countless aunts and cousins and never had a proper family of her own, she'd settled into our family remarkably quickly, welcoming the stability and routine. However, while I was very pleased with her progress, both at home and school, my biggest concern remained with her eating. She was an attractive girl, her long black hair and dark eyes coming from her father, who was Thai, but she was slim to the point of thin. At 5 feet 4 inches, she weighed only six and half stone and whereas when she'd first arrived I'd assumed she would put on weight once she'd settled into our family, she hadn't.

I'd mentioned my concern to Jill and also to Lucy's social worker, who in turn had taken advice from the looked-after children's nurse who is employed by the council to advise on the health of children in care. On her advice I was now monitoring (as far as I could) what Lucy ate, and also her weight, keeping my supervision very low key so it didn't become an issue. There was no evidence that Lucy was making herself sick after eating, or pretending to eat and then throwing the food away, so we were optimistic that she wasn't suffering from an acute eating disorder such as anorexia or bulimia. But over the last four months since I'd started monitoring Lucy she hadn't put on any weight but had grown in height, which in real terms meant she'd lost weight. According to the height/weight chart the nurse had used, Lucy should have weighed eight stone, so she was one and a half stone (twenty-one pounds) underweight, which was obviously very worrying.

However, I was pleased to see that Lucy came downstairs with Paula for dinner. At the same time Adrian returned to the kitchen for an update on dinner.

'It's ready,' I announced. 'Sit down.'

I began dishing up while the three of them sat at the table in what we grandly call the breakfast room – the term used by the architect who drew up the plans for what is really an extension to the kitchen. Having plated up some of the casserole for Alice and left it to one side, I carried the other plates over to the table. All that could be heard for some time was the chink of cutlery on china. As we ate I was half expecting the phone to ring – the social worker telling me Alice had been found and they were on their way – or even the door bell to ring, if they came straight to me.

As we ate I was also watching Lucy out of the corner of my eye for, as often happened, she had begun well, eating four mouthfuls straight off as though she was ravenous, and then ground to a halt; she was now toying with her food. When Lucy had first arrived, I had told her, as I tell all children at their first meals, to eat what she wanted and leave what she didn't want, but when I'd realized just how little she was eating I'd started to encourage her: 'Can't you just eat half of it?' 'Another couple of mouthfuls?' 'Just the mashed potato?' I didn't know if I was doing the right thing, but as every mother knows it is excruciating to watch a child eating insufficient for their body's needs.

'Did you have lunch?' I asked Lucy as she continued to fork her food around the plate. I gave her money for lunch every day, but her secondary school ran a cafeteria system, so I'd no idea what, if anything, she'd bought or eaten.

'Yes,' she said as she usually did. 'I had a sandwich.' Which, as usual, I had to believe. But even if she had bought a sandwich and eaten all of it, her day's food intake was still very small and barely sufficient to maintain growth and health: a thin slice of dry toast for breakfast, a sandwich for lunch and now a few mouthfuls for dinner.

Lucy toyed with her food for a bit longer; then she laid her knife and fork on her plate, having finished. Paula laid down her knife and fork too, on a clean plate, and Adrian was looking for pudding.

'Are you sure you've finished?' I asked Lucy. She nodded, and I collected the plates. 'I've just got to make the custard,' I said and, leaving the three of them at the table talking about a television programme, I returned to the kitchen. I boiled the kettle and made instant custard; then I poured it into a jug and placed it on the table with a shop-bought apple pie. I told them to help themselves and surreptitiously watched Lucy take a small amount of custard but no pie. Then the phone rang and I jumped up from the table and went into the sitting room to answer it, fervently hoping it was Martha, Alice's social worker, phoning to say Alice had been found, safe and well, and they would be with me shortly.

It was Martha, but without good news. 'Nothing,' she said. 'Alice and her mother have completely disappeared. The police have searched all the addresses of friends and family we have given them, so I really don't know where they can be.' She sounded very weary. 'I'm off duty soon, but I shall be leaving my mobile on all night and the police have instructions to call me directly when she's found. Jill said it was all right to bring Alice to you, even it it's in the middle of the night.'

'Yes, of course. I'm a light sleeper – I'll hear the phone or the door.'

'Alice will be very distressed,' Martha warned.

'I know. Don't worry. I'm an experienced foster carer. I'll settle her and make sure she's all right.' Sometimes the social workers need as much reassuring as the children.

'Thanks, Cathy.'

'Have they found her?' Paula asked as I returned to the dinner table. Adrian and Lucy looked at me, puzzled, unaware there was a problem.

'Alice, the little girl who was supposed to be coming this afternoon, is missing with her mother,' I explained.

'Oh,' Adrian said. 'I thought she'd just got delayed.'

Lucy nodded, clearly having thought the same as Adrian. In the past children had been delayed, for all sorts of reasons, arriving a lot later than expected – even the following day.

'No,' I said. 'Unfortunately not, but I'm sure Alice will be found soon. If you hear the phone or front door bell go in the night, try to go back to sleep. Alice could arrive at any time, and you've all got school tomorrow. You'll be able to meet her first thing in the morning.'

They nodded, accepting my assurance and believing, as I did, that at some point during the evening or night Alice would be found safe and well, and be brought to us, when I would tuck her into bed and sit with her and comfort her until she finally dropped off to sleep.

If only that had happened!

Chapter Two

Am I to Blame?

At 10.00 p.m. we were all in bed, Lucy and Paula asleep, Adrian reading for half an hour, while I had the radio on, although I wasn't listening to it. My thoughts were with Alice and her mother, and I was very worried. I hadn't heard anything further during the evening, so I had to assume they were still missing. It was the end of March and although we'd had a few mild days the nights were very cold, with a ground frost. I sincerely hoped Alice and her mother were indoors, having been given a bed for the night by a friend or relative who perhaps didn't know about the court case or that the police were looking for them. Or perhaps, I speculated, Alice had been found and was being brought to me at this very moment. At 11.00 I switched off the radio and dozed, but I was listening out for the phone and doorbell, every so often raising my head to glance at the luminous hands on my bedside clock.

Acutely aware of every street noise, shortly after 2.00 a.m. I heard a car pull up outside. My bedroom is at the front of the house, overlooking the road, and immediately I got out of bed and peered through the window, ever hopeful. A taxi was outside with its engine running and as I looked I saw my neighbour, Sue, and her family get out, with their suitcases, having returned from the airport after a week in Turkey. Sue looked up and, seeing me, gave a little wave. Aware that I fostered, she saw nothing too unusual in my peering out of my bedroom window at two in the morning, possibly waiting for a teenager to return, or for the police to bring a child under an emergency protection order.

I returned to bed and dozed fitfully until 6.00 a.m. Then I declared the night over and, slipping on my dressing-gown and slippers, went downstairs to make coffee. On the work surface in the kitchen, almost as a testament to Alice's disappearance, was the dinner I'd plated and covered the night before. If Alice had arrived hungry, as children often do, I could have easily reheated her dinner in the microwave, whatever time of night. Now I removed the cover from the plate and, scraping the congealed casserole into the bin, put the plate in the dishwasher. Dear Alice, wherever could she be? She had been missing for twelve hours now, which is a long time for a child of four. She and her mother – who I knew from the referral was called Leah and was twenty-three – had vanished into thin air. Where could they have gone? Then I wondered if they had been found and Alice had been returned to her grandparents, in which case Leah would now be in police custody, for I knew that despite any sympathy I had for Leah's desperate bid to keep her daughter, snatching a child, especially a child protected by a court order, is a very serious offence and Leah would be prosecuted and very likely sent to prison. It was all so very sad.

At 7.00 a.m. my speculation and worries had to be put on hold as I swung into action at the start of the school day. It was Friday, thank goodness, and I was looking forward to the weekend. Apart from getting out of the routine of school for two days we were all going to a birthday party on Sunday afternoon – a friend of mine was forty and was having an open house to celebrate. Fuelled by a large mug of coffee and the prospect of the weekend, I went upstairs and woke everyone with a cheery 'Good morning'. As I went into each of the children's bedrooms I was met with a question or statement about Alice.

'Is Alice here?' Paula asked.

'I didn't hear you in the night,' Lucy said.

'She must have been very quiet,' Adrian commented.

I had to tell each of them that Alice hadn't arrived and I hadn't heard anything further.

The routine of school took over for the next hour, culminating in my waving Adrian, Lucy and Paula goodbye at the front door with 'Have a good day'. Adrian had a ten-minute walk to school, Lucy had a twenty-minute bus ride and Paula, in her last year of primary school, had recently persuaded me to let her walk to school by herself. It was only ten minutes, with one road to cross, and I knew I had to give her this responsibility in preparation for her going to secondary school in September when she, like most of her class, would be catching the bus to school without their mothers. And Paula wasn't actually walking to school alone but was knocking on the door for a friend who lived halfway down our street.

Having seen everyone off I cleaned up and, checking on the whereabouts of our cat, Toscha, left the house to do a supermarket shop. I couldn't wait in all day on the off chance that Alice might arrive. I'd left the answerphone on and the social services had my mobile number. Also, I was pretty certain that if Alice was coming to me during the day the social worker would phone me first before bringing her, as opposed to during the night, when it wasn't unusual for the police to take a child straight to the carer.

As it was, Friday passed and the only person who phoned was Jill, asking if I'd heard anything from the social services, which I hadn't. Apparently she'd tried to contact Martha but had been told by a colleague she had back-to-back case conferences and was therefore unavailable for most of the day. 'It's not very good practice,' Jill said. 'Someone from the department should have phoned you or me with an update, even if it was to say there was no news. We'll keep the foster placement with you open over the weekend and hope that Alice is found, but we can't hold it open indefinitely.' Jill wasn't being heartless but practical: if Alice wasn't coming to me then another child would. It's a sad fact that so many children need fostering that in most areas in the UK the demand for foster placements outstrips the number of available foster carers.

'I was wondering if Alice had possibly been found and allowed to stay with her grandparents?' I suggested to

Jill. 'They were looking after her before Leah snatched her.'

'I'm sure someone from the social services would have told us,' Jill said. 'Although I agree it wouldn't be the first time arrangements had changed and no one had thought to notify us. If Martha doesn't get back to me today I'll phone her first thing on Monday.'

'OK. Thanks, Jill,' I said. Then I asked the question that had been troubling me since I'd first read Alice's details on the referral. 'Jill, why wasn't Alice allowed to stay with her grandparents instead of being brought into care? According to the referral she'd been there for six months and was very happy.'

'I'm not sure. I think there were issues about the grandparents allowing Leah to see Alice.'

'So Leah wasn't allowed to see her own daughter?' I asked, surprised. 'That's very unusual.'

'Very,' Jill said. 'I don't know the reason.'

I didn't hear anything about Alice on Saturday, although I was half expecting to, hoping every phone call was to say Alice had been found safe and well. I had another restless night, listening for the phone or the doorbell as I had done the previous night. Jill had been right: an update to keep me in the picture, even if there was no news, would have been preferable to hearing nothing. I suppose I should have been used to not knowing, for foster carers are often left in the lurch and not included in the loop of information circulating among the professionals involved in a case. Although sharing information and keeping all professionals informed in childcare cases has improved since I first started fostering, largely because of the passing of the Children's Acts, there is still a way to go. Often foster carers are bottom of the list when it comes to being kept informed, but when information is urgently required by a social worker about a child in care – for a report or court case – the carer is suddenly very popular, for we know the child better than anyone and have the information required to hand.

What I didn't know at the time, but found out later, was that no one was being kept informed – not the social services, the grandparents, who were beside themselves with worry, the Guardian ad Litem, or any of the other professionals connected with Alice's case – because of a 'news blackout'. The police, fearful for Alice's safety, were in sensitive, on-going and secret negotiations with her mother, via text messages, to try to persuade her to leave Alice in a public place where she could be collected.

Tired from two nights of little sleep and much anxiety, but determined to go to the party, at twelve noon on Sunday I changed out of my jeans and jumper and into a dress, stockings and high heels.

'Blimey. Mum's got legs,' Adrian remarked dryly.

'You look nice,' Paula said.

'Shall I do your make-up?' Lucy asked, which I took as a compliment – that I was worth the effort and not beyond hope, as my tired reflection in the mirror sometimes suggested.

Half an hour later, all in our Sunday best, and me with a professionally applied mascara and eye shadow (Lucy wanted to be a beautician), and clutching a present and bottle of wine for the hostess, we piled into the car and headed up the M1. Once again I had left the answerphone on, and my mobile was in my handbag; if I was needed I could be home in twenty minutes. But it was true to say that my concerns for Alice had lessened during the morning because I was sure Alice must have been found by now and was with her grandparents, and that no one had thought to tell me. I simply couldn't see how a mother with a young child could have avoided the police for all this time.

We had a really good time at the party and my mobile didn't go off during the afternoon or evening. The house was overflowing with old friends and families with children my children knew. There was a disco in one room, and the older children kept the younger children entertained. There was plenty to eat and drink, although as I was driving I had only one glass of wine early on and then kept to soft drinks. We all enjoyed ourselves tremendously, but with school the following morning we said our goodbyes, as most other families did, just before 9.00 p.m., and we arrived home at 9.30.

As soon as I opened the front door and stepped into the hall I saw the light flashing on the answerphone, signalling a message. Close up, I saw that the indicator showed I had four messages. Without taking off my coat, and while Adrian, Paula and Lucy went through to the kitchen to get a glass of water each to take up to bed, I picked up the receiver and pressed play.

The first message was timed at 8.30 p.m., a male voice, stern sounding and quite terse: 'Message for Mrs Glass.

This is the out-of-hours duty social worker, please call me immediately on … I was informed you were to be the carer for Alice Jones.' My heart missed a beat at the mention of her name, as the answerphone continued to the second message, timed at 8.47 p.m. It was the same male voice, now very impatient, almost demanding: 'It's the duty social worker again. I've already left a message. Would Mrs Glass phone immediately?' He repeated the number and hung up. In his third message, timed at 9.05 p.m., I could hear his anger: 'I've phoned twice. Alice has been found. Call me immediately.' And in his last call, timed at 9.16 p.m., he was rude: 'What the hell is going on!' he demanded. 'Where are you? You were supposed to be looking after Alice. Phone immediately. It's not good enough!' He hung up, the line went dead and the answerphone clicked off.

With my heart racing and my fingers shaking, I quickly took my mobile from my handbag and checked for messages and missed calls. There were none. If he was angry, I was upset, and my legs trembled. I prided myself on being a good carer, experienced and professional, and now it seemed I had failed in my duty.

Adrian, Lucy and Paula came into the hall, with a glass of water each, en route to their bedrooms. The colour must have drained from my face. 'What's the matter?' Adrian asked. Lucy and Paula had stopped too and all three were looking at me, very concerned.

'Alice has been found,' I said, picking up the receiver, ready to dial. 'The duty social worker has been trying to contact me for the last hour. But no one called my mobile.'

'And you're surprised?' Lucy asked sarcastically, remembering her own experiences with the social services before coming into care.

I shook my head. 'I don't understand it.'

Still in my coat, I quickly dialled the duty social worker's number, as Adrian, Lucy and Paula continued upstairs to take turns in the bathroom. Not only was I upset by the duty social worker's manner and rudeness, but he had made it sound my fault, as though I was solely to blame. Had I done wrong in going out for the afternoon and evening, even though I'd had my mobile on? Neither Jill nor the social worker had told me to stay at home; in fact no one had told me anything. But as I listened to the phone ringing, waiting for the duty social worker to answer, I knew the real reason I was upset was because I hadn't been there for Alice. The poor child: whatever must she be thinking? I had badly let her down even before I'd met her.

Chapter Three
Stretched to the Limit

'So you're there, at last!' the duty social worker snapped, finally answering the phone. 'I've been trying to get you all evening. Alice has been found.' I didn't know the duty social worker and, as far I was aware, I hadn't had any dealings with him before. He would probably be from an agency, covering out-of-office-hours calls.

Ignoring his gross exaggeration of 'all evening' – his first call had been timed at 8.30, fifty minutes before – I held my voice steady as I said: 'I'm sorry you were unable to reach me. Why didn't you phone my mobile?'

'Wasn't aware I had your mobile number,' he said, no less tersely. Then, clearly having found it on the paperwork, he added dismissively: 'Oh yes, but it's not obvious. At least you're there now.' I thought an apology wouldn't have gone amiss but, aware Alice was waiting somewhere, waiting to be brought to me, I didn't pursue it. 'The child is at the police station,' he said. 'I'll have to bring her to you, but it won't be straight away. I'm stretched to the limit here.'

'Do you want me to collect Alice from the police station?' I offered.

'You can't,' he snapped. 'It needs an SW' – social worker – 'to place a child who's on an Interim Care Order.' It was a technicality, but I realized he was probably right. As a foster carer I couldn't simply go to the police station and collect Alice; procedure dictated a social worker or police officer should bring her to me.

'Is Alice all right?' I asked anxiously. 'Where's she been?'

'No idea. Mum snatched her, and then disappeared, that's all I know. I'll get to you as soon as I can, but I'm the only one on duty.'

'How long do you think you'll be?' I asked, mindful that little Alice, after three days missing and goodness knows what else, was now waiting at the police station instead of snuggled in her bed upstairs and being comforted by me.

'As soon as I can,' he snapped. 'Why? You're not going out again, are you?'

That was the final straw. I'd had enough of his rudeness and intimidating manner. 'No, of course I'm not going out,' I snapped back. 'It's nearly ten o'clock. But I'd have thought, given Alice's age and what has happened to her, it should be a priority for you to get her to me.'

It went quiet for a moment, then he said stiffly: 'I'll be with you as soon as I can, Mrs Glass. You do your job and I'll do mine.' And he hung up.

I remained where I was by the phone for a second and then replaced the receiver with more force than was necessary. 'Ignorant pig,' I muttered. Overworked he might be, but that was no reason to be rude. I glanced up the stairs and saw Lucy and Paula watching me from the landing, looking very worried.

'It's all right,' I reassured them. 'That was the duty social worker. He's bringing Alice to us as soon as he can.'

'Terrific. Is she OK?' Paula said.

'I think so, although the social worker didn't know much.'

'Do they ever?' Lucy said disparagingly.

'Now, now,' I cautioned lightly. 'They're under-staffed.' Lucy took every opportunity to criticize social workers and I knew she had to start letting go of the anger from her past and look to the future. 'Alice is safe at the police station,' I said, 'but I don't know what time she will be here. I want the two of you to get ready for bed, and if you're still awake when Alice arrives you can see her. Otherwise you'll see her in the morning.'

Lucy and Paula disappeared into their bedrooms to get changed, ready for bed, and I went upstairs to draw the curtains in what would soon be Alice's room. The room was ready, as it had been since I was first told to expect Alice. There was a brightly coloured Cinderella duvet cover on the bed with a matching pillowcase, cuddly toys propped on the chair and posters of rabbits and kittens on the walls. I knew virtually nothing about Alice – only that she was small for her age and of average intelligence. More details would follow in the essential information forms, which Martha should bring when she visited Alice – presumably on Monday. What trauma Alice had suffered since going missing I couldn't begin to guess, but clearly she was going to be very distressed, and I anticipated being up most of the night comforting her. For when all was said and done Alice was being brought to the house of a stranger (albeit a well-meaning one), in the middle of the night, by a man she didn't know, having somehow got to the police station after going missing for three days. I thought she had a right to be upset.

Perhaps the duty social worker had heeded my comment about prioritizing his workload, for he must have left his office straight after we'd spoken. Thirty minutes later the doorbell rang and, with a mixture of apprehension and anticipation, I ran to answer it.

Standing in the porch was a very tall man, over six feet, cradling a small bundle in a pink blanket.

'Oh my,' I said, peering into the bundle, and holding the door wider so that he could come in. 'Oh, bless her, poor little mite.'

I looked closer at the child the duty social worker held as he stepped into the hall. With only her little face showing, Alice looked just like a sleeping doll. A few strands of light brown hair wisped around her delicate features, and one little hand lay pressed against her chin.

'She fell asleep in the car,' he said amicably.

For a moment I couldn't say anything; I just gazed at Alice, nestled deep in the blanket, so peaceful and vulnerable in sleep, and so, so beautiful – she looked just like an angel. My heart went out to her in a rush of love and pity.

'We'll put her straight to bed,' I said, coming to my senses. I closed the front door and led the way upstairs and into what was now Alice's room. The duty social worker's previous animosity towards me appeared to have gone now and he carried Alice into her room, where I helped ease her from his arms and on to the bed. She didn't wake. 'I'll just remove her coat for tonight,' I whispered. 'I'll leave her to sleep in her clothes – save disturbing her.'

'She hasn't come with a change of clothes,' he said quietly.

'It's all right. I have spares.'

While the duty social worker supported Alice's back, floppy in sleep, I carefully slipped her arms out of her coat. I noticed that although her coat had dried mud on it, it was of very good quality and also new, as was her little dress and cardigan. My first impression was that Alice wasn't undernourished, and her face and hands were clean; her chin-length hair looked well groomed. In fact, apart from the mud on her coat, she appeared clean and well cared for.

Having taken off Alice's coat, I gently eased her head on to the pillow. As I did, her long black eyelashes fluttered and her eyes opened. Huge brown eyes looked at me in surprise and fear. 'It's all right, love,' I soothed, stroking her little forehead. 'My name is Cathy. I'm going to look after you for a while. You are in bed in my house and you are safe. There is nothing to worry about.' Her eyes remained wide, staring at me: she was so innocent, so overwhelmed and so worried, I could have wept. 'It's all right,' I soothed again.

'I'll get the paperwork from my briefcase in the car,' the duty social worker said, clearly pressed for time.

I nodded. 'I'll ask one of my children so stay with Alice and I'll come down.'

He left the room and I sat on the edge of the bed, stroking Alice's forehead. She looked at me with big wondering eyes. 'It's OK,' I continued to reassure her. 'My name is Cathy, I am a foster carer and I look after children. You are safe now.'

I half expected her to burst into tears and sob hysterically, but I think she was so tired and traumatized she didn't have the energy. She lay on her back under the duvet with her pink blanket loosely draped on top, her huge eyes still staring at me. Then she licked her lips. 'Do you want a drink?' I asked softly, but she didn't answer, her eyes not daring to move from my face. 'Oh pet,' I said. 'Please don't worry. Everything will be all right now.'

Lucy and Paula, in their pyjamas, appeared at the bedroom door and hesitated, uncertain if they should disturb us.

'Come in and say hello to Alice,' I said quietly.

They crept in, to the side of the bed, and gazed down at her. Their gasps said it all. 'Oh! Oh, look at her. She's so sweet.'

Alice's big eyes moved from my face to theirs.

'This is Lucy and Paula,' I said. 'They live here too.'

'Hi, Alice,' the girls whispered. They knelt beside her bed.

I heard the front door close as the duty social worker returned from his car. 'Could you stay with Alice for a moment while I speak to the social worker?' I asked the girls. 'I shouldn't be too long.'

It wasn't a question that needed answering. Lucy and Paula immediately took over, Lucy soothing Alice's forehead as I had been doing, while Paula took hold of her little hand, which still lay against her chin.

'I'm just going downstairs to speak to the man who brought you here,' I said to Alice. 'Lucy and Paula will stay with you.' While it might have been obvious to us and an older foster child what was happening, it wouldn't necessarily have been obvious to a traumatized four-year-old, who might have thought I was disappearing for good and that Lucy and Paula would follow me, leaving her alone in a strange room.

Alice's gaze briefly flickered to me as I stood, and then returned to Lucy and Paula.

Downstairs I found the duty social worker already in the sitting room, seated in the armchair and using his briefcase to rest on as he completed a form.

'What's your full name, and postcode?' he asked as I entered, his terseness returning. I told him. 'And I placed Alice at ten twenty-five p.m. on 25 March,' he said, glancing at his watch.

I nodded and sat on the sofa.

'Who else is in the house?'

'Just my children and me,' I said, surprised.

'I need their names for this form.'

'Adrian, Lucy and Paula. Lucy is my foster daughter.'

'And their ages?'

'Fourteen, twelve and ten.'

He wrote, and then asked: 'No husband or partner?'

'No.' Had Alice been placed during the day, all this information should have been available, supplied by Jill or the social services, but without access to the file I assumed he was completing a placement form for his agency.

He wrote some more, I didn't know what, and then put the form in his briefcase and snapped the lid shut. 'Alice's social worker will contact you on Monday,' he said and stood, ready to go.

'Do you not have any other information about Alice?' I asked quickly.

'No. Don't you?'

'All I have is the original referral, which doesn't say much. Do you know if Alice has an allergies or special needs?'

'I don't know,' he said with a shrug, 'so we'll have to assume she doesn't, although I should go easy on the peanut butter.' I didn't appreciate his stab at humour. Even if a child arrives in the middle of the night as an emergency I'm usually told of anything that could affect the child's health like allergies or asthma. And given that Alice's move to me hadn't been an emergency but had been planned (although it had gone badly wrong at the end, with Alice being snatched), I'd have thought Martha would have had time to print out the essential information and leave it with the duty social worker – or was that expecting too much?

'I've got to go,' the duty social worker said, heading towards the sitting room door. 'A runaway teenager has been found on the other side of the county. I'm the only one on call to collect him.'

I nodded, but while I sympathized with his obviously very heavy workload, my concerns were with Alice, and I persisted in trying to find out more about her background that might help me to look after her. 'Who took Alice to the police station?' I asked, following him down the hall.

'Mum's boyfriend, I think,' he returned over his shoulder; then, hand on the doorknob, he let himself out.

'Goodnight,' I called after him as he went down the front path, but he didn't reply. He was already taking his mobile from his jacket pocket and answering the next call.

'Yes, I'm on my way,' he snapped. 'But I can't be in two places at the same time.' I thought that if I ever won the jackpot on the lottery I'd use some of the money to fund more social workers so they could do their jobs properly and didn't have to be in two places at the same time.

Chapter Four

Normal?

Upstairs again, I joined Lucy and Paula at Alice's bedside. I stood for a few moments gazing down at Alice as Lucy stroked her forehead and Paula held her hand. Alice's expression still held the same wide-eyed bewilderment and amazement, but I thought she looked slightly less anxious, and at least she wasn't crying. The girls were talking to her gently, telling her their names again and that she would be staying with us for a while, and reassuring her it was a nice house and she would be happy. Alice stared at them with her big brown eyes, occasionally shifting her gaze from one to the other, as she had to me when I'd come into the room, but she didn't speak.

Nestled beneath the duvet and pink blanket, with only her little face peering out, she reminded me of a little babushka doll, swaddled, with her cheeks red against her pale skin. I was going to leave the pink blanket on her bed, for although it wasn't needed for warmth (she had the duvet), I assumed the blanket was familiar to her and would therefore be a source of comfort now everything else was unfamiliar. But I wondered where the blanket had come from, for Alice had been staying with her grandparents when she'd been snatched, and according to the duty social worker, she'd been taken to the police station by her mother's boyfriend. I'd no idea where he lived or how he fitted into Alice's life.

Adrian's bedroom door opened and he appeared in the doorway of Alice's room in his pyjamas and dressing-gown. 'Mum, do you know it's nearly eleven o'clock?'

I nodded. 'Come and say hello to Alice. Then we'd all better try and get some sleep.'

At fourteen years of age I'm sure Adrian would have preferred it if a boy his own age had come to stay, but when he saw Alice his face melted. 'Hi, Alice,' he said with a little wave. 'I'm Adrian.'

Alice's eyes flickered from the girls to him and the briefest of smiles crossed her lips.

'She likes you,' Paula exclaimed, and I wondered if Alice's extended family had included a boy of Adrian's age with whom she'd had a close bond, so she now felt comfortable with Adrian. I knew from the referral that Alice didn't have any siblings; perhaps there'd been a cousin, or perhaps her mother's boyfriend had helped in her care?

'Adrian is my son,' I explained to Alice. 'He lives here too.'

Alice's eyes darted to me and then returned to Adrian. He smiled and waved again and she smiled back. The four of us then stood for a moment, grouped around the bed, gazing down at Alice. The poor child was the star attraction but she didn't seem to mind.

'I think we need to get some sleep soon,' I said presently, as reluctant as the children were to leave.

Adrian made a move first and, giving Alice another little wave, said, 'Goodnight, Alice.' Alice's gaze followed him out of the room.

'And you two,' I said to Lucy and Paula, who I'm sure would have happily spent all night with Alice, petting and reassuring her.

'Goodnight,' they said at last, and took it in turns to kiss her forehead.

Alice's big round eyes blinked, her long dark lashes dusting her cheek like a butterfly's wing. 'They're going to their bedrooms to sleep now,' I explained to Alice. 'You'll see them in the morning.'

Lucy and Paula kissed Alice again and, with more goodnights, finally moved away from her bed. Alice's gaze followed them until they were out of her line of vision and they left her room.

'OK, love,' I said gently to Alice, leaning over the bed. 'I want you to try and get some sleep. You must be very tired. I'll leave your bedroom door open a little so I can hear you if you wake in the night. Do you usually sleep with your light on or off?' Although I didn't expect a reply – Alice was too overwhelmed to make a decision about lighting – I always ask the children I foster this on their first night, for so many are afraid of the dark. 'I'll leave the light on low,' I said. 'Is that all right?'

Her big eyes blinked, but she didn't say anything.

'All right, pet, I'll see you in the morning. I'm going to my bed now.' I kissed her forehead, tucked her in and moved away from the bed.

She watched me as I walked slowly to the door and I smiled. 'Night, love. See you in the morning.'

Dimming the light to a level that allowed her to see but wouldn't keep her awake, I said a final goodnight and came out, leaving the door half open. I waited on the landing, expecting her to cry out now she was alone, but she didn't. She was very quiet and didn't make a sound. From where I stood on the landing, with her door half open, I could see her, although she couldn't see me unless she turned her head. She lay on her back, very still, and as I watched, her long eyelashes flickered and then closed in sleep. She was utterly exhausted, which was hardly surprising considering what she had been through.

I now crept along the landing and into Paula's room to kiss her goodnight.

'I feel so sorry for Alice,' Paula said as I perched on the bed, her face clouding. 'She's so little to be without her mummy.'

'I know, love, but we'll look after her and make sure she's all right.'

Paula's face immediately brightened. 'Yes, we will. And I'll get up tonight if she's upset and look after her. You can stay in bed.'

I smiled. My family were used to disturbed nights when a child first arrived, but they didn't always offer to get up. 'That's very kind of you, love,' I said. 'But it's important you get your sleep, with school in the morning. There'll be plenty of opportunity for you to help look after Alice – after school and at the weekends.' I paused. 'But Paula, you do realize that I don't know how long Alice will be with us? It could only be a few weeks.' For already I could see that my family were going to get very attached to Alice, and very quickly.

Paula nodded. 'I know, Mum, but I hope she stays a long time.' Then she yawned.

'OK, love, off to sleep now.' I kissed her goodnight, tucked her in, and then came out and went into Lucy's room.

Lucy was propped in bed, listening to her Discman. 'Lucy, it's far too late to be listening to that,' I said. 'You've got to get up for school in the morning.'

She immediately switched off her music and took out her earpieces – a vast improvement from when she'd first arrived, nearly a year before, when she'd bucked against authority and argued and debated about absolutely everything I (or her teachers) had asked her to do. Now she placed the Discman and headphones on her bedside cabinet and snuggled down, ready for me to tuck her in and say goodnight.

'I wonder why Alice has come into care.' Lucy said as I kissed her forehead.

'I'm not sure exactly. Her mother couldn't look after her, so she's been staying with her grandparents.'

"Well, they've done a good job. She looks normal.'

'What do you mean "normal"?' I asked, smiling.

'You know, like someone has looked after her. Not like I was. My aunts didn't care a toss. They didn't do anything about my nits, even when the school nurse sent me home with a letter. It was awful going to school and scratching my head the whole time. All the other kids laughed. I remember sitting in lessons and trying not to scratch, but in the end I had to 'cos it itched so much. And I stank. I knew I did. My clothes were filthy. I tried to wash them at home but I was only allowed to use cold water.'

I took Lucy's hand between mine, as I had done so many times during the past year, when she'd wanted to talk about the sad memories of her deprived childhood – the severe neglect she'd suffered for as long as she could remember. 'I can only guess how awful that time must have been for you,' I said quietly. 'But thankfully it is past now, and will never return. You did so well coping with all of that. I'm sure I wouldn't have coped so well.'

'You would if you had to,' Lucy said thoughtfully. 'You just get on with it and take each day as it comes. I always made sure I found one good thing in each day. It didn't matter how small it was as long as it was good and made me happy. One day a girl at school gave me a crisp from her packed lunch – that was a really good thing. And another time I was chosen by the teacher to collect the brushes at the end of the art lesson – that was a very big good thing. But sometimes it was the small things that were good, and maybe you wouldn't notice them if you weren't looking for something to make you happy. Like the bud of a flower just about to open in spring, or a bird flying off with a twig in its beak to make a nest, or writing a poem you're really pleased with. There are so many good things in the world to make us happy, but sometimes you have to look very hard to find them.'

I pressed Lucy's hand between mine and swallowed the lump rising in my throat. Lucy had such a beautiful way of putting things, I wondered if it was as a result of her suffering, if it had sharpened her senses, for I doubted the average twelve-year-old would have such insight. 'Nevertheless, Lucy,' I said, 'you had a lot to cope with, and you coped very well. I'm just so pleased that that time is past and you found your way to me.'

'So am I,' she said. Throwing her arms around me, she gave me an extra big hug.

Having said goodnight to Lucy and come out of her room, I hovered on the landing again, outside Alice's door. It was quiet but I wanted to check on her so, easing the door open, I crept in. She was still on her back, fast asleep, with one little hand pressed to her chin. Relaxed in sleep, her lips were slightly parted, and I could hear the faintest whisper of her breath. What memories of her past would Alice have, I wondered; not only of the days when she was missing but from the four years before that? – her short life to date. Would her memories be like Lucy's, which were similar to those of many of the children I'd looked after? – memories of severe neglect and abuse. I doubted it. Something told me Alice's story would be very different, although I doubted it would be any less upsetting.

Chapter Five
'Mummy Things'

Convinced I'd have a disturbed night, after checking on Alice I went straight to bed, hoping for a couple of hours' sleep before she woke, distressed at finding herself in a strange room. I woke at 1.30 a.m. and, although I couldn't hear Alice crying, I wondered if she'd called out and I'd subconsciously heard her. But when I went round to her room she was fast asleep, now curled on to her side, but still with one little hand pressed against her chin. I returned to bed and woke again just after 4.00. I immediately checked on her, but she was still asleep. At 6.00, when my alarm clock went off, Alice remained asleep, having slept far better than I had.

It was Monday, a school day, so I needed to get going – showering and dressing, and then making the two packed lunches before I woke Adrian, Paula and Lucy. However, I also wanted to be with Alice when she woke so that I could reassure her, for I could imagine how frightening it would be at her age to wake from a deep sleep, alone in a strange room. She probably wouldn't even remember how she got there the night before. I continued my normal weekday morning routine but interrupted it every ten minutes or so to check on her. Quickly showering, and with a towel wrapped round me, I checked on Alice. I hurriedly dressed in my bedroom and then checked on Alice. I went downstairs, fed Toscha and put the kettle on; then I returned upstairs to check on Alice. I made the packed lunches and checked on Alice. Then at 6.45, as I again peered into her room, I was rewarded by seeing her eyes flicker open, followed by a big yawn.

I had been right to be concerned. The second Alice woke and saw unfamiliar surroundings she sat bolt upright in bed and cried, 'Nana!', her voice tiny with fright.

I was immediately by her bed. 'Hello, love,' I smiled. 'It's all right. You're safe. I'm Cathy. You came to my house late last night.'

Alice looked at me with the same wide-eyed amazement she had the night before. She was completely overwhelmed, and probably wondering why and how I'd been summoned into her life like a genie from a lamp.

'There's nothing for you to worry about,' I continued, kneeling by the bed and taking one of her little hands in mine. 'You are staying with me for a while. I'm a foster carer. Do you remember seeing Adrian, Lucy and Paula last night? They are in their beds, still asleep.'

She looked at me and blinked. 'Nana?' she asked in the same small voice, her eyes widening further. 'Where's my nana and grandpa?'

'They're fine, love, they'll be at home in their house. I expect they are waking up, just like you.' I'd obviously no idea where her grandparents were or what they were doing, but this seemed the most likely option and would, I hoped, reassure Alice. 'Nana and Grandpa know you're here,' I added, feeling she should know this and that it might help.

Alice blinked again and then her face began to crumple. 'I want Nana and Grandpa,' she cried, tears springing from her eyes.

'Oh, love, don't be upset,' I soothed, putting my arm around her and holding her close. 'You'll see Nana and Grandpa soon.' Again, I had to assume this would be so for, given that Alice's grandparents had been her main carers for the last six months, I expected the social services to arrange contact so that Alice could see them within the next day or so. My reassurance seemed to help. The tears stopped and Alice's face brightened a little. 'That's better, love,' I said, and I cuddled her.

Aware we would be having a very busy day, as soon as I'd woken the rest of the family, I would get Alice dressed and ready. When a child arrives, the first few days are always hectic. Apart from settling the child into our home, all the professionals connected with the case would phone or visit; clothes and toys would need to be collected from home if at all possible, or I would go out and buy new clothes; school and contact arrangements would be clarified; and if there was any reason to believe the child had been physically harmed or was in bad health then an emergency medical would be arranged.

Alice had arrived with only the clothes she had on and I'd already sorted out a tracksuit and underwear from my emergency supply, which I kept in an ottoman in my bedroom. But now, seeing Alice properly for the first time, I realized that the tracksuit I'd selected was far too big. Although Alice was four she was so dainty I guessed she was probably wearing three-year-old clothes. 'Just wait here a moment, love,' I said, standing, 'and I'll find you something to wear until we can get your own clothes.'

She looked up at me, wide eyed and incredulous, and, not for the first time since I'd begun fostering, I wondered how on earth these children coped with all the turmoil and upheaval in their short lives; I doubt I would have coped so well. Before I left the room I took one of the cuddly toys I'd arranged on the chair in Alice's bedroom and tucked it beside her on the bed. 'Ben will keep you company,' I said. 'I won't be a minute.' Alice slowly blinked, her long black eyelashes fluttering gracefully; she really was a beautiful chid, and despite everything that had happened to her she seemed to have a natural inner peace.

Going round the landing en route to my bedroom to change the clothes for Alice, I knocked on each of the children's bedroom doors and then poked my head round. 'It's seven o'clock, time to wake up,' I called, adding, 'Alice is awake,' which I hoped might provide the incentive for them to leap out of bed.

In my bedroom, I rummaged in the large ottoman, where I found another tracksuit, pale blue, which looked more like Alice's size. I also took out some smaller-sized socks and pants. Closing the lid, I returned round the landing, again poking my head into the children's bedrooms. 'It's seven o'clock,' I repeated. 'Time to get up. Alice is awake.' And whereas before I'd been met with silence, I now heard murmurs and groans suggesting they were awake and might even get up.

Alice was exactly as I'd left her, sitting up in bed and staring at her surroundings, with the cuddly toy at her side. 'All right, love,' I said, 'let's get you dressed. You can have a bath later, tonight.' Had she arrived dirty, as some children do, I would have bathed her straight-away, but Alice looked clean and it was preferable she got to know me a little before I started bathing her. 'You can wear these today,' I said, showing her the tracksuit. 'I'll wash the clothes you have on and you can wear them again tomorrow.' For in the new and unfamiliar world in which Alice now found herself, she might have thought I was taking away her own clothes for good.

Alice remained sitting up in the bed, just looking at me, and I gently eased back the duvet. 'If you get out of bed, I'll show you where the toilet is,' I said. 'I expect you want to go.'

She continued to look at me in wonder but didn't move. I gently eased her legs out of bed and helped her to stand. 'This way,' I said cheerily, taking her hand. 'The toilet is round here.' I led her from the bedroom and round the landing to the toilet, where I opened the door.

She stood looking in, making no attempt to use the toilet. 'Can you manage by yourself?' I asked. 'Or do you need some help?' At her age she should have been able to manage the toilet alone, although I'd looked after many children who couldn't. 'Do you want some help?' I asked again.

Alice slowly shook her head and began to raise her dress. I held the door to, giving her some privacy, and waited for her to finish. Hearing it flush, I went in, ran some water in the sink and helped her to wash her hands. I guessed Alice probably had these self-care skills but was so overwhelmed at present she needed help. I dried her hands on the towel and then led her back along the landing towards her room.

Paula appeared from her room. 'Hi, Alice,' she called, smiling and giving a little wave.

Alice started, unblinking and overawed.

'This is Paula, my daughter,' I reminded her. 'You remember you saw her last night?' A little smile crossed Alice's face. 'She remembers,' I said to Paula. 'She's just very shy at present.'

'See you at breakfast,' Paula said. 'I'm going to shower and dress.'

She gave another little wave and Alice very cautiously raised one hand and gave a little wave back.

At the age of four a child should normally be able to dress him or herself, apart from tricky bits like doing up buttons and shoelaces. But as Alice had come into care with so little information, I'd no idea what she was capable of doing. And given that she was clearly over-whelmed, if not traumatized, I told her I would help her dress. She cooperated by raising her hands so that I could easily draw her dress up and over her head. As I changed her into the clean clothes I also, unfortunately, had to keep a lookout for any marks or bruises which might have suggested she'd been physically abused, and which I'd have to tell the social worker about as soon as their offices opened. Alice, like all children coming into care, would have a medical but it might not be arranged for another two to three weeks.

I'll never forget the time, in my early years of fostering, when I stripped an eighteen-month-old toddler ready for his bath only find his torso covered in angry bruises and red weals, which turned out to be cigarette burns. It was late in the evening on the day he'd arrived and I was completely shocked. I quickly wrapped him in his clothes again and, leaving the bath, fled to Accident and Emergency at our local hospital. They examined and X-rayed him and kept him in overnight (I stayed with him). The paediatrician's report showed that the toddler had eighteen recent bruises, thirteen cigarette burns and two (old) fractures to his ribs. I'd been so shocked and horrified that anyone, let alone a parent, could inflict such cruelty on a small child that the memory of that night had stayed vivid. But as I now changed Alice thankfully there were no marks of any description and she looked very clean and well cared for.

Once I'd helped her into the new tracksuit I sat her on the bed and, kneeling at her feet, began putting the socks on her. As I worked I could feel her large eyes looking at me, probably wondering who on earth this strange woman was, who was nothing like her nana. I could hear the rest of the family getting ready: Lucy's music was on, Paula had finished in the bathroom and was now in her bedroom getting dressed, and Adrian was in the shower.

'OK, love,' I said. 'Ready.' I lifted Alice off the bed. 'Let's go downstairs for some breakfast and you can tell me what you'd like to eat. We've got lots of different cereals, or you can have toast, or egg, or whatever you like.' (Within reason, I thought.)

Alice looked up at me, her little mouth slightly open in wonder; then she slipped her hand into mine. I smiled, and we went out of her bedroom and towards the top of the stairs. Before we began downstairs she drew me to a halt, and I looked down into her big brown eyes.

'Cathy?' she asked quietly, and innocently. 'Are you going to be my mummy now?'

I could have wept. 'Oh, love,' I said, bending down so I was at her height. 'I'm not your mummy, but I will be doing mummy things for you. While you are with me I'll look after you – make your meals, take you to nursery, play with you and take you to the park. Is that OK?'

Alice considered this for a moment and then said, 'Is that what mummies do?'

'Yes, love, usually, or perhaps it was your nana and grandpa who did those things for you?'

She gave a small nod. 'Yes, my nana and grandpa did mummy things, while my mummy was ill. I miss my nana and grandpa. Can I see them soon?'

'Yes, I hope so, love.' And again I wondered why Alice hadn't been allowed to stay with her grandparents, who seemed to have done a good job of looking after her and were obviously much loved.

Chapter Six

Sleeping with Wolves

Alice was very quiet at breakfast, which was hardly surprising, given the unfamiliarity of everyone and everything around her. Between the children and me we'd managed to coax from her that she'd like cornflakes for breakfast, 'Like I have at my nana's,' she said. Relieved that I could give her some continuity, even if it was only breakfast, I'd tipped cornflakes into a child's china bowl decorated with Beatrix Potter characters, added milk and a sprinkling of sugar, and joined the rest of the family at the table. I'd had to rummage in the cupboard under the stairs for the child booster seat which Alice now sat on so she could reach the table – it was some time since we'd fostered a child as young as Alice. Now she sat at the table at the right height with her spoon resting in the untouched bowl of cornflakes and stared at us in amazement.

I was sitting next to Alice and as I ate my breakfast I encouraged Alice to eat hers. I filled the spoon with cornflakes and left it on the edge of the bowl for her to put it into her mouth – she was too old to be fed as a baby or toddler. But invariably the spoon never left the bowl; or if it did it stopped en route to her mouth; or when she did manage a mouthful, she chewed for so long she almost forgot what she was doing. Alice, bless her, was mesmerized by us, overwhelmed and in a complete daze. She hardly took her eyes from Adrian, who was sitting diagonally opposite her. He had eaten three wheat biscuits, and was now on his second slice of toast and jam.

'Perhaps you could encourage Alice to eat?' I said quietly to him across the table.

Adrian looked at Alice and smiled kindly. 'Come on Alice, eat up. You want to be a big strong girl, don't you?'

Alice's eyes characteristically widened and she continued to stare at Adrian, mesmerized, the spoon still resting on the bowl. 'Come on, eat up,' he tried again. 'I'm winning.'

Alice grinned at Adrian, which I supposed was something, but her spoon lay untouched. Presently I filled it and then, with her holding the end of the spoon, I guided it to her lips. I was sure, as I had been previously about Alice knowing how to dress herself, that she had these skills but was simply overawed. Breakfast was therefore very slow and piecemeal. Adrian and Paula finished and left the table to get ready for school, which left Lucy sitting opposite Alice, and me at Alice's side. Ironically, it was Lucy, whose eating I had grave concerns about, who finally persuaded Alice to eat her cornflakes.

'Let's eat our cereal together,' Lucy said gently, smiling at Alice from across the table. 'Do what I do, and copy me. Dip your spoon into your bowl, like this,' she said, showing her. 'Now scoop up the biggest spoonful ever, and pop it in!'

Alice laughed, and then to my great relief she followed Lucy's example with a spoonful of her own. Five minutes later both bowls were empty.

I thanked Lucy as we left the table. 'Well done, love. That was a great idea.' But I thought I should also have thanked Alice, for it was the first time since Lucy had arrived that she'd eaten all her breakfast!

Alice and I waved Adrian, Lucy and Paula off to school at the door; then I told Alice we would go upstairs and I would help her have a wash and brush her teeth. I'd already found a new child's toothbrush, face flannel and towel in my emergency supply and had placed them in the bathroom, ready; but as at breakfast Alice was too mesmerized by her new surroundings to do anything other than stand and gaze at everything in the bathroom, including me. I washed her face and hands, brushed her teeth and then brushed her hair, which was chin length and very clean and shiny. All the time I talked to Alice, explaining what I was doing and reassuring her: 'This is your towel; I'll hang it on the rail next to mine. We'll put your toothbrush in the glass here. Now we'll go downstairs …' and so on.

Although Alice didn't say much I could tell she was taking it all in. Her gaze alighted on everything I pointed out or mentioned, and after a while I began to sense she was feeling more comfortable with me. Her little hand, which she'd tucked into mine, relaxed and she seemed to be less tense. Downstairs, I left the clearing up from breakfast for later and steered Alice into the sitting room. 'Would you like a story?' I asked. She nodded. I showed her to the bookshelves, where the children's books are kept on the lower shelves within reach. 'Choose some books,' I encouraged.

Alice spent a few minutes squatted down, going through the books, before selecting three – *The Very Hungry Caterpillar* and two books about teddy bears. We sat on the sofa and Alice immediately snuggled into my side, ready for the story. I put my arm around her and felt her head gently pressing against me, completely relaxed.

'Did Nana and Grandpa read you stories?' I asked, as I opened the first book.

Alice nodded. 'I like stories.'

I smiled. 'Good, because I like reading stories too. So do Adrian, Paula and Lucy.'

I read the first book about bears with Alice sitting very still and quiet, apparently engrossed in the story as I turned the pages, but as I finished and closed the book she said, 'Can I see my nana soon?' So I wasn't sure what she'd been thinking about.

'I hope so, love,' I said. 'Your social worker should phone me today and tell me when you are seeing them. Do you know Martha, your social worker?'

Alice nodded. 'Not that man last night?'

'No, he brought you to me because it was very late and Martha wasn't at work. I'm sure it will be Martha who phones us later.'

'I don't like Martha,' Alice said quietly.

'Oh?' I looked at her. 'Why?'

'She made my nana cry. She told her I'd have to go into care and my nana was very upset.' Although Alice spoke quietly, now that she was talking more I could hear just how good her diction was. She pronounced her words clearly, as a much older child would, and was fluent, suggesting someone had spent a lot of time talking to her.

'Well, you're in care now,' I said gently, 'and it's not so bad, although I understand why your nana was upset. I should be meeting Nana soon, so I'll be able to reassure her and tell her you are fine; then she won't be upset.' I assumed I would be meeting Alice's grandparents – either at contact or at the placement meeting (the meeting held within five days of a child coming into care). It is usual for a foster carer to meet the child's family or main carer and I was expecting Martha to phone later with the details.

'I love Nana and Grandpa,' Alice said, reluctant to let go of the subject and listen to another story.

'I know, pet, and they love you, lots. It's just that the social worker felt it was better for you to come into foster care for now.' And I thought for goodness' sake don't ask me why, because I've no idea.

'I wanted to stay with Nana and Grandpa,' Alice said. 'I was upset when Mummy took me away, but I love her too.'

I hugged her. Then I thought that, as Alice had touched on the subject of her mother taking her from her grandparents, and was now clearly more at ease talking to me, I could ask her what I knew the social worker and all the other professionals connected with the Alice's case would eventually want to know.

'Alice, love,' I said, 'you remember when Mummy took you from Nana's a few days ago, before you came here?' She nodded. 'Where did Mummy take you? Do you remember?'

Alice snuggled closer into my side and tucked her arms under mine, as though seeking reassurance. 'To McDonald's and the shops,' she said, 'then to Mummy's friend.'

'And where did you sleep at night?'

'With the wolves,' she said, and shivered. 'I was very frightened. It was dark and I didn't want to see the wolves. They made a horrible noise at night.'

Now, whereas I usually believe what children tell me until it is proved differently, and while I knew Alice was trying to tell me something, I also knew she hadn't slept with wolves. We don't normally have wolves roaming the UK and the nearest zoo – over an hour drive away – didn't have wolves, and even if it had I was sure they wouldn't have just let them loose.

'Wolves?' I asked gently. 'Can you tell me what they looked like?'

'I didn't see them. I heard them bark. Mummy said they weren't dogs but like wolves. She told me what they were called but I forgot.'

'Alice,' I said, looking at her. 'Did your mummy call them foxes?'

'Yes. That was the name. It was so dark and I could hear them bark. I was very scared.'

'I'm sure you were, love.' I felt my heart start to race as I realized what Alice could be trying to tell me. 'Alice, when you heard the foxes at night, were you in a house or outside in the open?'

'Outside,' she said. 'It was very dark and I'm frightened of the dark.'

Dear God, I thought, surely not? 'Alice, did you sleep outside at night?'

She nodded. 'I was tired and it was cold. I couldn't sleep, I was so frightened.'

I hid my shock as Alice snuggled even closer into my side at the recollection. 'Do you know how many nights you were outside?'

'Three,' she said without hesitation.

'How do you know it was three?' I asked, for I would have thought that at her age, and with the trauma of it all, she wouldn't have known precisely.

'Mummy cried and said we had slept outside for three nights and she couldn't do it any more. It wasn't fair on me. She said she would take me back.'

'And that's what happened?'

Alice gave a little nod. 'Mummy phoned Mike and he came and got us in his car and I fell asleep in the back.'

'Who's Mike?'

'Uncle Mike is Mummy's friend.'

'I understand. So what happened after that? When you woke up? Do you remember?'

Alice gave a little nod and her face clouded. 'When I woke up Mummy and Uncle Mike had gone and I was with the policemen.' Which fitted in with what I knew of Alice being taken to the police station late on Sunday evening.

'It's all right, love.' I held her close.

Alice's account had a nasty ring of truth and I was almost convinced she was telling me the truth,. Almost, for I couldn't believe a mother would sleep out in the open for three nights when the temperature had been down to two degrees centigrade, as it had for the last few nights. Was it possible Alice had seen something similar on television? Or maybe someone had put her up to saying this, although I couldn't imagine who or why.

'You must have been very brave,' I said. 'It's not right for a child to stay out all night.'

'I had my coat on and Mummy cuddled me,' Alice said, almost defending her mother. I remembered the dried mud I'd seen on Alice's otherwise new, clean coat.

'Still, it's not right and you won't ever be sleeping outside again,' I reassured her, as this was not necessarily obvious to Alice if she'd done so for three nights. 'Alice, do you know where it was you slept for those nights?' I was guessing she wouldn't know, but she nodded.

'In the hide at the quarry,' she said clearly.

I felt my heart lurch. I knew exactly where she meant. A couple of miles away there is a disused quarry which, some years before, had been filled with water and turned into a nature reserve. Anglers, with a permit, were allowed to fish in it during the day, and part of the surrounding land had been made into a bird sanctuary with a hide for watching the birds. The hide was no more than a wooden shack with small openings in one side, through which you could observe the birds. While it had a roof on it, the cold wind ripped through the observation slits and there was no door. I'd taken the children up there one bright spring morning the year before to watch the birds nesting and it had been cold even then. However, while all this was true – there was a quarry with a hide – I also knew that since vandals had got in and terrorized the nesting birds the area had been patrolled by security at night.

I looked at Alice and wondered: could she have made it all up? Would a mother really take her child up to that cold, remote spot to sleep for three nights? I supposed she might if she was unstable, or desperate, or both. Then, as though hearing my doubts, Alice looked up at me and said, 'We lay on the benches in the hide, but I couldn't sleep. The benches were too hard. And when the man came with his torch, we had to lie on the floor, under the benches, and keep very still until he went away.' At that point I knew Alice was telling the truth, for there was no other way she could have known and described in such detail the night security patrol unless she'd been there at night.

Chapter Seven

Accused

'Snatched from her nana! On the run for four days, and three nights sleeping at the quarry! It's a wonder she's not more traumatized than she is,' I said. 'Alice is quiet, but not obviously disturbed.'

'It might come out later,' Jill warned. 'The poor child must have been petrified. But you say she's been well cared for?'

'She appears to have been. She hasn't got any of her own possessions with her, but what she was wearing was new and clean. Her hair has been well looked after and she seems very bright, although naturally she's still wary of us. When Alice talks she has a wide vocabulary and she's very polite. The grandparents' influence, I expect.' It was 9.45 a.m. on Monday and Jill, my link worker from the fostering agency, had phoned for an update. I'd been doing most of the talking.

'Martha should be in touch soon,' Jill said. 'I haven't had any more information. Have you?'

'No. The duty social worker who placed Alice didn't have the paperwork. I guess Martha will bring the essential information forms when she visits.'

'I'll phone her when we've finished and remind her. If possible I'd like to be there when Martha visits to check and sign the placement forms.' Jill paused. 'Cathy, the duty social worker who placed Alice?'

'Yes?'

'Was there a problem?'

'What do you mean, "problem?" He was a bit rude on the phone. I think he was stressed. He said he was the only one on duty on Sunday night for the whole of the area.'

Jill paused again, as though uneasy about what she had to say. 'Unfortunately, Cathy, he's put in a complaint about you.'

'What?'

'I'm sorry, but apparently the police were concerned that Alice was left at the police station for so long before she was collected. They complained to the social services manager, who contacted the duty social worker through his agency. He said the delay was because you refused to take Alice straightaway.'

'What!' I exclaimed again. 'You must be joking! That's not true. I even offered to collect Alice from the police station.' Alice, who was sitting at the coffee table a little way in front of me doing a jigsaw, looked up on hearing her name. 'It's all right, love,' I reassured her; then I lowered my voice as I spoke again to Jill on the phone. 'He was the one who delayed collecting her, not me.'

'I'm sorry, Cathy, but I'm going to have to ask you for some details. The manager wants a full report. I've already told him you are one of our longest-serving foster carers and that you've never had a complaint made against you before.'

'Thanks,' I said, tightly, glancing at Alice again. Little wonder there was a shortage of foster carers, I thought, with an annual drop-out rate of over 10 per cent, if we were treated like this!

'Let's start at the beginning,' Jill said. 'Go slowly, because I'm taking notes. I understand you were out when the duty social worker first phoned?'

'Yes. I'd been waiting for Alice to arrive since Thursday evening and hadn't heard a thing,' I said, forcing myself to speak slowly. 'So on Sunday afternoon we all went to a friend's birthday party. I had my mobile with me but no one phoned.' I paused to allow Jill to write. 'When we got home, it was about half past nine and there were four messages on the answerphone from the duty social worker. I remember the first was left at eight thirty and I think the last was about nine fifteen, and he was quite rude. I phoned him back straightaway and asked why he hadn't phoned my mobile.'

'Hold on a minute,' Jill said. I waited as she wrote. Alice looked at me again, and I raised a smile. I wasn't happy going through all this in front of her, but I couldn't do anything else. Jill needed this information now and Alice wasn't confident enough yet to be left in a room by herself. 'Right,' Jill said after a few moments. 'What happened then? Why didn't he phone your mobile?'

'He said he didn't have my number.'

'That's not true,' Jill said. 'It was included in your details, sent to his agency.'

'Yes, he found it when he looked further, but said it wasn't obvious.'

Jill tutted. 'I'll check, but I'm sure it is included on the front page. Then what happened?'

'He told me Alice had been found, and was at the police station. He said he'd collect her as soon as he could but it wouldn't be straightaway as he was the only one on duty. He was obviously stretched to the limit, so I offered to collect Alice myself, but he said it needed to be a social worker. He was pretty short tempered on the phone, but by the time he arrived with Alice he seemed to have calmed down and was just a bit terse.'

'And what time was that?'

'About half past ten.'

Jill paused again and I heard her sigh. 'I can see why the police were concerned. Alice was taken to the police station just before eight. The police informed the duty social worker at eight fifteen, but Alice wasn't collected until ten. The poor child was at the station for over two hours.'

'Jill, if I'd had any idea Alice had been found I'd have left the party immediately and gone straight home. Of course I wouldn't leave a child sitting at the police station, but I'm not clairvoyant. If the duty social worker had phoned my mobile when he first knew Alice had been found at eight fifteen, I could have been home by the time he'd collected her from the station; we were only twenty minutes away.' I felt hot and shaky – a mixture of anger and upset. Alice shouldn't have been left all that time at the police station, and although

I was angry that the duty social worker was blaming me, I was also thinking I shouldn't have gone to the party, for it was my absence that had caused all this.

'It's not your fault,' Jill said. 'You acted properly. You had your mobile with you and switched on. Even though you were on standby to receive Alice it didn't mean you had to stay in the whole time; you just had to be contactable and within easy reach, which you were. I think the duty social worker is trying to cover up for his mistake. He didn't see your mobile number and now he is blaming you.' I didn't say anything. 'Don't worry, I'll put what you have told me in my report,' Jill said. 'I'm sure it will be fine.'

I mumbled my agreement, but I was far from reassured. Jill apologized again for having to question me, and said that as soon as she'd spoken to the social services manager, she'd phone Martha and find out when she was planning to visit.

We said goodbye and, replacing the receiver, I remained on the sofa for some moments, deep in thought. I loved fostering, even with all the meetings, training and paperwork, but I really didn't need the worry of being investigated. I knew how long these investigations could take, and how 'mud could stick' once thrown. And while the allegation levelled against me was comparatively minor, and I knew it was in Jill's capable hands, I still felt pretty bad. It had undermined my professionalism as a foster carer, which I take very seriously, as well as bringing into doubt my own personal integrity.

But I also knew that what I was being accused of, while hurtful and damaging to my reputation, was minor compared to the allegations made against some carers. During their careers approximately 35 per cent of foster carers will be accused of some misdemeanour, and if a child is angry, or a parent is angry that their child is in care, they can make up the most appalling allegations, which can sometimes result in a police investigation.

Leaving the sofa, I joined Alice at the coffee table and, putting aside my own worries, praised her. She had just completed a complicated jigsaw, aimed at ages five to eight, without any help whatsoever.

'Who taught you to do jigsaw puzzles?' I asked, impressed.

'My mummy and grandpa,' she said. 'They played with me lots. And my nana. Will you let me see them soon, please?'

'Oh, love,' I said, taking one of her little hands in mine. 'It's not my decision when you see your family. Let me try to explain.' Although I had touched on my role when Alice had first arrived, I thought that now she was more relaxed it might be easier for her to understand. 'I am a foster carer,' I said, gently. 'I look after children when they can't live with their own mummies, daddies or grandparents. I look after children but I don't make the decisions about where they live or when they can see their families. The social worker and judge make those decisions and I am sure they will say you can see your family soon.' I smiled. 'Do you know what a judge is?'

Surprisingly, Alice nodded. 'The judge tells people what to do,' she said, 'and he made my nana cry. I didn't see him, not like the social worker – I saw her. But the judge and social worker made my nana cry because they said I had to leave Nana and come here.'

I nodded thoughtfully. Alice's explanation might not be politically correct but it was honest – a child's-eye view of being brought into care.

'Why did they do that, Cathy?' Alice asked, her eyes widening in disbelief. 'Why did the judge and Martha make me go away from my nana and grandpa? Why are they being horrid to my mummy?'

I looked at her and my heart twisted. This was going to be difficult to explain. 'They aren't being horrid, darling,' I said, gently rubbing her hand between mine, 'although it might seem like it. The judge and social worker are doing what they think is best for you at present. And they think it is best for you to come and stay with me for a while.' Had Alice been abused or neglected it would have been easier to explain: I would have had concrete examples as to why she'd been brought into care, and indeed some children who have suffered badly at home are relieved to be in care. As it was, all I had was the original referral, which said Alice's mother, Leah, had mental health problems exacerbated by using illegal substances, and Alice's grandparents had been looking after Alice. There was no suggestion that her mother or (heaven forbid) her grandparents had abused Alice.

'I'll find out more when I speak to your social worker today,' I said, trying to reassure Alice as best I could. 'You're being very brave.' I patted her hand and then gave her a hug. 'Would you like to do another puzzle or play something different?'

'Another jigsaw, please,' she said. 'I like jigsaw puzzles. Mummy used to play with me lots.' I fetched another couple of puzzles from the toy cupboard and sat with Alice while she completed them. As she worked she talked easily of her mummy, nana and grandpa, mainly describing happy memories of their time together but also expressing anxious thoughts as to where they were now, and if they were upset. I continued to reassure her as best I could, telling her that Nana, Grandpa and Mummy would all be looking after each other. I noticed Alice hadn't mentioned her dad. The referral contained the name, but no other details, of Alice's father, Chris, so I assumed Alice had been brought up by her mother and maternal grandparents. Alice didn't say any more about the four days and three nights she had been missing with her mother and I didn't ask her. She would tell me in time, as she felt more relaxed.

As I played with Alice I was waiting, hoping, for the social worker to phone with, among other things, the arrangements for Alice to see her family. When a child first comes into care, contact is usually set up immediately – often the same day or certainly the next day, so that the bond between the child and the parents (or whoever the main carer has been) doesn't suffer. But when Martha phoned an hour later, I was shocked, and at a complete loss to understand the reasoning behind what she told me.

'There will be no contact with mum,' she said. 'And none is planned for the future. Contact with the grandparents will be for one hour every two weeks, supervised at the family centre. Contact with Alice's father will be twice a week, increasing to include overnights, until Alice goes to live with him next month.'

Chapter Eight

When Can I See My Mummy?

'The first contact with dad and his new wife, Sharon, will be tomorrow,' Martha, Alice's social worker, continued. 'At the family centre, from two to four p.m. Contact is being supervised at present, but only for the time being. Alice will be at nursery, so you will need to collect her early on the days she has contact. I'll give you the other details when I see you later today. I'll also try to get some of Alice's clothes and toys from the grand-parents. I assume you're in all afternoon?'

'I can be. I thought I might take Alice to the park for a while, as it's a nice day. Do you know roughly what time you'll be coming?'

'No,' Martha said. 'I've got a lot to deal with here first. This case has taken over, with the abduction and the police being involved. Your link worker told me what Alice said about sleeping at the quarry. Thank God Leah didn't do anything silly. Although any chance she might have had of having Alice returned to her has now gone.'

'Has it really?' I asked. 'Alice seems to have a very strong bond with her mother. She has lots of happy memories. And Leah seems to have done a good job of parenting Alice in the past. How did it all go so badly wrong?'

'I don't know,' Martha said. 'I've only been on the case two weeks, but I know enough to know that the sooner Alice is settled with her father the better. I'll see you later. I expect it will be after four.'

'Could you bring the essential information forms with you, please?' I asked quickly before she finished. 'And a copy of the care plan.'

'Unfortunately not. I told your link worker that our computer is down. I'll tell you what you need to know when I see you, and the rest will follow. How is Alice after her ordeal?'

'Coping very well, considering …'

'Good. Say hello to her from me. See you later. Bye.'

I replaced the receiver and went down the hall. I had answered the phone in the sitting room, but when I'd realized it was the social worker, I'd told Alice I'd be just down the hall if she needed me – I didn't want to keep talking about her in front of her. Now I returned to the sitting room, thinking about the contact arrangements, which seemed at odds with Alice's needs. From what Alice had been saying all morning she appeared to have a strong attachment to her mother, whom she wouldn't be seeing, a strong attachment to her grandparents, whom she would be seeing for only one hour every two weeks, and no attachment to her father whom, with his new wife, Alice would be seeing twice a week and with whom she would be going to live within a month. Knowing very little of Alice's background, I could only assume I'd misinterpreted what Alice had been telling me, and that there were sound reasons for the decisions that had been made.

Alice looked up from the toy box as I entered, and I smiled. 'That was Martha, your social worker,' I said. 'She's coming to visit us this afternoon.'

'When can I see my mummy?' Alice asked, aware Martha was responsible for when she saw her.

'I'm not sure,' I hedged. It wasn't my position to tell Alice she wouldn't be seeing her mother; that was the responsibility of her social worker, who should have built up a relationship with Alice and, with the details of Alice's background, could explain to her why she wouldn't be seeing her mother and answer her questions. 'But you will be seeing your dad and Sharon tomorrow,' I added.

'And Nana and Grandpa?' Alice asked. 'When can I see them?'

'We'll ask Martha when we see her this afternoon. But you will be seeing them before too long.' That was all I could say, but even then, knowing so little, I instinctively felt uncomfortable that Alice was not seeing her mother, and very little of her grandparents, when they had been her main carers. Alice was clearly very close to them and was missing them badly.

It was now 11.20 a.m. and I wondered about taking Alice to the park. It was only fifteen minutes' walk away, and if Martha wasn't coming until 4.00 p.m. there would be plenty of time. But, aware Martha had been vague about the exact time of her visit and not wishing to risk being out again when a social worker called, I decided to leave the park for another day. I exchanged one box of toys for another and sat with Alice while she played. She seemed a very self-possessed child: although she liked it when I joined in her games she didn't continually seek my attention but was happy to play alone, preferably in the same room as me. As she played she made little comments about the toys, which were obviously all new to her, and mentioned the toys she had at home with her mum and also at her nana's house. I told her I hoped we would be getting some of her own toys and clothes soon, as Martha was going to see Nana.

'I hope she doesn't make my nana cry again,' Alice said.

'No, she won't,' I reassured her, but I thought that when her grandmother learned of the very limited contact arrangements cry was exactly what she was likely to do.

Jill phoned to say she'd spoken to Martha and as Martha wasn't sure what time she'd be with us, Jill would have to leave visiting us until another day. 'You know to check and sign the forms,' she reminded me. 'Although if their computer is still down Martha won't have the placement forms.'

At 1.00 p.m. I asked Alice what she would like for lunch. 'A cheese and chutney sandwich, please,' Alice said, 'like my nana makes.' I thought I would be setting myself up for failure if I tried to replicate Nana's sandwich alone, so I suggested to Alice that she help me and she could show me how her nana made the sandwich.

Alice stood on a stool beside me in the kitchen and gave instructions on how thick to cut the bread, how thin to grate the cheese, how much chutney to put in and, once the sandwich was closed, how to cut it diagonally into four triangles.

'It's nearly right,' Alice said as we sat at the table and she took her first bite. 'I think Nana might use different chutney.'

I smiled. 'When I meet your nana, I'll ask her what type of chutney she uses and I'll buy some the same.' I dearly hoped it wasn't home-made, which would have been right out of my league. 'You're going to nursery tomorrow,' I said as we ate. 'Do you like nursery?'

Alice nodded. 'Is Nana taking me?'

'No, love, I'll be taking you. Did your nana used to take you?'

'Yes, and sometimes my mummy and sometimes Grandpa, and sometimes they all took me, and I had lots of people.' She gave a little smile, happy at the recollection. 'Why can't they take me to nursery now?' she suddenly asked, her face serious.

'Alice, you remember we talked about how I shall be doing "mummy things" for you while you're living with me – those things Mummy, Nana and Grandpa did for you?' Alice nodded. 'Well, taking you to nursery is one of those things, as well as making your meals, and helping you to clean your teeth and have a bath.'

'Mummy used to give me a bath,' Alice said. 'And sometimes Nana did. But Grandpa didn't. He said it was because I was a young lady.'

I smiled at this image of a pleasant, normal, loving family, and wondered again how it had all gone so badly wrong. I obviously knew nothing about Alice's grandparents, but from the memories Alice had shared with me they seemed lovely people who had clearly been an important part of Alice's childhood and doted on her. They must be devastated, I thought, at having their grandchild brought into care. It all seemed so very, very sad, and if I was honest it didn't make much sense.

'I shall be collecting you early from nursery tomorrow and I'll take you to the family centre to see your dad and Sharon,' I explained. 'I think you have seen them there before.' Alice continued eating, her expression blank, as though these arrangements were of little interest to her. 'Is that OK, then?' I asked.

'Don't mind,' Alice said and changed the subject. I felt a stab of unease. Usually when a child first comes into care, they can't wait to see their parents, but then from what Alice had said so far it was her mother and grandparents to whom she'd been close and for whom she now pined, not her father and his new wife, Sharon.

Four o'clock is not the best time for a social worker to visit, as it is the time when children arrive home from school, badly in need of a drink and snack, and all talking at once with their day's news. I could only say a brief hi to Adrian, Paula and Lucy as they came home, and had to let them get on with it while I showed Martha through to the sitting room, where Alice was watching some children's television. 'We'd better switch that off for now,' I said gently to Alice. 'I think Martha would like to talk to us.'

Alice didn't complain at having her viewing interrupted, but gave a small stoical nod. I switched off the television and hovered. Aware that social workers usually spend some time alone with the child – to discuss any issues the child might not feel comfortable talking about in front of the carer – I said to Martha, 'Shall I leave you two alone now or later?'

I was expecting Martha to say later, as it would have been reassuring for Alice to see the social worker and me chatting and getting along before I disappeared, but she said, 'Yes, now, please. Oh, and remind me before I go that I've got some of Alice's things in the car.' Then turning to Alice: 'I've been to see your nana.'

Before I left the room I caught a glimpse of Alice's face at the mention of her nana and my heart went out to her. Her little face brightened for a moment and then saddened as she asked: 'Is my Nana still crying?'

'No,' Martha said. 'She's fine and sends her love. You'll see her next week, and you can phone her on Saturday.' I dearly hoped Alice didn't know the days of the week, for she'd just been told it would be five days before she could speak to her nana and seven until she saw her – an eternity in a young child's life.

Chapter Nine
Pass the Parcel!

I busied myself in the kitchen with the preparations for dinner until I heard the sitting-room door open and Martha call me. She and Alice had been in the sitting room for thirty minutes, and I'd no idea what they'd been talking about. When I went in, Martha asked if Alice could go and play somewhere else while she spoke to me. I called upstairs to Lucy and Paula, and they appeared on the landing from their bedrooms, guessing what I wanted. Alice scampered up the stairs and I returned to the sitting room.

'Alice is too young to know her own mind,' Martha said as I closed the sitting-room door so we couldn't be overheard. 'I asked her who she wanted to live with but she didn't answer.'

'I think she's completely overwhelmed with everything that's happened,' I said, sitting on the sofa. 'Has Alice got a choice where she lives, then?'

'No, but it's always nice to hear the child's views.' So I thought that asking Alice who she wanted to live with had been rather a pointless exercise.

'Alice has been talking a lot about her mother and her grandparents,' I offered. 'She's very close to them. And they seem to have done a very good job parenting Alice in the past. She's a delightful child – intelligent, well mannered and very engaging.'

Martha looked at me, mildly surprised. 'Mum abused Alice,' she said, as though I should have known.

'Really? It wasn't mentioned on the referral and Alice's memories of her mother are all very positive.'

Martha shrugged. 'The neighbours reported hearing Leah shouting and screaming when Alice was in the house. Coupled with Leah's mental health problems and drug habit, there's no chance of Alice returning to her mother, although I understand Leah says she's kicked the drug habit now.'

'I see,' I said slowly. 'And where is Leah now?'

'Don't know. Leah's boyfriend took Alice to the police station. Leah is wanted by the police for abducting Alice. She's been given forty-eight hours to hand herself in. She can't hide forever.'

I shook my head sadly. 'And Alice won't be seeing her mum in the future? Even if the contact is supervised?'

'Leah isn't stable enough,' Martha said. 'The department has tried to set up a meeting with her but she won't engage. She screams down the phone, completely out of control, and won't listen to reason. We're concentrating all our efforts on getting Alice settled with her father and his new wife as soon as possible.'

'I see,' I said again, but I was reluctant to let go of the subject of Alice's mother. 'And Leah isn't on any medication to help her? I know that many people with mental health problems function very well with medication.'

'I've no idea what's she's taking, prescribed or otherwise,' Martha said tartly. Then she changed the subject: 'Now, Alice's father, Chris, and his wife, Sharon, are being assessed with a view to parenting Alice. So far the assessment has been very positive. As soon as the assessment is complete we'll move Alice to them. They're a nice couple and unfortunately Sharon can't have children of her own. Alice will make them a lovely daughter. We're in the process of re-homing them; they're in bed and breakfast at present.'

'Does Alice's mother have a home?' I asked.

'A flat. We won't be giving her your address, although there is no reason why Chris and Sharon shouldn't have it, assuming you have no objection?'

'No, that's fine.' Parents of a child in foster care are usually told where their child is staying unless there are concerns for the child's safety. 'But you're not telling Mum where Alice is?' I queried.

'No, nor the grandparents, in case they pass it to Mum. There is a risk that Leah could snatch Alice again.'

I nodded. 'Does Alice have a relationship with her father and Sharon?' I was trying to glean as much information as I could while I had the chance. 'She hasn't spoken of them so far, although she chats about her mother and grandparents.'

'From what I know, Dad didn't have much involvement in Alice's life before all this,' Martha said, 'so it's fortunate for Alice that he wants her now. Contact with Dad and Sharon will be Tuesday and Thursday, and with the grandparents on alternate Wednesdays. Alice can also have phone contact with her grandparents on Saturdays, but I want you to monitor it. Do you have a speaker phone?'

'Yes,' I said, surprised she felt it was necessary. 'I can put that phone on speaker.' I pointed to the phone on the table in the corner of the sitting room.

'Good. I've told the grandparents what they can and can't say to Alice, and that you will stop the call if you're not happy with anything you hear. You're experienced enough to know what is acceptable.'

'Yes,' I said. While I'd monitored many phone conversations in the past it had always been in cases where a child might be frightened or intimidated by abusing parents. In all my experience as a foster carer I'd never before had to monitor the phone conversation between a child and what appeared to be loving grandparents.

'Is there a suggestion the grandparents have abused Alice?' I asked.

'No, not at all, but they're in cahoots with Leah, and we need to know what they're saying. The grandparents haven't been entirely honest with us, so we're not taking any chances.' Martha didn't elaborate and it wasn't for me to press for more details. She then passed me a handwritten sheet of paper with the contact arrangements: the address of the family centre where Alice would be seeing her dad and grandparents, and the grandparents' telephone number.

'Have you been able to print off the placement agreement form?' I asked.

Martha shook her head. 'The computer is still down. I'll leave a note on the file that you haven't received the placement form or the essential information form. I'm off the case now.'

'Oh, are you? That's a pity. Alice will have to get to know a new social worker. Do you know who it will be?'

'No, but whoever it is will print out the forms you need when the system is up and running again. I think that's everything.' She made a move to go.

'Have you told Alice she won't be seeing her mother?' I asked.

'I've told her it's not possible at present, but that she'll be seeing lots more of her dad and Sharon to make up for it.'

'And what did Alice say?'

'Nothing. She just looked at me with those amazingly large eyes. She's a very attractive child, but far too young to understand.'

I went with Martha to her car, where we lifted two large suitcases from the boot – Alice's possessions from her grandparents. We took them into the hall and then Martha called 'Goodbye, Alice,' up the stairs. There was no response.

'She's playing with Lucy and Paula,' I said. 'Shall I fetch her so she can say goodbye? I don't expect she'll see you again if you're off the case.'

'No, there's no need. She hasn't known me very long. Just say I said good luck.'

I saw Martha out and closed the front door. Then I went upstairs to check everyone was all right. Far from playing with Lucy and Paula, as I'd assumed, and far from 'being too young to understand', as Martha had assumed, Alice had understood that she wouldn't be seeing her mother and was completely distraught. I found her sitting on the bed in her room, sobbing quietly, with Lucy and Paula either side, trying to comfort her.

'She wants her mummy,' Paula said as soon as I entered. She looked close to tears herself.

'That old bag told her she couldn't see her mum,' Lucy said bitterly, referring to the social worker.

'Lucy,' I cautioned. 'That won't help. Let me try to explain to Alice.'

I sat on her bed and took Alice on to my lap, with the girls either side of me, and held her until she was calm enough to hear what I was saying. Although I couldn't give Alice false hope, I could at least try to explain and also focus on the positive. I explained that Mummy wasn't well enough to see her at present but that she was being looked after, so there was nothing for her to worry about. I emphasized that she would be seeing and phoning her grandparents, and she would also be seeing lots more of her dad and Sharon.

'I don't want my dad and Sharon,' Alice said fretfully. 'I want my mummy and Nana.'

'There! Told you!' Lucy put in.

'Why can't she see her mum?' Paula asked.

'Alice's mother is unwell,' I said, looking pointedly at Paula and Lucy. 'She isn't up to it at present. But Alice will be seeing her grandparents and I'm sure they'll tell Alice how her mummy is.'

Lucy snorted. 'Oh yeah. Right. In supervised contact?' she said cynically, having experienced supervised contact. 'As soon as her gran mentions her mum she'll be stopped from saying anything. You're not allowed to talk about other people at contact, especially those connected with the case.' While there was an element of truth in this, Lucy was exaggerating the situation and her attitude wasn't helping Alice, who was now crying again.

'It will be fine for your nana to tell you that Mummy is OK,' I reassured Alice. 'And when I next speak to your social worker I'll ask if we can have a photograph of Mummy, and I'll frame it, and we'll put it on that shelf.' I pointed to the bookshelf in the recess by her bed.

Alice brightened a little. 'And can I have a photograph of Nana and Grandpa?'

'Yes. And they can all watch over you while you sleep.' Alice finally wiped her eyes. I always try to obtain photographs of the child's parents (or main carers) as soon as possible after a child arrives. It is surprising just how much comfort having these photographs gives a child, and the child often kisses the photograph good-night.

'Why don't you phone the social worker now and ask her to get them?' Paula asked.

'Martha is leaving the case, so as soon as we have a new social worker I'll ask.'

'All change!' Lucy said disparagingly, referring to Alice's change of social worker and all the changes of social workers she'd experienced. 'Pass the parcel!'

'Enough!' I said to Lucy. She was in rather an antagonistic mood and while I appreciated why, she needed to stop it, as it wasn't helping Alice. I'd noticed before that when a new child arrived it had an adverse effect on Lucy for the first few days. Although Lucy went out of her way to help settle in the new arrival, as did Paula, it reminded Lucy of her own unsettled past and painful memories resurfaced. I knew she would be fine in a day or so.

I decided to leave unpacking Alice's suitcases until after dinner and, with everyone helping, we sat down to eat thirty minutes later. But unlike at breakfast, when Lucy had set a good example and had encouraged Alice to eat, Lucy now toyed with her food and ate virtually nothing. Alice seemed to be copying her and I found myself having to encourage them both to eat, my own eating interspersed with sideways glances and 'Come on, eat up.' Out of the two it was Lucy I was most concerned about, for I knew Alice had had a reasonable lunch – sandwich, yogurt and fruit – but I'd no idea what, if anything, Lucy had eaten. I also knew that if I asked her she'd become evasive and it would turn into an issue.

Eventually I began collecting together the plates. 'Are you sure you've had enough?' I asked Lucy and Alice. They both nodded. Apart from being concerned that Lucy wasn't getting enough for her body's requirements, I was also concerned that Paula might copy her example. Adrian had always been a good eater and he was that much older, but Paula was at an impressionable age and looked up to Lucy. In all other respects

Lucy had settled in very well, was coming to terms with her past and was growing very close to Paula, Adrian and me. It was a shame there was still the issue of her eating.

Chapter Ten

Brian the Bear

Before I ran Alice's bath, Adrian took the two suitcases upstairs and into Alice's bedroom. I lay one
flat on the floor and opened it, leaving the other standing by the wall. Opening a child's bag or case is always
a poignant moment: a bittersweet reminder of the life
the child has left behind. Sometimes the bag contains
no more than a handful of ragged dirty clothes which
aren't of any use, and I make do with clothes from my
emergency supply and then go shopping at the earliest
opportunity to buy new. But as I opened the first of
Alice's two cases my heart ached: rows and rows of her
little clothes, washed and neatly pressed, and smelling
of a fabric conditioner which, while unfamiliar to me,
would be very familiar to Alice. I looked through the
case and found skirts, jumpers, dresses, pyjamas, dressing-gown, slippers, little jogging outfits, coat, gloves
and scarf, and shoes wrapped in a plastic bag. It was like
a suitcase packed for a holiday where, unsure of the
weather, all eventualities had been catered for. I knew
how much love and care had gone into that packing;

Alice's nana had wanted to make sure Alice would be comfortable and have everything she needed. I also knew the pain it must have caused her nana to pack her cherished granddaughter's belongings for a holiday from which she would never return.

Alice, who had been watching me, wide eyed and in silence, now began diving into the case, taking out the little bundles of her clothes and pressing them to her face. The smell and feel was a welcome reminder to her that at least some of her past had come with her. She took out another bundle of clothes and an envelope appeared. 'To the Carer' was written on the outside and I quickly picked it up. Directing Alice towards the wardrobe so she could begin putting away some of her clothes, I moved to one side and slit open the envelope. My eyes filled as I read the short handwritten note: 'Dear Carer, Please take good care of our beloved granddaughter. She means everything to us. God bless you. Janice and Martin Jones.' I looked at the note and then at Alice. I dearly wished I could have phoned Alice's grandparents there and then and tried to reassure them. But the social worker had clearly stated that phone contact should take place on Saturday evenings, and I knew I couldn't go against her instructions.

Tucking the note into my pocket, I joined Alice in unpacking. She was engrossed in the task and, while many of the clothes would need refolding later if they weren't going to be badly creased, she was happy in her work and, with her clothes in the wardrobe, it was starting to look more like home. I was conscious of the time: I needed to get Alice into bed before long, as she would have to be up early in the morning for nursery, and she hadn't had her bath yet. I suggested to her that we left unpacking the second case until the following day.

'Can we just find Brian?' she asked.

'Yes,' I smiled, guessing that Brian was a favourite toy rather than a stowaway. 'I hope Nana has remembered to pack him,' I said.

'She will,' Alice said. I shared her confidence: Alice's grandmother had remembered to pack everything else that Alice could possibly need, so I was sure she would have remembered a favourite toy.

Closing the empty suitcase I stood it on the landing, ready for putting away later. I laid the second case on the floor in Alice's bedroom and unzipped the lid. Sure enough, to Alice's delight, there lay Brian: a cuddly teddy bear, resplendent in a Nottingham Forest football kit.

'Who supports Nottingham Forest?' I asked.

'My grandpa,' Alice said, smiling, and, scooping up the bear, clutched him to her. 'Grandpa bought him at an away match when they won,' Alice explained knowledgeably. 'Brain Clough was the manager and Grandpa said he should have a bear named after him because he had done so well with his team. You can say hello to Brian the Bear if you like.'

'Pleased to meet you,' I said, shaking his paw.

We assume our lives are pretty constant and that our surroundings and routine will remain constant too, but for a child who is taken into care all continuity vanishes when the child is suddenly uprooted and set down in a strange environment, with strange people and customs. Now that Alice had been reunited with Brian the Bear and her clothes I could see she was already starting to feel more at ease. There were more toys in the second suitcase, and books, a set of towels, a wash bag, and a throw-over bed cover with a big picture of Barbie doll. I took this out, together with the wash bag, one of the books and a towel. Although I had plenty of towels I would use the one Alice's grandmother had sent, which was familiar to Alice.

Closing the case, I stood it to one side and then removed the pink blanket Alice had arrived in from the bed and draped the Barbie cover over it. I then took Alice through to the bathroom, where I ran her bath. I squirted in a few drops of the child's bubble bath her nana had included in Alice's wash bag, and used the sponge and face flannel that were also in the bag. I washed Alice's back and she did the rest. Then I lifted her out and wrapped her in the bath towel her nana had sent. It was fragranced with the same fabric conditioner as her clothes and Alice pressed it to her face as I helped dry her. I helped her into her Sleepy Cat pyjamas, squirted toothpaste on her toothbrush and waited while she brushed her teeth.

In her bedroom Alice snuggled beneath the duvet and Barbie cover and looked much more relaxed and at home. 'All right, love?' I asked. She nodded. 'You're doing very well.' I perched on the edge of the bed and, lightly stroking her forehead, ran through what we would be doing the following day: I would take her to nursery, collect her after lunch, take her to the family centre to see her dad and Sharon, and then collect her and bring her home. Although I'd already told Alice this I repeated it, as children can get very confused when they first come into care with so many new things and routines to adjust to. Alice didn't make any comment, but she looked quite tired. I asked her if she wanted a story before she went to sleep. She nodded so, still sitting on the bed, I read the book I'd taken from the suitcase – *Favourite Nursery Rhymes*, which I guessed her nana had read to her many times, for Alice was word perfect.

When I finished the book I went on to the landing and called downstairs that Alice was ready to say goodnight. Lucy and Paula broke off from doing their homework in the dining room and came up, and Adrian appeared from his bedroom. They took it in turns to say good-night to Alice; the girls kissed her cheek while Adrian blew a kiss and gave a little wave from the door. 'See you in the morning,' they chimed as they left, and Alice smiled.

As Adrian, Paula and Lucy returned to their home-work, which they knew had to be completed before they watched television, I returned to sit on Alice's bed for a moment, stroking her forehead and just looking at her little face. 'You're doing very well,' I said again. 'I know it isn't easy, but you'll find it gets a bit easier as time goes on. There's nothing for you to worry about. If you've got any questions or there is anything worrying you, ask me, won't you?'

Alice's gaze went to the window where the curtains were drawn. 'Is it dark outside?' she asked in a small voice.

'Yes, love. But I'll leave your light on low, like I did last night.' I assumed she was worried by the dark, as she had been the night before.

Alice paused and thought for a moment. Then she asked seriously: 'Can we go to the quarry now it's dark?'

'No, love,' I said, surprised. I'd have thought that would have been the last place she'd want to go. 'The quarry is closed. It's night-time. We don't go to the quarry at night.'

'But my mummy might be there,' she said. 'I want to see my mummy. I want to sleep with her in the shed at the quarry. Why can't we go?'

'Oh, love, Mummy isn't at the quarry now. People don't normally sleep at the quarry; they sleep in their beds. Your mummy will be sleeping in a bed now.'

I continued to stroke her forehead. Despite the trauma of being snatched and taken to the quarry at night, where the sound of the barking foxes had terrorized her, Alice would risk it all again just to be with her mother.

'Where is my mummy?' Alice asked after a moment, her large eyes finally moving from the window to me.

'I'm not sure, love, but I do know she isn't at the quarry. I expect your nana is looking after her.' Clearly I had no idea where Leah was, but this seemed enough to reassure Alice. I continued to sit with her, stroking her forehead until her eyes finally closed in sleep.

Chapter Eleven

Precious

I always feel like the 'new girl' at school when I walk into a playground for the first time. I don't know the layout of the school or where the child's classroom is, and I feel other mothers are looking at me, wondering who I am. Without any further instructions from Martha, other than I had to take Alice to nursery on Tuesday, I had decided to do what I usually did on the first morning: introduce myself at the school's reception and ask for directions to Alice's classroom. Alice, however, bright as a button and happy at the prospect of seeing her friends again at nursery, wanted to go straight to her classroom.

'It's this way,' she said, pulling me across the playground. 'I'll show you.' She led me to the side of the main school building and to a separate entrance with a door marked 'nursery only'. 'We can go straight in,' Alice explained. 'The older children have to wait in the playground until the bell goes.'

I pushed open the door, then followed Alice down a short corridor and through another door into the actual

nursery. It was a large, brightly lit room, with gaily
coloured mobiles hanging from the ceiling and children's artwork decorating all the walls. The floor was
covered with toys, floor cushions and themed mats;
around the edge of the room were tables containing all
types of activities. There was a home corner, an 'office'
corner with a couple of desks and chairs and two small
computers, and further along two large fish-tank-like
bowls for sand and water play. A couple of children
were already seated at one table, modelling dough.

I had purposely come early so I could introduce myself
to Alice's teacher and have a brief chat with her before
all the children arrived. A lady in her mid-forties
dressed in slacks and a jumper approached us.

'That's Mrs Davis,' Alice said, smiling at her.

We shook hands. 'I'm Cathy Glass, Alice's foster
carer.'

'Pleased to meet you. Margaret Davis.' Then to Alice:
'Would you like to hang up your coat and find an activ-
ity while I talk to Cathy?' Mrs Davis waited until Alice
had gone to hang up her coat and was out of earshot
before she asked, 'How is Alice? We were all so
concerned. Thank goodness she was found safe and
well.' From which I assumed she knew Alice had been
missing.

'Alice is doing very well,' I said, 'considering all that
has happened. She came to me late on Sunday. I expect
her new social worker will be in touch with the school
soon.'

Mrs Davis nodded. 'All the staff have been very
worried. Leah hasn't been well for some time. I do hope

she can get the help she needs now. How long do you think Alice will be with you?'

'I don't think it will be very long. I understand the social services want her settled with her father as soon as possible – in about a month, I think.'

Mrs Davis frowned, puzzled. 'Really? So she's staying with her father until her mother is well again?'

I glanced at Alice, who had joined in the dough modelling. 'No, I understand it will be permanent.'

'What?' Mrs Davis asked, clearly shocked. 'I wasn't even aware there was a father on the scene. Are you sure? He's certainly never been to the school.'

Not knowing how much the school had been told about Alice's background, and not really knowing enough myself to be able to add anything that would reassure Mrs Davis, I said the social worker would be the best person to ask; then I moved on to the practical arrangements.

'I'll need to collect Alice at one thirty today and on Thursday,' I said. 'Alice has contact with her father. I understand she usually has a school dinner?'

'Yes. She'll be finished by one o'clock.'

'That should work out fine. We'll go straight from school to the family centre. Shall I go into the office and advise them of the arrangements, and also check that they have my contact details?'

'Yes please,' Mrs Davis said.

'Is there anything else I need to do or know about the school?'

'I don't think so. The office can give you a copy of the term dates.'

'Thanks. I'll see you at one thirty, then.'

I went over to say goodbye to Alice as Mrs Davis greeted another parent and child. Alice was busy dough modelling. As I said goodbye Alice pursed her lips, wanting to kiss me. I lowered my head and she kissed my cheek.

'Goodbye, love,' I said. 'Have a good day. I'll see you just after lunch.'

'Bye,' Alice said. Then, turning to the child sitting next to her, who was eyeing me suspiciously, she announced: 'That is Cathy, my carer.' I smiled, pleased, for so often children are embarrassed about being in care and having a carer, but Alice had made me sound like an acquisition to be coveted.

'Bye,' I said to the other child.

She grinned, and as I left I heard her asking Alice where you got a carer from.

Before I left the school I went to the office and introduced myself. The school secretary was aware that Alice was in foster care but hadn't been given my details. She handed me a form and I filled it in with my name, address, telephone numbers, plus the contact details of the person who should be called in an emergency if I wasn't available. Because Alice was a looked-after child I filled in the second contact details with those of the social services; then I told the secretary that I would be collecting Alice at 1.30 p.m. today and on Thursday.

On the way home I stopped off quickly at the supermarket; then when I got home Jill phoned for an update. I told her how well Alice had been doing but that she missed her mother and grandparents. I also told her of the contact arrangements and that I still hadn't received any paperwork. Jill said she would chase up the paperwork, and then made an arrangement to visit us – after school the following day, Wednesday, when Alice wouldn't have contact. I told Jill that Martha was now off the case and Jill said she would try to find out who was taking over.

Once I'd said goodbye to Jill I grabbed a quick coffee, put the washing in the machine, and then went upstairs and finished unpacking Alice's second suitcase. It contained toys, cuddly dolls, books and another towel. I put the towel in the airing cupboard and arranged Alice's personal possessions on her bookshelves. Now her bedroom was full of her things it looked very cosy and inviting and I hoped it would make her feel comfortable and more at home.

I stowed the two suitcases in the cupboard under the stairs; when I spoke to Alice's grandparents I would ask them if they wanted them back. Aware of the passing time, I pegged the washing on the line, then had a sandwich lunch while I wrote up my log. All foster carers keep a log which is a daily account of the child they are looking after. They record everyday events like going to nursery, the child's mood and behaviour, if they are sleeping and eating well, and anything significant – positive or negative. Once I'd brought my log up to date I shut it safely away in a drawer. Then I sent Toscha out for a run, put on my coat and shoes and returned to the school for 1.30. Because it wasn't home time the gate to the playground was security locked and I pressed the buzzer. A voice came through the intercom; I gave my name and the gate released.

I could see Alice in the nursery section of the playground, playing hopscotch with a friend. As soon as she saw me she came bounding over with another child in tow.

'This is Cathy,' Alice said proudly to her friend, 'the carer I was telling you about.' Clearly I was getting something of a reputation!

'Hi,' I said. 'I'm looking after Alice. How are you?'

The girl grinned shyly; then the playground supervisor, spotting a stranger in the playground, came over and I explained who I was. The supervisor had been told by the office that Alice was being collected early and that it would be by her foster carer, Cathy Glass, but having never met me before she sensibly asked to see my ID. All foster carers are supposed to carry their ID and it's not only for going into government buildings, where security is strict, but also for situations like this where they are collecting a child and the person responsible for the child doesn't know them.

'Thanks,' she said as I took my ID from my bag and showed it to her.

Alice already had her coat on, so there was no need to go into the school. We said goodbye to the supervisor and Alice's friend, and then crossed the playground to the gate, where I pressed the security buzzer to exit.

'Have you had a good morning?' I asked as we walked hand in hand up the road to where I'd parked the car.

'Yes, but I wanted to stay at nursery all day.'

'You can tomorrow, but this afternoon you're going to see your dad and Sharon,' I reminded her.

'When am I seeing Nana?' Alice asked, as she had done that morning.

'Wednesday next week, which isn't too far away.'

Alice didn't say anything further and it was impossible to know what was going through her mind. She still hadn't spoken of father – all her thoughts and memories of home were of her mother and grandparents.

The traffic was light in the early afternoon and we arrived at the family centre five minutes early. I knew the family centre from having taken other children I'd looked after there for contact with their families. It's a single-storey building with an office, kitchen, gardens and play area, and six rooms furnished like sitting rooms where children see their parents with a supervisor present. The rooms are very comfortable and designed, as much as possible, to feel like home, with pictures on the walls, carpets, sofas, curtains at the windows, table and chairs, a television, board games and so on. In fact the family centre is so comfortable, warm and inviting that some parents don't want to leave, and hang around chatting to the staff long after contact has finished and their children have gone home with their carers. Some parents have been known to pop in even when they are not scheduled to see their children, feeling that the contact centre offers more in the way of home than their own homes, which is very sad.

Alice knew the centre from having seen her father and Sharon there a few times while she'd been staying with her grandparents. I parked in the small car park at the side of the building and then got out and opened Alice's car door which, as always, was child locked. Alice slipped her hand into mine and we went up the short path to the front door, where I pressed the security buzzer. The CCTV camera overhead allowed the office staff to see who was at the door and a moment later the lock released and we went into reception.

Before I had a chance to sign in the visitors' register or say hello to the office staff, a very fashionably dressed woman in her late twenties, with jeans tucked into red knee-length boots and long flowing hair, appeared from the waiting area.

'Hi, precious!' she cried at the top of her voice to Alice and, rushing over, scooped Alice into her arms. 'I've missed you so much! How are you, my precious?' In a flurry of hair and perfume she began planting kisses all over Alice's head, face and neck while Alice just lay in her arms, expressionless. Then as quickly as she'd picked up Alice she set her down again. Alice staggered for a second before she got her balance. Turning to me, the woman smiled and offered her hand.

'I'm Sharon, Chris's wife and Alice's new mother.'

I glanced at Alice and her look said it all: this woman isn't my mother and won't ever be.

Chapter Twelve

A New Mummy

Embarrassment, confusion and something close to resentment flickered across little Alice's face. Then she looked past Sharon to a man who was coming into reception from the direction of the waiting room. Alice didn't run to him but remained where she was, beside me.

He came up to her and, without any display of emotion, said, 'Alice. How are you?'

'This is my husband, Chris,' Sharon said. 'Alice's daddy.'

I smiled and shook his hand. Alice hadn't said anything but remained by my side, silently watching her father and Sharon.

'We really wanted Alice to come straight to us,' Sharon said in a rush. 'But the social services said she had to go into care first while our assessment was being completed.'

'That's usual,' I confirmed.

'Seems a waste of time to me,' Sharon continued. 'I mean we're in our house now. Before, when we just had one bedroom, I could understand it. But Alice has got her own room. It's all ready for her. So how's she been since she came to you?'

It's usual to give parents or relatives a brief update before or after contact, to reassure them the child is well and happy, but I didn't want to do so in the main reception area where other parents could pass and overhear, and neither did I want to talk about Alice in front of her if it could be avoided.

'Just a minute,' I said to Sharon. 'I'll see if the contact supervisor is free to look after Alice for a moment.'

I put my head round the office door and, having exchanged hellos with the two staff who were in there, I asked who the contact supervisor would be for Alice.

'Lyn,' the receptionist-cum-secretary said. 'She'll be here soon. Is everything all right?'

'Yes. I just need someone to look after Alice for a few minutes while I update her dad and Sharon.'

'Bring her in here. I'll look after her and keep her amused.'

'Thanks. You're a gem.'

I showed Alice into the office and said we wouldn't be long. Then I went with Sharon and Chris to the waiting room, which was empty.

'We were so worried,' Sharon said as soon as we sat down. 'We weren't told a thing. All that time Alice was missing we didn't know what was happening. She could have been dead for all we knew. No one kept us informed. I kept phoning the police and the duty social worker, but they said they didn't know anything. It was only when I phoned the social services on Monday morning that I was told she'd been found on Sunday! I've told Chris we should put in a complaint.'

I glanced at Chris, who nodded but didn't say anything. 'I wasn't kept informed either,' I said. 'So I can understand how worried you must have been.'

'I didn't sleep all weekend. It was awful,' Sharon continued. 'I'm so angry, I'm going to speak to my solicitor about suing them. We should have been told; we had a right to know.' I noticed Sharon did all the talking while Alice's father sat beside her, occasionally nodding in agreement but not adding anything. They were both the same height, about 5 feet 8 inches and fashionably dressed – Chris in designer sportswear. His spiky haircut was gelled in place, and I knew from the referral that he was twenty-five and Sharon was a few years older. Clearly Sharon was the more assertive of the two, and from what she was saying she appeared to have shouldered most of the responsibility (and possibly worry) during the time Alice had been missing.

'That woman's got a lot to answer for,' Sharon said, referring to Alice's mother. 'She was always a bit odd but now she's off her trolley.'

'You know Leah?' I asked, surprised.

'Sort of. She used to live in the same road. The social worker, Martha, said when they find Leah she'll be prosecuted and put inside. Do you know if she's been caught yet? I hope she has for what she did to Alice.'

'I don't know,' I said. I wasn't going to be drawn into discussing or condemning Leah. While snatching Alice had been completely unacceptable and had caused everyone, including Alice, untold anxiety, part of me felt sorry for Leah. From what I had seen so far of Alice, Leah – with the support of her parents – had done a good job of parenting Alice, and I couldn't help but view her act of snatching her daughter as that of a mother desperate to keep her child.

'Now, I expect you will want to spend your time with Alice,' I said. 'So let me quickly tell you how she's been. Alice came to me late on Sunday and although she was overwhelmed by everything that had happened, she settled remarkably well.' They both nodded. I continued to tell them that Alice had been eating and sleeping well, that she had been to nursery, and that there would be a placement meeting before the end of the week when the social worker would be present to answer any queries they might have.

'She's not fit to be a mother,' Sharon said as soon as I finished. 'And those grandparents are no better. They've poisoned Alice against me and Chris. Alice hardly knows her father.'

I'd noticed in reception there was a coolness between Alice and her father, but whether this was a result of Alice being 'poisoned' against her father or whether it was simply distance – from him not being involved in Alice's life – I'd no idea.

'Thankfully, Alice is safe now,' I smiled, 'and I understand she will be seeing quite a lot of you both. Have you any questions about her care? Or is there anything you can tell me that will help me to look after Alice – for example, her likes and dislikes?'

They both thought for a moment; then Chris shook his head, and Sharon said: 'Alice calls me Mummy now.

I told her to. I can't have children, so Alice can be my daughter, which is nearly as good.'

I looked at Sharon. Apart from 'nearly as good' settling uncomfortably with me, I thought how confusing it must be for Alice to be calling Sharon Mummy when she had a strong bond with her own mother. One of the reasons foster carers don't encourage foster children to call them Mummy or Mum is to avoid such confusion, and divided loyalties. If the child is with the carer permanently and has little or no attachment to his or her own mother, then over a period of time the child might naturally start referring to the carer as Mum, which is very different from being told to do so.

'How long have you known Alice?' I asked Sharon.

'Nearly five weeks,' she said. 'But I knew Chris had a child right from the beginning. He told me straightaway. We don't have any secrets. It's all happened so quickly. We met six months ago, got married three months ago, and now I'm in a new house and will soon have a daughter of my own! I think the reason Alice has loved me so quickly is because her own mother is crap. Ooops, sorry.' She turned to Chris and grinned girlishly. 'I shouldn't swear now I'm a mother.'

I looked at Chris, who smiled indulgently, while I kept my own thoughts to myself. 'Well, if there's nothing else,' I said, 'I'll just say goodbye to Alice and leave you to enjoy your time together.' I turned and led the way from the waiting room and into reception, where Alice and Lyn, the contact supervisor, were just coming out of the office. I said goodbye to Alice and told her I would come back in two hours to collect her. She

pursed her lips, wanting to kiss me goodbye as she had
done at nursery that morning. I bent down so she could
reach my cheek, but before Alice had the chance to kiss
me Sharon intercepted.

'Come and give your mummy a kiss instead,' she said.
Kneeling down, she turned Alice towards her.

I straightened as Alice reluctantly kissed her cheek.
'Goodbye, love,' I said, and came away.

In the car I sat for a moment staring through the windscreen, deep in thought. Dear Alice: she seemed so
vulnerable and in need of protection that I could see
why Sharon was all over her. Yet Sharon came across
as dominating, a force to be reckoned with, and if I had
felt overwhelmed by her, goodness knew what little
Alice felt. I was sure Sharon had the best intentions, but
from what I'd seen she was going about becoming
Alice's stepmother the wrong way. She needed to stand
back and let Alice take the initiative on how fast she
wanted their relationship to build. Sharon was trying
too hard – being the classic over-zealous step-parent –
and I knew Alice was resenting it.

The same certainly couldn't be said of Alice's father,
Chris, who had hardly said a word to her. When a child
comes into care and can't be returned home, as in Alice's
case, another suitable relative willing to parent the child
is usually considered the next best option. But from
what I'd just seen, Alice's father had no relationship
with Alice, and didn't seem to know how to make one,
while Sharon, who had only known Alice five weeks,
was the other extreme – obsessed with making Alice

her daughter. And what no one seemed to be taking into account were Alice's feelings and wishes. She loved her mother and grandparents, and if she wasn't going to be able to live with them again, as Martha has said, then someone needed to explain exactly why to Alice; I didn't know enough to do this. As soon as the new social worker took over I would ask him or her to clearly explain to Alice the reasons for their decision. Alice was old enough to understand and had a right to know.

Chapter Thirteen

Placement Meeting

'There is no way Alice can see her mother at present,' Martha said with a sigh. 'When I phone Leah she screams at me down the phone – the whole office can hear. If she can't talk sensibly I can't help her, which means Alice doesn't get to see her mother.'

It was Friday morning and, having taken Alice to nursery, I was in the placement meeting at the social services' offices. Although Martha had officially left the case, as the new social worker wasn't in place yet she had stepped in just for this meeting. A placement meeting – the meeting that has to be held within five days of a child being placed with a foster carer – is usually informal, without a chairperson. It allows those connected with the child to meet and share information so that everything that can be done is done to help the child settle. Apart from Jill, me and Martha, the only other people present were Sharon and Chris. Alice's mother and grandparents had been invited but had sent their apologies, saying they didn't feel able to attend if Chris and Sharon were present – such was their mutual animosity. The health visitor and Guardian ad Litem had also been invited, but because of the short notice – Martha had phoned us at four o'clock the previous afternoon – they hadn't been able to attend and sent their apologies. This was reasonable and their attendance at the placement meeting wasn't as essential as it would be at some of the meetings to be held in the future – Alice's review, for example.

Given that I had already met Sharon and Chris twice – at contact on Tuesday and Thursday, when I had updated them – and with them knowing so little about Alice we didn't really have much information to share. If Alice's mother and grandparents had been present, the meeting would have been far more productive and worthwhile. They could have told me of Alice's routine, her likes and dislikes, and anything I could do to help Alice settle; in turn I could have reassured them. As it was, the meeting quickly became a platform for Sharon to criticize Leah and extol her own virtues as a mother, which of course had yet to be proved. 'Did you know she …!' prefaced many of Sharon's derogatory comments about Leah. Or 'How could she! I don't believe it!'

'The sooner Alice is with me,' Sharon concluded, 'the sooner she can forget Leah and we can all get on with our lives.'

I saw Jill flinch at this last comment and I knew she couldn't let it pass without saying something. 'Children of Alice's age don't forget a parent they've had a close relationship with,' Jill said gently but firmly. 'Indeed it is important, for Alice's sake, that she doesn't forget her mother. Her mother's memory needs to be kept alive, and in a positive way, especially if she isn't seeing her.'

'But I'll be her mother soon,' Sharon put in quickly.

'You will be her stepmother,' Jill corrected, 'which is a very important role, and one that will complement the role of Alice's natural mother.' Jill had a very diplomatic way of phrasing things that diffused a situation when feelings were running high.

'But I understand what Sharon is saying,' Martha said, leaping to her defence (not for the first time). 'Alice desperately needs the security Chris and Sharon can offer so she can move on with her life. The department is very grateful that Chris and Sharon are prepared to give Alice a home; she is a very lucky little girl.' Martha and Sharon smiled at each other. 'Alice has had so much upset in her short life,' Martha added.

'But has she?' I asked, finally voicing my concerns. 'I appreciate being snatched by her mother was shocking and should never have happened, but apart from that Alice seems to have been very happy living with her mother when she was well, and then her grandparents. It's a long time since I've looked after a child who appears to have come from such a loving and, for want of a better word, normal home. She's showing no signs of the disturbed behaviour you'd expect from the type of childhood that has been described here.'

Between Martha and Sharon I'd heard that Leah had been a drug addict since the age of sixteen, had supplemented her benefit money with earnings from prostitution, had neglected Alice and was often incoherent and irrational; and that the screaming and crying coming from Leah's house when Alice had been living there were so dreadful that the neighbours had called the police. Where all this information had come from wasn't clear. Martha had been on the case for only two weeks prior to Alice coming into care, and admitted she hadn't familiarized herself with 'the file' and that it wasn't worth her doing so now because she was 'off the case'. Sharon's information seemed to be titbits of gossip she'd picked up from the estate where, prior to being re-housed, she had lived in the same road as Leah. I thought there was a grave danger of fact and hearsay becoming confused.

'Alice's disturbed behaviour may come out later,' Martha said. 'She's probably internalizing her pain or maybe she's in a state of shock,' which I couldn't disagree with.

'I appreciate that,' I said. 'I've looked after children in the past who kept their emotions under wraps and then suddenly exploded into anger or depression. But usually there is some indication in the child of the trauma they've suffered, even if it's utter silence. Alice speaks freely of her mother and grandparents. She has happy memories of their time together, as you would expect from a normal loving family, not an abusing one.'

'Alice has been brainwashed,' Sharon said, 'by Leah and those grandparents. They hate us.'

'Why do you think they hate you?' Jill asked.

'No idea,' Sharon said. Chris shrugged.

'Alice has probably made up these "happy" memories,' Martha said. 'She won't be the first child to fantasize about the idyllic childhood she has been denied.' Which again was certainly possible.

Changing the subject, Jill asked Sharon and Chris if there was anything they could tell me about Alice that could help me care for her, but there wasn't, simply because they didn't know Alice. Sharon took the opportunity to say that the reason Chris didn't know anything about Alice's routine or her likes and dislikes was that Leah had stopped him from seeing Alice and from being a father to her. Martha didn't confirm or deny this – she probably didn't know. Then Sharon continued with her diatribe against Leah, who, according to Sharon, had wanted nothing to do with Chris once Alice had been born, and had turned violent to Chris when he'd asked to see Alice. Chris nodded in agreement. What I wanted to ask, but couldn't, because it was none of my business, was why it had taken Chris four years to do anything about trying to see his daughter. Why hadn't he applied for contact? I half suspected the answer: that he hadn't really been bothered about seeing Alice until Sharon, desperate to have a child, had arrived on the scene and taken the initiative. It had been their 'luck' that at the same time as Sharon had come into Chris's life Leah's life had fallen apart to the point where she could no longer parent Alice.

Martha asked Sharon and Chris if they had any questions. Sharon wanted to know when Alice could start staying with them at weekends with a view to moving in within the month. Martha said that as soon as the new social worker was in place a timetable for the move would be drawn up. Sharon then said that she'd heard Leah was back on the drugs and also on the game to fund it, which added nothing to the meeting and was clearly designed to further smear Leah's character.

To my surprise Martha then divulged what I thought should have been confidential information. 'We've asked Leah to do a hair-strand test,' she said, 'but she's refusing at present.' Jill and I exchanged a pointed glance. Testing a strand of hair is now a reliable and widely used method of determining (among other things) if a person has taken illegal drugs in the last six months and it can identify what those drugs were. It is often used in childcare proceedings, for sadly many children come into care as a result of their parent(s) being drug addicted, and one of the issues is often whether the parent is now clean of drugs as they are claiming.

'I know why Leah's refusing to be tested,' Sharon said smugly. 'It's obvious. She knows she'll be caught out and test positive.'

'Will you be testing Chris and Sharon?' Jill sensibly asked Martha.

Sharon looked horrified while Chris said nothing, as he had been doing for most of the meeting.

'I thought your two tests had already been requested?' Martha said, looking at Sharon.

'No! Why?' Sharon said, her voice rising.

'Hasn't your solicitor asked you to go to the clinic for a hair-strand test?' Martha asked. 'I'm sure I read some-where on the file that the forms requesting the drug tests had gone out.'

'No!' Sharon cried; then, turning to Chris, 'We haven't heard anything, have we?' Chris shook his head.

'I'll leave a note on the file for it to be chased up,' Martha said calmly, writing on her pad. 'Sorry, it must have been overlooked. I'm the third social worker on this case and things are getting lost.' She shook head. 'You will both need to have the hair-strand test because of Leah's allegation that Chris got her into drugs.'

'Bitch,' Sharon cursed under her breath.

'Don't worry,' Martha said. 'I didn't believe her, but the judge will ask for the test. Now, is there anything else?'

'Paperwork,' Jill said as Sharon seethed. 'We still haven't had the essential information forms, or a copy of the care plan.'

'I'll put a note on the file for the new social worker,' Martha said. I didn't say anything but Martha had already said she was putting a note on the file to that effect, and I thought the new social worker was going to be reading a lot of notes when he or she finally took up the position.

Before winding up Martha confirmed the contact arrangements: Alice was to see her father and Sharon on Tuesday and Thursday, and her grandparents on alternate Wednesdays, beginning the following week; and she was to have phone contact with the grandparents on Saturdays, beginning the following day. Martha closed the meeting, thanking us for coming, and we all stood. Sharon and Chris hung back to talk to Martha as Jill came away with me.

'Sharon is certainly a woman with purpose,' Jill remarked dryly as we walked down the stairs towards reception.

I nodded. 'I just hope the novelty of being a mother doesn't wear off once Alice is living with them,' I said. 'I mean Sharon's got fourteen years of parenting before Alice is an adult and I don't think Chris is going to be contributing much.'

'No, I got that impression. But then again, if what Sharon is saying is true, and Chris never got the chance to be a father, he might shine and come into his own once he's in that role.'

'Yes, he might,' I agreed. I paused at the bottom of the stairs and turned to Jill. 'But you know, I can't help feeling there's something wrong here. If Leah is as dreadful as we've been told, why don't I see something in Alice? She was living with her mother for the best part of four years. You'd have thought it would have had some effect on her. Alice loves her mother; she hasn't been neglected and I'm convinced she hasn't been abused either.'

'We'll know more when the new social worker is in place,' Jill said as we left the building. 'And having the essential information forms will help.' Before we said goodbye in the car park and went to our cars Jill said: 'Oh, yes, and Cathy, about the complaint the duty social worker made against you: I've sent in my report, and we should hear in a couple of weeks. But don't worry, I'm sure it will be fine. '

'Thanks,' I said. 'Although to be honest, I haven't had time to worry about that. I've been more concerned about Alice. I hope living with her father and Sharon is the right thing. Alice is such a little treasure, I feel very protective and want what's best for her.'

'Fortunately it's not your decision,' Jill said, which was her way of gently telling me to concentrate on looking after Alice and stop worrying about things over which I had no control.

And I tried to do as Jill had said, until Saturday evening, when I phoned Alice's grandmother for Alice's telephone contact and heard her breakdown and sob.

Chapter Fourteen

A Beam of Love

'I'm so sorry,' Alice's grandmother said, between sobs. 'Alice can't hear me, can she?'

'No, don't worry,' I reassured her. 'Alice is in another room. I'll fetch her when you're ready, and we've finished talking.' As I usually did, I'd made the first contact phone call out of earshot of the child so that I could answer any questions about the child without them hearing. But as soon as I'd introduced myself to Mrs Jones, she'd broken down in tears.

'Take your time,' I said. 'There's no rush. Alice is playing. I'll call her only when you're ready. I appreciate how upsetting all this is.'

'Oh, do you?' Mrs Jones said gratefully. 'Bless you, dear. How kind you must be. This is tearing us apart. Grandpa and I really aren't coping with losing Alice, not at all.' I heard her take a deep breath as she tried to control her tears; I really felt for her. Mrs Jones had a warm and gentle voice with a very slight Yorkshire accent. It was the voice of a doting grandmother, kind and caring.

'I'm so sorry,' she said again, after a moment, her voice slightly more even. 'I'm all right now. I promise I won't cry when I speak to Alice. The social worker told me not to, and what I can and can't say.'

Tactfully, I hoped. 'Please don't worry,' I reassured her. 'I'm sure you know what to say. Would you like me to put Alice on now and we can have a chat after you've spoken to her? She's been looking forward to speaking to you and Grandpa all week.'

'Has she?' Mrs Jones said. 'Bless her.' I heard her voice catch again. 'Yes please, put her on. I'll be fine. Thank you so much.'

I laid the receiver beside the phone and went into the breakfast room, where Paula had been keeping Alice amused with a puzzle. I'd already explained to Alice that I would be speaking to her nana first, and I'd also given Alice a demonstration of how we'd use the phone when it was set to speaker. I now took Alice into the sitting room and she scrambled on to the sofa. I sat beside her and, pressing the 'handsfree' button to engage the speaker, I replaced the receiver.

'Say hello to your nana,' I said, which Mrs Jones could now hear.

'Hello, Nana,' Alice said in a little voice, leaning towards the phone as she spoke, although it wasn't necessary.

'Hello, Alice,' her nana said, putting on a very brave voice. 'How are you, love?'

'I want to come home,' Alice said. 'I love you, Nana.'

'We love you too, pet. Very much. Are you being a big brave girl?'

Alice nodded, although of course Nana couldn't see that. 'I only cried on the first night,' Alice said.

'And you're all right now, pet?'

Alice gave a very small, 'Yes.' My heart went out to her.

'Good girl. Have you got your clothes and toys? I sent them with the social worker.'

'Yes,' Alice said quietly. 'I helped Cathy put them in my bedroom.'

'That's good. And you've got Brian the Bear to watch over you at night?'

'Yes,' Alice said again. Then she drew a deep breath.

'Yes?' Nana prompted. 'What were you going to say, love?'

'Nana, why can't I live with you and Grandpa any more? Don't you want me?'

I heard Mrs Jones's silence and knew she was fighting back her tears as indeed I was. Dear little Alice, so very innocent, asking her nana if she no longer wanted her: it was heartbreaking. I also guessed Mrs Jones would be struggling with what to tell Alice, given that the social worker would have warned her to keep off the subject of why Alice was in care, so I stepped in and offered some help.

'It's natural that Alice will need a lot of reassurance,' I said. 'When Alice asked me the same question earlier in the week I told her that you, Grandpa and her mum love her very much but it's not possible for you to look after her at present. I've explained to Alice that I look after children who can't live with their own parents or grandparents until everything is sorted out.'

'Yes, that's right, Alice,' Mrs Jones agreed; then she added, 'It wasn't our decision, love.'

'Nana, Martha told me it was because you were too old to look after me,' Alice said.

'Grandpa and I don't think we're too old, but perhaps Martha meant that nanas and grandpas usually have their grandchildren come and visit, not live with them all the time.' Which I thought was very well put. Mrs Jones then changed the subject, steering it away from Alice being in care, and asked Alice about nursery and her friends and teacher.

I felt so sad, sitting beside Alice and listening to their conversation, as her nana struggled to keep their talk on safe ground and they both fought to control their emotions. I looked at Alice, her eyes round with innocence and not really understanding why she couldn't be with her beloved nana instead of having to make do with talking on the phone – their first contact since she'd come into care. I listened to Mrs Jones, having to deny her own feelings because the social worker had told her not to cry and upset Alice. I felt it was intrusive and demeaning for her to know I was listening to everything she said and I wondered if my monitoring the phone call was really necessary. The social worker had told me to use the speaker phone, so I had to, yet I struggled with the notion that Alice's doting nana could say anything remotely detrimental to the well-being of her cherished granddaughter.

After about ten minutes of chatting with her nana Alice looked up at me and said: 'Am I allowed to speak to my Grandpa?'

'Of course you're allowed to,' I said, concerned that Alice should think otherwise.

'I'll fetch him now,' Mrs Jones said, and we heard a small clunk as she set down the receiver.

I put my arm around Alice and gave her a hug. 'You're doing very well,' I said. 'You'll be seeing Nana and Grandpa next Wednesday, which isn't long now.'

Alice just looked at me with those big brown eyes. I knew my reassurance was of no consolation – she was yearning to be with her grandparents now. We heard another small clunk as the receiver was picked up, and then Grandpa's voice came on.

'So how's my Alice?' he said with forced brightness. 'And how's Brian the Bear? Has he won any matches lately?'

'I don't play with him now,' Alice said quietly.

'But you've got him with you?'

'He's in my bedroom.'

'Well, that's good. He'll be keeping you safe at night. Have you told Cathy he sits with you when you watch the football?'

'I don't watch the football here,' Alice said.

'But you've got a television there?' Mr Jones asked. 'Can't you ask to have it on?'

Alice nodded, which obviously Mr Jones couldn't see, so I thought I should say something. 'Hello, Mr Jones,' I said. 'Cathy here, Alice's carer.'

'Hello, Cathy, pleased to meet you.'

'And you. We can talk more later, when you've finished speaking to Alice, but if you could tell me a bit more about the football Alice watches, I can make sure she doesn't miss it in future.'

'That's kind of you, Cathy,' Mr Jones said. 'Thank you for looking after Alice.' I didn't say anything. I always feel uncomfortable when someone thanks me. 'I hope we'll have the chance to meet you soon.'

'Next Wednesday,' I confirmed. 'I shall be bringing Alice to contact at the family centre.'

'That's good. Now, about the football and Brian the Bear. Alice might have told you I am a football fan and I used to support Nottingham Forest. I don't go to the matches any more, but Alice and I always watch the football on television on a Saturday afternoon. And we always have Brian the Bear, our lucky mascot, with us. We've been doing this since Alice was a toddler, even before she came to live with us. Alice's mum, Leah, used to visit every Saturday afternoon and while she was talking to Nana, Alice and I would watch the football. I've always watched it with Alice, always.' He paused and took a breath. 'I couldn't put the television on this afternoon,' he said. 'Not alone. I couldn't watch the football without Alice.' His voice broke and I heard a sob; Alice heard it too.

'Don't cry, Grandpa,' she said, her own voice quivering. 'I'll watch the football with you again soon, I promise.'

There was a moment's silence as Mr Jones fought to regain control. Then in a broken voice he said: 'Sorry, love, I'll put Nana back on.' He left the phone in tears.

I hugged Alice, who was close to tears herself. She rested her head against me as I swallowed the lump in my throat. It's never easy when a child first starts having to speak to their loved ones on the phone, especially for a young child who isn't used to using a phone, but this was one of the most upsetting phone contacts I'd ever been party to, and I'd monitored plenty during my years of fostering.

After a few moments we heard Nana pick up the phone. 'Hello, Alice,' she said, her own emotion carefully under control. 'Grandpa's a bit tired. He's gone for a lie-down. He sends his love and he'll see you on Wednesday.'

Alice nodded.

Mrs Jones then talked about subjects that were neutral and not likely to upset them – nursery, what Alice was wearing and what she'd had to eat. Mrs Jones asked Alice if there was anything she would like her to bring with her on Wednesday. Alice shook her head sadly; then suddenly she brightened and said: 'Chutney. I have cheese and chutney sandwiches here, but there's something wrong with the chutney.'

'You shouldn't say that,' her nana cautioned. 'It's not polite.'

'Ask Nana which brand it is,' I whispered to Alice, 'and I'll buy some the same.'

Alice did. 'It's home-made,' her nana said proudly. My spirits fell, but then rose again as Nana added, 'I've a pot left. I'll bring it with me on Wednesday and you can have it at Cathy's.'

'Thank you very much,' I said, loudly enough for Mrs Jones to hear.

'You're very welcome. Alice loves that chutney. I'll have to make some more. That's the last pot. Is there anything else you need?'

'I don't think so,' I said, 'but when you've finished speaking to Alice perhaps we could have a chat and you can tell me about Alice's likes and dislikes?'

'Yes, love, that would help put my mind at rest.'

Mrs Jones talked to Alice for another five minutes or so, again searching for safe, non-emotive topics, which wasn't easy: they were missing each other so much that all topics seemed to lead back to their separation and loss. Mrs Jones asked Alice if she'd like her doll's pram with her but Alice said, no, she wanted to leave it at her nana's house so she could play with it there again. Presently her nana wound up. 'Well, love, I expect it's getting near your bath and bedtime. We'll see you on Wednesday. I can't kiss you goodnight, so shall I send a big kiss down the phone?'

'Yes please, Nana,' Alice said.

'Be ready to catch it, then.'

'I will,' Alice said. She moved to the edge of the sofa and, leaning forward, towards the phone, cupped her little hands in front of her, ready to catch the kiss.

'Are you ready?' her nana said. 'Here it comes. Don't miss it.'

We heard Nana blow a kiss and we waited as it flew down the phone, transported on a beam of love, and landed into Alice's little outstretched hands. Closing her hands around the kiss, Alice carefully drew it to her face before letting it go on her cheek.

'I've caught it, Nana. I've got your kiss.'

'Good girl. Have you got a kiss for me, love?'

'I have,' Alice said. Again she leant towards the phone, then said: 'Are you ready, Nana? Are you ready to catch my kiss?'

'Yes, I'm ready, love. I'm here.'

Alice pursed her lips and, drawing a deep breath, blew a big kiss down the phone. We saw it disappear. Borne on the same beam of love that had carried Nana's kiss to her, Alice's kiss winged its way down the telephone line to her beloved grandmother, who was waiting to catch it at the other end. 'Did you catch it, Nana?' Alice asked after a moment, having given it time to arrive. 'Did you catch my kiss, Nana?'

'I did, love, I did. I'll share it with Grandpa. Night, love, see you on Wednesday.'

'Night, Nana.'

Chapter Fifteen

A Dreadful Mistake?

I took Alice into the breakfast room to continue playing with Paula and returned to the sitting room, where I closed the door so I couldn't be overheard. When I picked up the receiver, the speaker phone automatically switched off. 'Alice is with my daughter in another room,' I assured Mrs Jones.

I'd intended that we'd spend some time talking about Alice, when I would reassure Mrs Jones as best I could and she would tell me of Alice's routine and her likes and dislikes, so that I could make Alice's time with me more comfortable; but Mrs Jones needed to unburden herself and all I could do was listen. She began immediately, with the day Leah had snatched Alice.

'I told Leah it was the wrong thing to do,' Mrs Jones said. 'But she wouldn't listen. She was so desperate that they'd take Alice away and give her to Chris, and she'd never see her again. I told her she should let Alice go into care and then get her solicitor to sort it out, but she wouldn't listen.'

'Yes,' I agreed. Mrs Jones had given Leah sound advice.

Mrs Jones then went back over the six months Alice had been living with them, prior to coming into care. 'We were doing all right,' she said. 'I know we're a bit old to be parenting a young child, but we always made sure Alice was at nursery on time, clean and well fed. Our biggest mistake was to ask that social worker for some help. I had a hospital appointment and Martin – Alice's grandpa – was going to take me. We asked the social worker if someone could take Alice to nursery that morning. They took it as a sign we couldn't cope.'

'Usually the social services are pleased to put in help to keep families together,' I said.

'I don't know,' Mrs Jones sighed. 'Perhaps this was the excuse they were looking for to take Alice away. We didn't get any help, just more visits from social workers, leading up to the court cases. You know, they took us back to court three times. I've not been well and I was physically sick with worry each night before we had to go. The first two times we went to court the judge wouldn't grant them the court order to take Alice away. He said there was insufficient reason. But the third time he did. I don't know what was different, other than that we'd asked for help with the hospital appointment, but by then we were too exhausted to put up a fight and Alice had to go into care.' Mrs Jones stifled a sob.

'You can't blame yourself,' I reassured. Certainly the first part of what Mrs Jones had said fitted in with what

I knew: the social services had returned to court three times before the Interim Care Order had been granted, although the reasons for this I didn't know.

'We did our best for Alice,' Mrs Jones continued. 'But it wasn't good enough. We've lost her and I think Leah is blaming us.' She stopped again to catch her breath.

'It's very difficult for me to comment,' I said. 'I don't know enough about the circumstances that brought Alice into care. But what I do know, and what I have said to the social worker, and will be saying again, is that Alice has been very well looked after. She is a delightful child and a great credit to you and your daughter. You should all be very proud of her. It's a long time since I've looked after a child who's been so well brought up.'

It was a moment before Mrs Jones could speak. 'Thank you, love, so much,' she said, her voice faltering. 'That means a lot to me.'

'Before Alice came to live with you,' I asked, 'did Leah look after her?'

'Yes, although we've always played a big part in her life.'

'I can tell. Alice has many fond memories of you and Grandpa, as well as her mother.'

'Cathy, can I speak frankly to you? I'm not saying anything I haven't told the social workers, but Alice's father is a very wicked man. He was the one who got Leah into drugs; he deals in them, or used to. He treated Leah dreadfully; he beat her up more than once. He's never been a father to Alice, and now they are going to send Alice to live with him and that Sharon woman. It's shocking, and Leah is so desperate I'm frightened she will do something silly.'

I hesitated. I didn't know what I should or could say, for while I knew Alice's father hadn't been involved in her life in the past, I didn't know the truth of Mrs Jones's claim of him beating Leah or starting her on drugs.

'Has Leah been found now?' I asked.

'Yes. She handed herself into the police on Wednesday.'

'Is she still in police custody?'

'No. Thankfully they let her off with a caution, although she's been told not to go to the nursery or try to contact Alice. The police were very fair. They said they recognized that snatching Alice was an act of desperation, so they wouldn't prosecute her, but they told her to get medical help.' I was relieved that good sense had prevailed. 'I think it was me letting Leah see Alice that led to Alice being taken into care,' Mrs Jones added tearfully.

'I'm sorry, I don't understand. When was this?'

'When Alice came to us, six months ago, when Leah couldn't cope, the social worker – not Martha, but a different one – said that because of Leah's mental problems I mustn't let Alice see her, or speak to her on the phone. They said they would set up supervised contact so that Alice could see her mum, but it didn't happen – I don't know why. But tell me, Cathy, you're a mother: how could I stop my own daughter from seeing her child? Where is the milk of human kindness? I couldn't do it, so I used to let Leah into the house so she could see Alice. There was never a problem; Leah always behaved herself – I made sure of it. The one time she arrived having been smoking something I sent her packing. But the social services found out I'd been letting her in to see Alice and they told the judge, and also that we'd all spent Christmas together. And I'm pleased we did. We had a lovely time and I think it will turn out to be our last Christmas together as a family.' Mrs Jones stopped as her voice broke again.

What the truth of all this was I'd no idea, but given what I knew of Alice's case, I could accept what Mrs Jones was saying. I also knew that if Leah was going to stand any chance of having her daughter returned to her, she needed to get medical help, speak to her solicitor, and stop screaming at the social workers as Martha had said she had been doing. I waited until Mrs Jones had stopped crying before giving her the best advice I could.

'Leah must try to engage with the social workers,' I said. 'There is a new one taking up Alice's case soon, so Leah can start afresh. Also she must make sure her solicitor is aware of all the background information. It is important. Does he know what you've just told me about Alice's father's violence and drug dealing? Was it ever reported to the police?'

'I don't think so. Leah was scared of Chris. He threatened her.'

'Leah must tell her solicitor all this,' I said again. 'Also – and you can tell me to mind my own business – is Leah on any medication to help her?'

'She was, but I don't know if she still takes the tablets. She said they made her feel ill.'

'I really think she needs to go back to her doctor and talk to him about her condition. If Leah's been prescribed medication then she should be taking it. If she has problems with one tablet then her doctor may be able to prescribe something else. It's important if she is going to try to make a case for having Alice returned to her, which I assume she will.'

'Oh, yes. Alice is the most important person it the world to Leah. I know she's lost her way, but she loves her daughter dearly.'

What I said to Mrs Jones was common sense really, but so often when we're in a crisis we can miss the obvious. Mrs Jones thanked me and said she would speak to her daughter and tell her what I'd said. We said goodbye.

I replaced the receiver and sat for a moment thinking, before I went to run Alice's bath. It wasn't helpful for a 'them and us' situation to develop between the social services and the family of a child who was considered to be at risk. But this had clearly happened in Alice's case, where Mrs Jones (and doubtless Mr Jones too) and Leah viewed the social services as the enemy, who were against them. I could appreciate why. If what Mrs Jones had said was true, then no help or support had been given to keep Alice with her maternal family and, worse, Alice was now being fast-tracked to a father who appeared to have a history of violence and drug dealing. Possibly Mrs Jones was misrepresenting the situation out of loyalty to her daughter; or had a dreadful mistake occurred? In all my years of fostering I had always been able to see the reasons why a child had been brought into care, and that there had been no alternative if the child was to be kept safe. Now, I had serious doubts.

Chapter Sixteen
Breaking the Rules

The first thing Alice said when she woke on Wednesday morning was: 'Am I seeing Nana and Grandpa today?'

'Yes, you are, love,' I was finally able to say. 'This afternoon.'

I knew how long her wait had been – twelve days since she'd come into care, plus the three days before that when Alice had been missing with her mother. And the waiting, the gap in Alice's life, seemed to have been highlighted by the regular contact she'd been having with her father and Sharon. When I'd taken Alice to the family centre the day before to see her father, Alice had asked: 'Why do I have to keep seeing him, and not Mummy or Nana?'

I'd explained to Alice that Mummy wasn't well enough at present, and then I'd had to rely on 'You'll see Nana and Grandpa tomorrow,' for I didn't know *why* Alice hadn't been allowed to see her grandparents sooner. There was still no sign of the new social worker, and Jill was still chasing up the paperwork.

Now, as I arrived in the playground at 1.30 p.m. to collect Alice from nursery and take her to contact, her face was pure joy. She was looking out for me and as soon as she spotted me she ran over.

'She's talked about nothing else all morning,' the playground supervisor said, also coming over. 'Please give Mr and Mrs Jones my best wishes. They're a lovely couple.'

'You know them?' I asked, slightly surprised, as Alice tugged on my arm, eager to go.

'Only from them bringing Alice to nursery. They must be devastated by all this. They adore Alice.'

I nodded. 'I'll pass on your best wishes,' I said with a smile, and came away.

In the car, during the twenty-minute journey to the family centre, Alice talked excitedly, non-stop, of all the things she was going to tell her nana and grandpa when she saw them: about her nursery, friends, teacher, me, her bedroom, Adrian, Lucy and Paula, and our cat, Toscha. But as I parked outside the family centre and cut the engine she suddenly fell silent.

'Don't worry, love,' I said, guessing that nerves had got the better of her. 'Nana and Grandpa will be feeling a bit strange too. It will be fine once we're inside and you've all met again.'

'That's Grandpa's car,' Alice said, pointing to a grey Ford Fiesta, as we walked across the car park, so I knew Mr and Mrs Jones were already inside waiting for us.

I'm often nervous meeting a child's parents or relatives for the first time, wondering if they will be friendly or hostile, critical or appreciative, and if they will take to me, but now I felt unusually calm. Having spoken to Alice's grandparents on the phone and having heard Alice talk about them so lovingly, I had no concerns about meeting them; I just felt utter relief that Alice was finally seeing them, and they her.

Alice slipped her hand into mine as I opened the gate, and we walked up the short path to the door, where I pressed the bell and the security lock released. As soon as the door sprang open and we were inside we saw them, standing side by side watching the door, waiting for us to arrive. Alice immediately dropped my hand and rushed into their waiting arms, hugging them for all she was worth. First her nana, then her grandpa, then her nana again as Mr Jones, overcome with emotion, moved to one side to wipe his eyes. Mrs Jones clutched Alice to her as though she would never let her go and allowed her tears to fall freely.

'Oh, Alice,' she said over and over again, in her warm Yorkshire accent. 'Oh, Alice, my love. Grandpa and I have missed you so much.'

'I've missed you,' Alice said in a muffled voice, her head buried in her nana's shoulder.

After a while Mrs Jones moved Alice slightly away from her. 'Here, let me have a look at you. I'm sure you've grown a good inch, lass. You're a fine strong girl.'

I smiled and remained where I was – standing to one side. I doubted Alice could have noticeably grown since Mrs Jones had last seen her, but clearly Alice's growing was something her nana and she talked about, as many grandparents do.

Alice grinned. 'I've been eating all my meals, so I grow into a big strong girl,' she said proudly.

'I can see that,' Mrs Jones said, and I saw her face crumple again.

Alice then slipped one hand into her nana's and the other into her grandpa's, and just stood looking at them, as though she daren't believe they were actually real, and thought that they might at any moment disappear. The contact supervisor had appeared from the office and was hovering by my side, ready to accompany Alice and her grandparents to the room they would use for the hour's contact.

'I'll just say hello, and then I'll come back and collect Alice later,' I said to the supervisor.

Mr Jones looked over and stepped forward to greet me. 'Martin Jones,' he said, taking my hand warmly between both of his. 'You must be Cathy.'

I smiled. 'Pleased to meet you.'

'This is my wife, Janice,' he said, transferring my hand to hers. She shook my hand warmly and I felt her love and security as Alice had.

'Hello, Cathy,' she said, her cheeks moist. 'God bless you, dear.'

They appeared a lovely couple, just as they had seemed on the phone, and I immediately took to them. They had open, honest faces, and I suspected in other circumstances laughed a lot. Mr Jones was about four inches taller than his wife, and his grey hair was streaked with white. They were everyone's idea of the perfect grandparents – warm, loving, embracing of others and completely unassuming. If they'd had my sympathy before we'd met, my heart now ached for them. They had only one hour with their cherished granddaughter, and then a two-week wait for the next hour.

Aware their contact time was ticking away, I said: 'I won't keep you now. Spend your time with Alice, and I'll see you again when I collect her.'

The contact supervisor stepped forward and, smiling, led the way along the corridor as I called goodbye to Alice, but she was so engrossed in telling her dear nana and grandpa all her news, unsurprisingly she didn't hear me.

Having met Alice's grandparents, albeit briefly, all my worries and doubts as to why Alice had been uprooted and brought into care, instead of being allowed to stay with them, resurfaced. It's none of your business, I told myself sternly as I opened the car door and left reception. You are the foster carer, you look after the child; the rest need not concern you. But without any real background information – apart from what Martha had said, which hadn't been much – it was very difficult for me to see that Alice had been in danger of significant harm from her grandparents or that their parenting had fallen below an acceptable standard, which criteria are needed to bring a child into care.

Yes, I appreciated that Alice couldn't live with her mother, but for the life of me I couldn't see why she hadn't been allowed to stay with her grandparents, which was surely the next best option. I remembered Martha had said that the social services had thought the grandparents were in 'cahoots' with Leah, as they hadn't been entirely honest. I now guessed, from what Mrs Jones had told me on the phone, that this had resulted from Mr and Mrs Jones allowing Leah to see Alice and spending Christmas together. But that was hardly a good-enough reason for bringing a child into care. Sharon had said that Mr and Mrs Jones had poisoned Alice against her father, but I struggled with that too. Perhaps I was being naïve, but I just couldn't see how Alice's nana and grandpa could have intentionally 'poisoned' or misled anyone: they just didn't seem the type.

There wasn't enough time for me to return home before I had to collect Alice again at the end of contact so, leaving the car outside the family centre, I walked to the local shops to buy a couple of items we needed. I then returned to the car and sat inside with the radio on, gazing absently through the windscreen. If one hour went quickly for me, how much quicker it must have passed for Alice and her grandparents. Very soon the clock on the dashboard clicked up the last few minutes and the radio presenter began the three o'clock news. I switched off the radio, got out and returned into the family centre.

As I entered, the receptionist looked up and smiled at me. Opening the glass partition she said, 'They're in Yellow Room. It's time. You can go straight in.'

Crossing reception I pushed open the swing doors and went along the short corridor to the yellow-painted door, where a large sign decorated with sunflowers announced 'Yellow Room'. Aware how painful it was going to be for Alice and her grandparents to say good-bye, I steeled myself before knocking on the door and slowly easing it open. Alice was sitting on the sofa between her grandparents, a book open on her lap as her grandpa read the story. They all looked up and towards me as I entered.

I smiled and the supervisor said gently, 'It's time to go, Alice.'

It was impossible to say who looked more shocked and upset as the supervisor's words slowly registered and the three of them realized that their hour together had ended. Alice stared wide eyed at her nana and grandpa, hoping against hope that it wasn't true, while Janice and Martin Jones, too engrossed in Alice to notice time ticking by on the clock on the wall, looked horrified.

Mr Jones came to first and, clearing his throat, said in a small voice: 'I guess we'd better be saving the rest of this story for next time, Alice.'

Alice looked at him. 'Why?' she asked innocently.

'Because it's time for you to go with Cathy,' Mr Jones said gently, closing the book.

Although Alice had had the experience of contact ending at a set time with her father and Sharon, she clearly hadn't realized the same would happen with her grandparents, although I'd explained. Or possibly, and more likely, Alice had simply blanked it from her mind, the thought of having to say goodbye being too painful.

'But I want to go home with you,' she said to her grandpa, desperation creeping into her voice and her face puckering. 'I want to stay with you and Nana.' She snuggled closer into his side.

'I know you do, love,' he said gently. 'But it's not possible at present. I want you to be a big girl and go home with Cathy.' He took the book from Alice's lap as Mrs Jones sat motionless on the other side of Alice, too upset to say or do anything.

'Come on, Alice,' the supervisor said gently, going over to the sofa. 'You'll see Nana and Grandpa again next week.'

'The week after next,' I corrected. 'Alice is seeing her grandparents every other week.'

'Oh, sorry,' the supervisor said, flustered. I could tell from her expression that she thought, as I did, that an hour every two weeks wasn't enough, which was why she'd assumed contact was weekly.

'We'll phone on Saturday,' I said encouragingly to Alice, trying to sound as positive as I could. But I knew this was small recompense for Alice having to leave her cherished nana and grandpa and then not see them again for another two weeks.

'No,' Alice said bluntly, her face setting. 'I want to stay with them.' She grabbed hold of her grandpa's arm and clung to him for dear life.

The contact supervisor knelt in front of the sofa so that she was at Alice's height and, resting a hand on Alice's knee, began talking to her gently. 'Come on, Alice, Nana and Grandpa have to go now. Cathy is here. It will be your dinnertime soon. What are you having for dinner?' and so on. She continued for a good five minutes, trying to persuade Alice to let go of her grandpa, say goodbye and come away with me. Mr and Mrs Jones sat either side of Alice, offering little reassurances and persuasions of their own, while all the time fighting back their tears.

Eventually the supervisor stood and looked at me. 'I think you're just going to have to take her,' she said.

I nodded and felt my stomach churn. It wasn't the first time I'd had to take a child screaming from contact, but it didn't make it any easier. 'I'm sorry, love,' I said to Alice, 'we really do have to go now. Can you be a big brave girl and say goodbye to Nana and Grandpa?'

Alice shook her head and buried herself deeper into her grandpa's side. I knew the longer I left it the worse it would be for everyone. I leant forward and reached between her grandparents; then, putting my arms around Alice's waist, I began to draw her to me. She clung tighter to her grandpa's arm and screamed. Mrs Jones stood up from the sofa and moved away, unable to watch Alice's distress.

'It's all right, love,' I tried to reassure Alice. 'We'll phone on Saturday.' I slowly eased open her fingers to release her grip from around her grandpa's shirt. Then I continued bringing her towards me, sliding her off the sofa.

Although Alice was only slight there was a lot of strength in her as, desperate to stay, she began thrashing her arms and legs. As I held her firmly to my chest the supervisor helped me to straighten. I quickly turned and carried Alice towards the door as her grandparents called tearful goodbyes behind me.

I was just through the door when I heard Mrs Jones's voice again. 'Cathy, wait a minute! I nearly forgot.'

I paused, wondering what Mrs Jones wanted, and concerned that delaying our departure was only going to upset Alice even further. She was still struggling in my arms, trying to break free and sobbing her heart out. I held on to Alice as Mrs Jones came over carrying a small carrier bag, which she hooked over my arm. 'It's the chutney,' she said, through her tears. 'Alice wanted my home-made chutney. She mustn't go without that.'

'Thank you,' I said. Then to Alice: 'Look! We've got some of your nana's chutney.' But Alice was in a very sad and dark place and not even the promise of Nana's home-made chutney could lighten her mood. 'She'll be fine once we're home,' I reassured Mrs Jones over Alice's sobs, but I could see Mrs Jones was unconvinced.

There was nothing to be gained by prolonging the agony so, saying a quick goodbye, I came away, with Alice still struggling in my arms and her screams ringing in the air. I settled her into her seat in the car and sat beside her until she was calm enough for me to drive home. Alice was quiet but the tears had stopped and I periodically glanced in the interior mirror to check on her as I drove.

Adrian, Lucy and Paula had just returned home from school when we arrived, so there was a lot going on and plenty to occupy and distract Alice. By dinnertime she had more or less recovered, although she was still quieter than usual. However, I knew that while Alice had recovered, Mr and Mrs Jones, alone again, were likely to still be devastated and plagued by the last sight of Alice being carried screaming from the family centre. I wanted to reassure them, but our next telephone contact wasn't until Saturday – four days away.

That evening, once Alice was in bed, I did something I shouldn't have done and had never done before. I broke the contact arrangements set down by the social worker and phoned Mr and Mrs Jones to put their minds at rest. They were so grateful it was pitiful.

Chapter Seventeen

Warm and Cosy Inside

'I can't thank you enough,' Mr Jones said for the third time. 'We've been beside ourselves with worry, after seeing Alice so upset. Have you got time to speak to Janice? She'll be so relieved to hear from you.'

'Of course,' I said. I waited as Mr Jones passed the phone to his wife.

Having reassured Mr Jones, I repeated what I'd said to Mrs Jones: that Alice had recovered, had eaten a good meal and was fast asleep with Brian the Bear tucked under her arm. Mrs Jones thanked me for phoning, as her husband had done, and then thanked me again for looking after Alice. Her voice was thick with emotion as she said again how much they missed Alice, and that all the uncertainty surrounding Alice's future was tearing them apart.

While I sympathized with their position, very much, I could offer little reassurance. I said that I thought once the new social worker was in post things should start to improve, as we'd all be better informed. I felt Mr and Mrs Jones's pain personally and could empathize with their position. They reminded me of my own parents in their love and dedication to their grandchild, and I knew that had my parents been placed in a similar position – stepping in to look after a grandchild and then having the child taken away – they wouldn't have coped either. It was the stuff of nightmares and my heart went out to them.

At least reassured that Alice was no longer distressed, Mrs Jones began talking again about the background to Alice coming into care. Some of what she said she'd already touched on when we'd spoken on the phone on Saturday, while other things she said were new. I didn't think she was trying to win me over or prejudice me against others involved in Alice's case – it wasn't said vindictively; she just needed to unburden herself, and perhaps she thought that as I was an experienced foster carer I could give her some hope.

She said that her daughter, Leah, had had mental health problems but had been quite well on the tablets the doctor had prescribed until she'd met Chris, who had introduced her to drugs and alcohol. In Mrs Jones's opinion the drugs and alcohol had combined with the medication and made Leah's mental health problems resurface, which was certainly possible – it was a toxic combination. Mrs Jones said that the health visitor had been concerned about Leah last August and had persuaded her to seek help. Leah had gone to her doctor, the doctor had notified the social services (the correct procedure if he had concerns for Alice's safety) and a social worker had visited Leah at home. According to Mrs Jones, instead of giving Leah help so that she could keep Alice, the social worker had said she would start proceedings to take Alice into care. Alice would have gone straight into foster care had Mr and Mrs Jones not stepped in and looked after her. Mrs Jones blamed the social services for not helping Leah, and on the face of it, although social workers are often criticized for leaving children at home longer than would seem wise, it did appear that Leah hadn't been given the support that could have kept the family together, particularly when she'd done such a good job of parenting Alice in the past. But then again, quite possibly Leah's condition was so acute that removing Alice was the only viable option. Clearly I didn't know.

'It's shocking,' Mrs Jones wound up. 'Leah asked for help and was rewarded by having her child taken from her, and now they are giving her to that wicked, wicked man. We were looking after Alice well,' she added tearfully. 'She was happy here. I really don't understand.'

I didn't understand either but I didn't have the facts, and it certainly wouldn't have been professional for me to collude with Mrs Jones against Alice's father. The social services must have had good reason for making the decision to send Alice to her father and Sharon, and once the new social worker was in place I was sure all would become clearer. There was little I could say over what I'd already said, so I changed the subject and asked Mrs Jones, as I had intended to do at contact, if she had photographs of herself, her husband and Leah that I could put in Alice's bedroom. 'Children find it very comforting to have photographs of their loved ones with them,' I said. 'I'll frame the photos and put them on the shelf in Alice's bedroom.'

Mrs Jones said she'd find some photographs and bring them with her to the next contact. I then asked her about the suitcases which, again, I had intended to do at the end of contact, had Alice not been so upset. 'The suitcases you used for Alice's clothes,' I said, 'shall I return them at the next contact?'

There was a short pause before Mrs Jones answered quietly, 'Cathy, would you mind keeping them there, so that you have them ready if Alice is brought back to us.'

'That's fine,' I said, although I think Mrs Jones knew her hope of having Alice returned was unrealistic. Martha had said the care plan was to have Alice living with her father and Sharon by the end of the month, which was now less than two weeks away. Having not heard anything to the contrary, I assumed this to still be so. So too did Sharon, as I found out at contact the following day.

'When is Alice going to start staying with us for weekends?' Sharon almost demanded the moment Alice and I walked into reception at the family centre. 'Martha said at that placement meeting it would be soon.'

'I'm sorry, I don't know any more than you do,' I said, drawing Sharon to one side so Alice couldn't hear her. 'I know it's frustrating. What have the social services told you?'

'Nothing,' Sharon said, clearly annoyed. 'Alice hasn't been allocated a social worker and the team manager has just left. I keep phoning the social services and leaving messages but no one gets back to me. Can she stay this weekend?'

'I'm sorry, I can't make that decision,' I said. Clearly Sharon had an inflated view of my power. 'My role is to look after Alice. I don't make decisions about contact or her future.'

'I know your role is to look after her,' Sharon said, agitated. 'But it should be my role. Alice is getting far too attached to you. It's not good. I'm her mother now.'

'Alice understands I'm her foster carer,' I reassured Sharon. 'And that I look after her while she is with me. It's nice that she can feel close to me during this time but obviously she knows I'm not her mother.'

'She talks about you and your family all the time at contact,' Sharon said, still peeved, and apparently viewing Alice's attachment to us as threat to her relationship with Alice.

'It's only natural she talks about us. She sees a lot of us and it's important she feels included.'

'Here's the photo,' Sharon said ungraciously, changing the subject and thrusting her hand into a carrier bag. I'd asked Sharon and Chris at the last contact if I could have a photo of them for Alice's bedroom, as I had asked Mrs Jones when I'd phoned her the previous evening. Although it wasn't as important for Alice to have a photograph of her father as it was for her to have one of an absent parent – Alice saw her father twice a week – it would be nice for Alice to have photographs of all her family. Also, given the animosity between her parents it was important that I was seen to be fair and treat all parties equally.

'Thank you,' I said, looking at the photograph Sharon had handed me of her and Chris, heads together, smiling into the lens. 'I'll put it in a frame and stand it on the shelf in Alice's bedroom.'

Sharon nodded, slightly appeased.

While Sharon and I had been talking, Chris had been hovering with the supervisor and Alice to one side. Chris was a man of very few words and Sharon did the talking for both of them. I now went over to say goodbye to Alice and to tell her that I would collect her in two hours, but as I did I saw her bottom lip tremble and her face grow very serious.

'What is it, love?' I said, bending down so I was at her height.

'Are Nana and Grandpa here?' she asked in a small voice, clearly expecting them to be.

'No, love. You saw them yesterday.'

'I want to see them tonight,' she said. Rubbing her eyes, she began to cry.

The supervisor – the same one as the previous day – looked at me knowingly, for we both appreciated how very confusing and upsetting it must be for Alice to see her grandparents at the family centre one day and her father and Sharon the next.

'We'll phone Nana and Grandpa on Saturday,' I said, trying to reassure Alice. 'You're seeing your dad and Sharon this afternoon.'

'I don't want to see them,' Alice cried. 'I want to see Nana and Grandpa.' Out of the mouths of babes, I thought, but who could blame her? Alice was only saying what she felt; she didn't know that her loyalties and affection were supposed to be transferring from her mother and grandparents to her father and Sharon.

Sharon looked affronted and pretty indignant. 'The sooner she stops seeing them, the better,' she said, referring to Alice's grandparents. Chris said nothing.

The supervisor, bless her, then stepped in and, before Alice could upset herself further, gently took her by the hand and began steering her towards the contact room. 'Let's play that Hungry Hippo game,' she said, distracting her. 'I bet I can beat you.' I waited until they had disappeared through the swing doors and then I left.

That night as I tucked Alice into bed she glanced at the photograph of her father and Sharon, which I'd propped on her bookshelf.

'Cathy?' she asked innocently, her eyes growing wide and questioning. 'Who do I have to love?'

I stroked a strand of hair away from her face. 'Alice, pet, love isn't something you *have* to do. It's something that comes from your heart; that you feel deep inside. When you love someone that person becomes very special to you, so that you want to be with them lots. And when you are with someone you love you feel all warm and cosy inside.' Which I thought was pretty good for an instant explanation of love.

Alice looked at me and her little brow furrowed as she considered what I'd said. 'I feel warm and cosy when I'm with my mummy, and Nana and Grandpa,' she said. 'I love them and they are very special to me. But when I'm with Sharon I think about my real mummy, and I want to be with her. Is that wrong?'

'No, love, it's not wrong. You haven't known Sharon for very long. Perhaps in time you might grow to love her. I know she'd like you to.'

Alice frowned as she thought again. 'OK. I'll try to love Sharon. I'll try to feel warm and cosy when I think about her like I do with my mummy and Nana and Grandpa.' She closed her eyes, screwed up her face and held her breath as though in deep concentration. After a moment, she breathed out with a long sigh and opened her eyes. 'No. I don't feel warm and cosy about Sharon yet. I'll try again tomorrow.'

Chapter Eighteen
Bad Practice

In the absence of a social worker, all I could do was carry on as I had been doing and follow the routine that I'd established in the first two weeks. I took Alice to nursery each weekday and on the days she had contact I collected her at 1.30 p.m., when I took her to the family centre. At the end of contact Alice never had a problem separating from her father and Sharon but unsurprisingly continued to have great difficulty in saying goodbye to her nana and grandpa, although it was never as bad as that first time, when I'd had to carry her screaming from the family centre.

At the next contact Mrs Jones gave me the photographs I'd asked for – one of her husband and her, and one of Alice with her mother. They'd been taken the Christmas before, at the grandparents' house, and my heart ached each time I looked at their smiling faces. Alice was sitting on her mother's lap, and they wore the party hats they'd pulled from the Christmas crackers. The Christmas tree could be seen glittering in the background, and Alice and her mother were clearly having a great time at what had turned out to be their last family celebration all together. I put these two photographs in frames and stood them on the shelf in Alice's bedroom beside the framed photograph of her father and Sharon. I often found the photograph of her father turned to face the wall, while those of her mother and grandparents were at the front of the shelf, looking out over her bedroom – Alice's little statement of her needs.

I pushed the two empty suitcases belonging to Alice's grandparents to the very back of the cupboard under the stairs, for realistically Alice wouldn't be going anywhere until a new social worker was in place, and then it wouldn't happen immediately. Martha had said that the parenting assessment of Chris and Sharon was only half complete, so I guessed that it had come to a standstill and wouldn't be complete until the new social worker was in post. Once the assessment was complete, assuming it was positive, contact between Alice and her father would be increased to include weekend stays, in preparation for her going to live with them. From my previous experience, I estimated all this would take at least six weeks, if not longer, from when the new social worker took up post, and there was no sign of that happening yet. It wasn't good social work practice, but there always seems to be a shortage of social workers, so posts are left empty for far longer than they should be and cases are delayed.

Alice had been with me just over a month when Sharon phoned the social services, furious, demanding to know of the duty social worker what was happening and threatening to put in a formal complaint. I could understand her frustration, although I would have liked to hear the same commitment from Chris, who was after all Alice's father. The duty social worker phoned me (not the same duty social worker who'd reported me) and, having admitted she knew nothing about Alice's case and couldn't find the case file, asked me if I had a copy of the care plan and could I tell her what was happening. Lost case files should be a thing of the past now, as all the files at the social services are held on computer at a central database. I told the duty social worker I was still waiting for a copy of the care plan and the essential information forms, and then I told her what little I knew of Alice's case. She thanked me and went off to try to pacify Sharon.

The Easter holidays approached, and on the last day of term Alice's nursery had an Easter parade. All the girls went to school dressed in long flowing skirts, and blouses, reminiscent of fashion in the 1870s when the tradition of the Easter parade had begun. They wore Easter bonnets they'd made in class, which were tied under their chins with brightly coloured ribbon. The boys went as Easter chicks, with bright yellow headpieces they'd made in the shape of a chicken's head, and long brown beaks jutting over their foreheads. There was much laughter and excitement as parents and children saw each other and met on their way into nursery. I was getting to know some of the other mothers now and we smiled and laughed with our children.

As I entered the school gates I happened to turn and look back over my shoulder. I don't know why; possibly I'd sensed someone was watching me. As I looked, over to the other side of the road, standing half concealed behind the large oak tree, I saw Alice's mother. I recognized her immediately from the photograph Alice had in her room. Even from a distance Leah's slight frame, light brown shiny hair and big round eyes just like Alice's were unmistakable. I was shocked and concerned. Leah would have known she shouldn't have been there. But as our eyes met I sensed she hadn't come to make trouble, just to catch a glimpse of her daughter going into nursery all dressed up.

I didn't know how Leah knew it was the Easter parade; perhaps she had a friend with a child at the school who'd told her. Or possibly she didn't know and had waited outside the school before, hoping to catch a glimpse of her daughter, and I hadn't seen her. It crossed my mind to tell Alice her mother was there, so that she could at least see her and wave, or possibly even go over and say hello, for it was six weeks since Alice had seen her mother and she was missing her dreadfully. But I knew I couldn't. It would have been unsettling for Alice to suddenly see her mother after all this time without any warning, and I couldn't be sure Leah would be able to handle the meeting and act rationally – just saying hi, complimenting Alice on her outfit and then going. Added to which there were no contact arrangements in place for Alice to see her mother and I couldn't take it upon myself to establish contact. Had Alice been seeing her mother regularly and we had bumped into her in the street it would have been a different matter and we could have spoken. But for now I followed the acceptable, sensible and very sad option of continuing into nursery without Alice being aware her mother was close by.

When I came out again I looked for Leah, with the intention of speaking to her and reassuring her that Alice was all right – which was acceptable, as Alice wasn't with me. But as I emerged from the playground and looked over the road to the tree, and then up and down the street, there was no sign of her. It would be some weeks before I saw Leah again and then her situation had deteriorated badly.

I am not a great fan of football, but every Saturday afternoon I dutifully sat on the sofa with Alice and Brian the Bear and watched the football. Alice knew more about football than I did, and sometimes more than the referee, who she often felt was in need of her advice when it came to penalties. I guessed she'd learnt all this from her grandpa – they'd been watching the football together for as long as Alice could remember. So every Saturday Alice's whoops of joy and groans of disappointment echoed round our house as goals were scored or missed, and teams won or lost. If a player performed well Brian the Bear jumped up and down on Alice's lap and clapped his hands; if a player performed badly then Brian hid his head in shame. Lucy thought I'd totally lost the plot one Saturday when she came into the sitting room to ask me something and I hushed her and said unless it was an

emergency she'd have to wait until the penalty had
been taken.

'But you don't know anything about football,' Lucy
said, throwing me an old-fashioned look.

'But I'm learning fast, and I know you have to be quiet
when a penalty is about to be taken.'

Alice nodded furiously and put her finger to her lips
to hush us both. Lucy hovered by the sitting-room
door, and the three of us watched in silence as the
penalty was taken, and missed! Alice and I groaned;
Brian the Bear hung his head in shame; and Lucy
raised her eyes skywards. 'You'll be taking up knitting
next,' Lucy said – the next most unlikely pursuit after
my watching football, but if it made Alice happy of
course I would.

At 6.00 p.m. on Saturdays when we phoned Alice's
grandparents, the first thing her grandpa always asked
was, 'Did you see the football, Alice?' They then spent
some time chatting about the pros and cons of the game,
who had played well and which player hadn't been on
form. Watching the football and being able to discuss it
was providing a positive link for Alice between the life
she had left and was missing at her grandparents', and
the life she was now living with me.

One Saturday evening when I phoned, and before I'd
put the phone on speaker so that Alice could talk to her
grandparents, Mrs Jones said quietly to me: 'Don't put
Alice on yet. I need to close the sitting-room door. Leah
is with us, in the kitchen, and Alice mustn't hear her.'

It was sad that Alice couldn't speak to her mother and
vice versa, but with no contact arrangements in place,

Mrs Jones knew we couldn't just take it upon ourselves to instigate phone contact and let Alice speak to her mother. Mr and Mrs Jones had previously been told by Martha that phone contact was for her and her husband only, although obviously as Alice was no longer living with them they could have Leah in their home whenever they wanted. Such constraints on contact are put in place to safeguard the child, but without a social worker in post I was concerned that Alice's case wasn't being reviewed as it should, and that phone contact could have been established between Alice and her mother, but hadn't because there was no social worker to make the decision.

On Easter Sunday my parents joined us for lunch and we held our usual Easter egg hunt, which was confined to the house, as it was raining outside. We saw my parents every couple of weeks and Alice had immediately warmed to them and they to her. And while my parents were considerably older than Alice's own grandparents, she had clearly found an added security in being with them and looked upon them as surrogate grandparents. For their part they were soon doting on their new grandchild.

There were four chocolate eggs hidden for each of the children, and one each for my parents and me. Alice had already been given two eggs at contact – one from her grandparents, and one from her father and Sharon – and would have happily eaten the lot in one sitting had I not explained that this was inadvisable, as it was likely to make her ill. Lucy, on the other hand, had panicked at the sight of so much chocolate and, when my parents had gone home, tried to give her eggs to me.

'I won't ever eat all these; you have them,' she said, bringing her chocolate eggs into the kitchen.

I'd seen Lucy panic before when faced with too much food. When we went to my parents' for dinner I always plated up Lucy's food, giving her a little, which I knew she could cope with, rather than the very generous portions my mother dished out. Now, Lucy wasn't able to delight in the prospect of unlimited chocolate, as most children and teenagers would have done, but saw it as an insurmountable hurdle, and just wanted to get rid of the eggs.

'OK, love,' I said, not making an issue of it. 'Put your Easter eggs in that end cupboard and if you fancy a piece of chocolate you can help yourself. Otherwise I'm sure they won't go to waste.'

As it was, gradually, over the next couple of weeks, bit by bit Lucy ate her chocolate, and enjoyed it. As with many people with mild eating disorders (as I thought Lucy had), when presented with too much food or the expectation to eat, she felt out of control and panicked, rejecting it all. Left to her own devices Lucy could manage food, a little and often; the problem came with mealtimes, when you were expected to eat enough to see you through to the next meal. And with so much social-izing in our society centring around meals, mealtimes were a continual worry for someone like Lucy. Yet I felt that little by little we were getting there and although Lucy's eating still worried me she was slowly improving.

* * *

We had a few warm spring days during the Easter holiday from school and we made the most of the weather by visiting parks and having an away day to the coast. Two days before the weekend and the start of the new term, on Monday, Alice's health visitor phoned, having just heard that Alice had been taken into care. She was called Glenys and she said she'd visited Alice at her mother's, and also once at the grandparents'. She was phoning because it was time for her to make a routine visit, so we made an appointment for her to come the following day at 2.00 p.m. I was looking forward to meeting her; she'd been involved in Alice's life for the last three years, so I assumed she'd be able to fill in some of the missing background information which might help me better look after Alice, and also explain why Alice had been removed from her grandparents and was going to live with her father.

But the following day, once Glenys was seated on the sofa in the sitting room, with Alice being entertained by the girls in another room, she said: 'So when is Alice going back to her grandparents? I assume she's here on respite – to give them a rest.'

'No,' I said. 'Alice won't be returning to her grandparents. She's going to live with her father and his new wife, Sharon.'

'What!?' Glenys exclaimed, astonished. 'I didn't even know there was a father on the scene. There certainly wasn't during the three years when I visited Alice. Are you sure? There must be some mistake.'

Chapter Nineteen
A Quick Fix

Not only had the health visitor never met Alice's father but Leah had never mentioned him during any of Glenys's visits. Glenys's understanding was that Leah had become pregnant by accident, and was parenting alone with the support of her own parents, Janice and Martin Jones, but with no input from Alice's father. And while Glenys had realized the previous summer, when Leah's mental health had deteriorated, that Leah needed help, and had been relieved when Alice had gone to stay with her grandparents, she couldn't understand why Alice had been brought into foster care. She'd assumed, as I would have done, that Alice would have stayed with her grandparents for as long as necessary.

'I feel dreadful,' Glenys said, her face creasing with anxiety. 'I was one of the professionals who raised concerns about Alice, and was therefore responsible for her coming into care. But what could I do? Leah obviously wasn't coping. I never dreamt Alice would be taken away for good.' Blaming herself, she looked close to tears.

'You weren't the only one who had concerns,' I said. 'The doctor also contacted the social services.'

Glenys nodded. She went on to say that Leah had been a very good parent to Alice (which I'd guessed), and that although Leah had had mental health problems the medication had allowed her to function normally, which was what Mrs Jones had told me. Glenys also said that Leah was an intelligent girl who had put her own life on hold to raise Alice. 'Once Alice was settled at school, Leah was going to continue her education,' Glenys said. 'She hated being on benefits and wanted to get a good job. She wanted to do the best for Alice, and always put Alice first.'

I nodded. 'Did you know the neighbours had reported Leah for screaming at Alice?'

'No,' she said, surprised. 'I certainly never heard Leah raise her voice to Alice when I was there – far from it. She was always very loving and protective. I wonder how the neighbours could be certain it was Alice Leah was screaming at? There might have been someone else there.' She paused in thought. 'Leah suddenly started behaving oddly last August. Perhaps she did start screaming at Alice; I suppose it's possible. But what I don't understand is why Alice couldn't have stayed with her grandparents?'

'I really don't know,' I said again. 'Was Leah on drugs, or drinking to excess? Martha said these had been issues.'

'Not as far as I know. There was never any evidence of illegal drugs or alcohol abuse when I visited, or I would have said.'

I nodded.

Glenys was clearly a kind and caring person, conscientious in her role as health visitor and very upset at the outcome for Alice. She had acted correctly in alerting the social services and doctor when she'd had concerns for Alice's safety, but it didn't stop her feeling she'd been the instigator in the break-up of Alice's family. 'I feel so responsible,' she said again. 'And there's no chance of Alice going back to her grandparents?'

'I don't think so.' I couldn't allay Glenys's concerns for Alice's future and neither could she relieve my worries about whether it had been the right decision to bring Alice into care.

Once we'd finished talking I called Alice into the room and Glenys weighed her, measured her height and asked her how she was doing. Alice told Glenys she was now in foster care and I was looking after her, which obviously Glenys knew. 'But when I stop living with Cathy,' Alice continued, perhaps seeing salvation in Glenys, 'I have to go and live with a new mummy. She's called Sharon. But I don't want a new mummy, I want my old one. Can you get my old mummy, please?'

Tears welled in Glenys's eyes at Alice's naïve request. She looked at Alice and then at me, clearly not knowing what to say to reassure Alice. There was nothing I could say beyond what I'd already said, so I told Alice she was staying with me while 'everything' was being sorted out. Then I changed the subject and pointed to the jigsaw Alice had been doing.

'It's for a six-year-old,' I said proudly. 'Alice has nearly completed it. All by herself!'

'Well done!' Glenys said to Alice. 'That's very clever. You're going to be as bright as your mum.' She stopped and looked as though she could have bitten off her tongue.

'It's all right,' I said. 'We talk about Alice's mother. It helps keep the memory alive, that and her photograph.'

Glenys nodded, relieved, and, reaching out, gave Alice a big hug before going over and admiring the jigsaw.

Glenys was with us for over an hour, talking to Alice and then again to me – lamenting the break-up of Alice's family, for which she held herself responsible. Before she left Glenys said she would visit us again in six weeks if Alice was still with me, but if I had any worries in the meantime about Alice's health or development I should phone her at the clinic. Alice and I saw her to the door, and when she'd gone Alice told me she was a nice lady and her mummy had liked her.

I thought about what Glenys had said – that Leah was an intelligent woman and a good mother, who had wanted to give her daughter the best. I thought about Glenys's shock when I'd told her that Alice wouldn't be returning to her grandparents or her mother, but was going to her father and Sharon. I thought about it, and my doubts and misgivings increased. Something hadn't felt right at the start, when I'd first met Alice and realized she'd been loved and well looked after. Alice's nursery teacher and now her health visitor had confirmed this and clearly felt as I did that taking Alice from her grandparents and giving her to the father she'd never known didn't make sense. Either the grandparents were not the people they appeared to be and the social services had good reason to take Alice away, or a dreadful mistake had occurred and the family had been wrenched apart unnecessarily, causing untold pain and emotional damage. Was it possible, I wondered, that with all the changes of social worker (Martha had been the third) errors of judgement had occurred and a 'quick-fix' solution of sending Alice to her father had resulted?

When the Guardian Ad Litem phoned the next day to say she would like to visit us the following week I was very pleased. The Guardian ad Litem – appointed by the judge in childcare proceedings – has an in-depth knowledge of the case, having read the files and been in close contact with all parties. She (or he) advises the judge on what is best for the child. I knew the Guardian would be able to answer my questions and, I hoped, reassure me that the correct decision had been made. Her name was Carole and she made an appointment to visit us at 4.30 p.m. the following Wednesday, but when she came, far from allaying my concerns, she added to them.

Chapter Twenty
Nail in the Coffin

I told Alice that Carole would be coming to see us. Alice had some understanding of the Guardian's role in deciding her future, and had met Carole once before when she'd been living with her grandparents. But as usual after seeing her nana and grandpa, Alice was very subdued and clingy, and needed lots of cuddles and reassurance that it wouldn't be long until Saturday when she could speak to them on the phone. When the Guardian came, not realizing this, or forgetting that Alice had just had contact with her grandparents, she tried to chat to Alice, who was on the sofa, snuggled close into my side.

'How was nursery today?' Carole asked brightly, as one would normally, talking to a child. 'What did you do?'

Alice nodded glumly but didn't say anything.

'Don't you like nursery?' Carole asked. 'You used to. I remember you told me.'

'Alice is just a bit sad from having said goodbye to her nana and grandpa,' I explained. 'She saw them this afternoon,' I reminded her.

'Ah, right,' Carole said. 'Yes, of course.' Then to Alice: 'How are Nana and Grandpa? Did you play some games?'

Alice gave a small nod, but still wouldn't be drawn. Carole's well-meaning, jolly conversation wasn't really appropriate for the loss and sadness Alice was feeling, having parted from her dear grandparents an hour before. Then Alice lifted her head from where it had been resting against my arm and, looking at the Guardian, said defiantly: 'My nana and grandpa still love me. And they won't stop loving me!'

Carole was clearly taken aback. 'Of course they won't stop loving you,' she said uncomfortably.

'And my mum still loves me,' Alice added, with the same challenge to Carole to prove differently. 'Even though you won't let me see her!'

The Guardian looked even more uncomfortable, for it was clear Alice was holding her responsible for her loss. 'Can we talk privately?' Carole said to me.

I nodded and, taking Alice from the sitting room, called upstairs to the girls, who were in their bedrooms, relaxing after school. Lucy appeared on the landing and I asked her to look after Alice until I'd finished speaking to Carole. Alice scampered upstairs, pleased to be in Lucy's company rather than that of the Guardian.

In the sitting room, with the door closed so we couldn't be overheard, Carole said, 'I don't think Alice has a very good understanding of what is happening in her life.'

'No,' I agreed. 'And with so little information, and no social worker to ask, it's very difficult for me to explain to her. Indeed I'm not sure I understand myself. Why was Alice taken from her grandparents and brought into care? And why is she being sent to live with her father, whom she doesn't know? I've been a foster carer a very long time, and until now I have always been able to see the reasons for the decisions that have been made, but not with Alice.' I stopped and felt my cheeks flush with emotion.

The Guardian looked at me, puzzled. 'But I thought contact with dad and step-mum was going all right?'

'It's all right,' I said, feeling the Guardian was missing the point. 'But why is Alice going to live with them? From what I understand her father didn't have any involvement in her life until all this happened.'

'But he wants her now,' Carole said, almost with tunnel vision. 'And it's encouraging that Sharon is so enthusiastic in her new role as a parent.'

'Too enthusiastic,' I heard myself say. Carole looked at me. 'Sharon is all over Alice like a rash. But no one seems to mind that there is not the same enthusiasm coming from Chris.' By 'no one' I meant the decision makers – i.e. the Guardian, the social services and ultimately the judge, which I knew Carole would realize.

Carole remained calm and composed, to the point of being distant. 'I think it is generally accepted that Chris would never have sought custody of Alice had it not been for Sharon. So it's very lucky for Alice that Sharon wants her.' Which was what Martha had said.

'Alice is very resentful of Sharon trying to be her mother. I know Sharon probably means well, but she is going about it the wrong way. Sharon needs to back off, stop telling Alice to call her Mum and let Alice warm to her in her own time.' I was putting it bluntly, but I'd had two months of having to defend Sharon to Alice every Tuesday and Thursday before and after contact.

'I'll mention it to Sharon when I visit them,' Carole said. 'Thank you for bringing this to my attention. Obviously we want the transition to Dad and Sharon to go smoothly.'

Clearly the Guardian and I were viewing the situation from very different perspectives. I wasn't sure if she was being deliberately evasive or hadn't realized the depth of Alice's feelings. 'You know Alice has a very strong bond with her own mother,' I said. 'She desperately needs to see her.'

'It's not possible at present,' Carole said. 'Leah's not well. She wouldn't be able to hold it together for contact. She hasn't the self-control.'

'What about telephone contact?'

'The same applies.'

'So I assume as soon as Leah is well enough, contact will be set up so Alice can see or at least speak to her mother?' I said, championing what Alice needed.

Carole nodded, took a notepad from her bag and wrote what I assumed was a reminder.

'What I don't understand.' I persisted, 'is why Alice couldn't have stayed with her grandparents. She's very close to them and they appear to have done a very good job looking after Alice. She misses them greatly.'

Carole looked up, and her reply left me absolutely astounded. 'I wasn't sure about that either,' she said. I stared at her open-mouthed as she continued. 'The first social worker involved in Alice's case felt that Janice and Martin Jones were too old to offer long-term care to Alice. They're in their sixties now, which means they'll be in their seventies by the time Alice is a teenager.'

'And that was the reason for Alice being taken from them?' I asked, amazed. 'Their age in ten years' time?'

'Mainly.'

'But Alice won't need long-term care from her grand-parents. Surely once Leah is better she'll be able to look after Alice again, as she has done in the past?'

'I did raise that at the time, but the social worker felt going to dad was the best option. Then of course there was the issue of Mr and Mrs Jones failing to cooperate with the social services.'

'How did they fail to cooperate?' I asked – or rather nearly demanded. 'By allowing Alice to see her mother at Christmas?' I could feel my pulse rising and I knew I had to calm down.

'It wasn't just Christmas,' Carole said evenly. 'They allowed Leah into their house to see Alice at other times.'

'But Leah is their daughter, for goodness' sake! Alice is their granddaughter. How could they not allow them to see each other?'

'Precisely. That's what the social services said – another reason for sending Alice to live with father. He and Sharon won't have the same problem.'

'That's for sure. There's so much animosity between Chris and Mr and Mrs Jones that when Alice goes to live with her father I doubt she'll ever see her mother or grandparents again!' I took a breath and lowered my tone. 'Leah's not an ogre,' I said. 'By all accounts she was a good mother until she became ill last August. What support was put in to help her?'

'I don't think it was much,' Carole replied. 'Chris and Sharon were very eager to have Alice, and the social services thought it was the best solution. But to be honest the final nail in the coffin for Alice ever being returned to her grandparents was their role in Alice's abduction.'

'They didn't have a role in her abduction, did they?' I asked, amazed. 'I thought they were at home looking after Alice when Leah snatched her.'

'Yes, they were. That's the point. They didn't stop Leah from taking Alice.'

'What were they supposed to do? Fight off their daughter?'

Carole looked at me and was silent for a moment. I thought I had probably said too much. 'I appreciate your concerns,' she said after a while, in the same even tone. 'When we have a new social worker or team manager in place, I'll meet them and review some aspects of Alice's case. Would that put your mind at rest?'

'Yes, it would. Thank you. I only have Alice's best interest at heart.'

Carol nodded and made another note on her pad, perhaps reminding herself to meet the social services, or perhaps that I was becoming too involved, or above my station — who knew? But at least I had had my say and voiced my doubts, for I would never have forgiven myself if the wrong decision had been made, Alice's life had been ruined and I'd said nothing.

Carole then asked about Alice's health, her routine, her general disposition and if she'd ever mentioned an 'Uncle Mike'. I had to think for a minute, for the name rang a bell. I fetched my log notes and flipped back to when Alice had first arrived.

'Yes, I thought so,' I said, running my finger down the page. 'Alice said it was Uncle Mike who collected her and her mother from the hide at the quarry, where they'd been sleeping. She said Uncle Mike was Mummy's friend.'

Carole nodded and made another note. 'That's correct. He is Leah's partner and he played a vital role in finding Alice after Leah had snatched her. He acted as go-between, the intermediary, passing text and phone messages between the police and Leah as they negotiated for Alice to be returned. He is a positive influence on Leah and has stood by her.'

'Good,' I said. 'Are they are still together?'

'As far as I know.'

Before Carole left, she said she would be in touch again as soon as the new social worker was in post and she'd had a chance to speak to him or her, which she hoped wouldn't be too long. I hoped so too, for although clearly Alice wasn't in any danger, as a child in an abusive home would have been, it was unfair and emotionally damaging to Alice to leave her in limbo – in foster care. If she was going to live with her father, as seemed likely, then the social services needed to get her settled there as soon as possible so that she could get on with the rest of her life. At present her life was on hold, and if I wasn't very careful all the good parenting that her mother and grandparents had done would be undone by the uncertainty. Alice was old enough and intelligent enough to worry about what was going to happen to her.

Chapter Twenty-One

Kitty-cat

Caring for Alice was an absolute delight, and I knew the children and I were growing very attached to her. Apart from looking like an angel with her large innocent eyes, delicate features and silky hair, she had such a gentle and loving disposition you felt you just wanted to pick her up and hug her forever. Foster carers always form attachments to some degree to the children they look after – it's natural, and we're always sorry to say goodbye to the child, even when he or she is returning home or going to a loving adoptive family – but I knew we were all going to be heartbroken when the time came for us to say goodbye to Alice. Lucy and Paula had asked me more than once if Alice could stay with us permanently, while appreciating it wasn't possible, as she was going to live with her father and Sharon. And while Adrian didn't say much I knew he too would miss Alice dreadfully, for he had become like an older brother to her. Often Alice would seek out Adrian in preference to the girls or me, and the first thing she always asked me when she came home from nursery or contact was: 'Is Adrian home?' If he was she would scamper off to find him.

However, we didn't have to worry about saying good-bye to Alice yet, for without a social worker, Alice wasn't going anywhere. Two months rolled into three and while Alice was as happy as we could make her, she still bitterly missed her mother and grandparents, and pined for them daily. She often shared her many happy memories of their time together – helping Nana bake a cake, going swimming with Mummy, her last birthday, Christmas, etc. Alice still never mentioned her father and I naturally assumed the reason she had no fond memories of him was that she hadn't see him until Sharon had come into his life and Alice had come into care.

I began a Life Story book for Alice, as I do for all the children I foster for longer than a couple of weeks. It is a record of the child's time with us and includes photographs and memorabilia – for example, cinema tickets, the child's drawings and merit certificates from school. A Life Story book is a tangible aide-mémoire which the child takes with them when they leave to supplement their memories of their time with us.

Each evening when Alice was in bed I wrote up my log notes, although there wasn't much new to report, and a lot of repetition: 'Alice had a good day at nursery. Alice asked when she could see her mum and said she misses her lots. Alice told me about the time her mum took her to the fair. Alice was subdued after seeing her grandparents; she would like to see them more often' and so on.

Then one day Alice suddenly stopped talking about her mother. When I went into her bedroom I found the photograph of her mother had joined that of her father and Sharon at the back of the shelf. The first time it happened I assumed Alice must have moved the photograph by accident, for it was always at the front of the shelf. I returned it to its usual position – looking out over the room. The next day when I found it again facing the wall, I realized it probably wasn't an accident and Alice was making a statement: that she was feeling very rejected by her mother and was now rejecting her.

'Why isn't Mummy watching over you?' I asked Alice, glancing at the shelf, as I tucked her into bed that night.

Alice shrugged and pulled a face but didn't say anything.

'Alice,' I said, perching on the bed. 'Even though you are not seeing your mummy, she still loves you.'

'Does she?' Alice asked woefully. 'How do you know? You don't know she still loves me. I don't think she does. Otherwise she would get better quickly so I can live with her.' Her bottom lip trembled and her eyes filled with tears.

'Oh, Alice, love,' I said, taking her in my arms. 'I know Mummy loves you. I know she is trying her hardest to get better so she can see you. But sometimes things go wrong with us that take a long time to heal. Look at James in your class. He broke his leg weeks ago and it's still in plaster. It will get better eventually but it is taking a long time.'

'But James can still come to school with his bad leg,' Alice said with a sob. 'He can still see his friends, but I can't see my mummy while she is ill.' I knew I had chosen the wrong illustration.

'Alice, pet, sometimes when we are ill it can stop us doing the things we want to do – the things we would like to do when we are well. Some illnesses affect our bodies, like when you have a cold in winter, while others affect the way we think and feel, and sometimes the way we behave.' It was so difficult trying to explain mental health problems to a small child.

'Was it Mummy's illness that made her take me to the quarry to sleep?' Alice asked after a moment.

'Yes, love, that's right. She was very worried – what we call anxious. I think she's been like that for a while, which is why you were staying with your nana and grandpa. Mummy thought she was doing the right thing when she took you to the quarry, but it wasn't the right thing really. Her illness made it difficult for her to know what to do for the best.' Alice gave a little nod. 'Alice, I know Mummy loves you and I know you are probably angry with her for being ill, and not being able to see you, but try not to blame her. I'm sure she wants to be well so she can see you again. Don't be angry with her any longer, love.'

Alice gave a little nod, and then looked up at me from my arms. 'I'm not *very* angry with her,' she said. 'Just a little bit. I'll try and remember what you said.'

'Good girl.' I tucked her into bed and kissed her goodnight. Before I came out I rearranged the photographs in a line on the shelf so that they were all looking out over her bedroom and she could see them from her bed. The photographs of her mother and grandparents stayed in place at the front of the shelf but the photo of her father and Sharon soon found its way to the back again. I knew that once Alice had a social worker, and the timetable of Alice's move to her father had been drawn up, I would need to spend a lot of time talking to Alice, preparing her for going to live with her father and Sharon, for without it I could see there were going to be huge problems, with Alice rejecting Sharon, and Sharon feeling affronted and then rejecting Alice. The social worker would also talk to Alice and prepare her for the move.

It was early June, and Alice had been with me for three months when Jill phoned to tell me that I had finally been cleared of the complaint the duty social worker had made against me on the day Alice had arrived. Jill said that the complaint had been investigated and the department was satisfied I had acted correctly and responsibly, which was a great relief. Jill also said that on behalf of the fostering agency she had put in a complaint to the social services that Alice had been with me for twelve weeks, largely without a social worker, which was completely unacceptable. However, June was to turn into a month of complaints, for having just been cleared of one, I soon found myself faced with another!

Two days after Jill phoned to say I was in the clear, she phoned again to say that Sharon had complained to the Guardian ad Litem about me and the Guardian had phoned Jill. According to Sharon, I was undermining the relationship she had with Alice, sabotaging her efforts to be a mother and 'stealing her daughter'. Ludicrous as the allegations appeared to me (and Jill), I still had to disprove them, for if I had been intentionally undermining Sharon's role as stepmother, for whatever reason, it would have been viewed most seriously. As a foster carer I am expected to remain neutral and work with all parties in a case, in line with the care plan, sometimes having to put my own opinions and feelings to one side, which I hoped I had been doing.

Not for the first time I was pleased I'd kept detailed log notes. I went through my file and highlighted the many instances when I'd positively reinforced to Alice Sharon's role as stepmother, as well as the negative comments Sharon had made to me, suggesting she had problems with my role: 'She [Alice] likes you more than me. Why does she go to you? She keeps taking about you. I've told Alice to stop talking about you while she's with Chris and me,' and so on. It was a pity Sharon was so insecure in her role as stepmother that she viewed me, the foster carer, as a threat, instead of another professional who was working in Alice's best interest. Jill gave a verbal explanation to the Guardian substantiating what I'd said, and I didn't hear any more. However, I was very wary in my future dealings with Sharon, and maintained very detailed log notes of any conversation I had with her that could be misinterpreted or used against me. Sometimes, as with Alice, looking after the child was the easy bit; it was some of the adults connected with the child who caused the problems and hard work.

Whether it was Jill's complaint to the social services that Alice had been without a social worker for three months, or whether the position would have been filled anyway, I didn't know. But that same week, on Wednesday morning, when I answered the phone there was a female voice on the other end, introducing herself as Alice's new social worker.

'Good gracious!' I exclaimed. 'Really? I'm very pleased to hear from you.'

She gave a little laugh, then said her name was Kitty and apologized for Alice having been left for so long without a social worker, which I thought was a good start.

'It's not your fault,' I said.

'No, but I feel responsible. When I accepted this post I told the authority I wouldn't be able to take up position for three months. They should have brought in an agency social worker to fill the gap.' She was right, although I guessed the cost of providing an agency social worker from the authority's hard-strapped budget had convinced them they could get by without. 'I've familiarized myself with Alice's file,' Kitty continued. 'I see there are a number of appointments outstanding. It seems Alice hasn't had her medical yet.'

'No, she hasn't,' I said. 'Or a dental check-up.' All children brought into care have these check-ups, but they have to be initiated by a social worker.

'If you could arrange these appointments, I'll prepare the form for the medical.' This had to be signed by the social worker. 'And Alice's three-month review is due now,' Kitty continued. I was impressed: Kitty had been in the post for only twenty-four hours and was already abreast of Alice's case. The review Kitty referred to was a meeting where all parties connected with the child come together to make sure everything is being done as it should for the child's benefit and assess what needs to be done. 'I want to set up the review straightaway,' Kitty said. 'Are you able to attend tomorrow? I have found a room free here we can use, and a chairperson. I've booked them for ten o'clock.'

'Yes,' I said, even more impressed. 'I'll be there.'

'And I'll need to see Alice before the review. Can I come this evening at five? I know she sees her grandparents this afternoon, and I appreciate it's rather short notice, but I need some understanding of Alice before I go into the review.'

'Yes, that's fine with me, although Alice may be a bit tired.'

'I understand. I'll keep it short on this occasion and see her for longer next time. I'd appreciate it if you could update me, now please, from the time Alice came into care.'

I then spent twenty minutes bringing Kitty up to date: Alice's routine, nursery, her general disposition, her likes and dislikes, the love she felt towards her mother and grandparents, how difficult she was finding it to bond with her father and Sharon, and that Alice's greatest wish was to return home – to her mother or grandparents.

Kitty thanked me and asked if there was anything I needed. 'A copy of the care plan and the essential information form,' I said.

'You haven't been given them yet?' she asked, amazed.

'No, there's been no one there to send them. Every-thing was put on hold until you arrived.'

Kitty tutted. 'I'll chase it up A.S.A.P.'

'Thank you.' I hesitated, unsure if I should voice my opinion, but decided to go ahead anyway. I would be working closely with Alice's social worker and I thought she should know how I felt, although how much credence she gave my views was obviously up to her. 'Alice's grandparents are heartbroken at losing Alice,' I said. 'Mrs Jones often speaks to me on the phone after she has spoken to Alice and offloads. I appreciate what she tells me is likely to be prejudiced in favour of her daughter, Leah, but I do have concerns as to why Alice is in foster care instead of remaining with her grandparents, and also about the plans for Alice's future. Alice hasn't been abused, I'm sure of it; on the contrary, she was very well looked after. And if half of what Mr and Mrs Jones are saying about Alice's father is true, then there is real cause for concern.'

Without any hesitation Kitty said, 'From my under-standing of the case so far, I have concerns too. There are huge discrepancies in what the parties are saying and further investigation needs to be carried out. At present I'm not sure who is telling the truth, but if at all possible I shall find out.'

Kitty didn't say what exactly the discrepancies were, or what exactly needed to be investigated – I assumed it was confidential and not relevant to my looking after Alice – but I was considerably relieved. For three months I'd worried and angsted over Alice, feeling there was something badly wrong and that her case wasn't as clear cut as the social services believed. Now, with the arrival of Kitty, I felt I had something of an ally, and that Kitty would re-examine Alice's case and delve deeper into what members of Alice's family were saying.

Kitty finished our conversation as she had begun it, by apologizing for Alice not having a social worker for so long, then said she'd see us at 5.00 p.m., and would I tell Alice she was coming.

I told Alice in the car when I'd collected her from nursery and was taking her to see her nana and grandpa at the family centre. 'You've got a new social worker,' I said. 'She phoned me this morning and she sounds very nice. She's coming to see us later and she's called Kitty.'

Alice laughed. 'Kitty?' she chirped from the back seat. 'That's a funny name. Paula calls the cat Kitty sometimes.'

I smiled. 'Yes, but you'd better not tell your new social worker that. She might not be impressed.'

'No,' Alice agreed. 'I won't have time with all the other things I have to tell her – like I miss Mummy and want to live with her or Nana.'

Chapter Twenty-Two

'Just One Line'

Alice hadn't had a social worker for three months and now suddenly things were moving quickly. Kitty visited us as planned at 5.00 p.m. prompt and was as pleasant in person as she'd sounded on the phone. Alice, although tired, immediately warmed to her, as Kitty sat on the floor and joined in with the farmyard set Alice was playing with. I asked Kitty if she wanted some time alone with Alice, but she (sensitively) said that as this was her first visit, and Alice didn't know her, she'd prefer it if I remained in the room. I sat unobtrusively at one end of the sofa while Kitty played with Alice, and Alice told her, in no uncertain terms, that she knew she couldn't live with her mummy because she was ill, but why couldn't she live with her nana and grandpa because they weren't ill, and they loved her?

'That's what I'm trying to find out,' Kitty said.

'You don't know?' Alice demanded, looking up, a toy pig in one hand and a cow in the other.

'Not all of it, not yet. I've only just come into the job. I'm still learning all about you.'

'But that's disgraceful!' Alice reprimanded.

Kitty smiled. 'I completely agree and I promise to do better in future.'

But Alice's censure was nothing compared to what lay in store for Kitty the following day at the review. I'd never known a review to be arranged so quickly – usually it takes weeks to book a room and a chairperson, and send out invitations to the various parties. But at 10.00 the following morning I was seated, with six others, at a large rectangular table in one of the committee rooms at the social services' offices. I saw straightaway that Leah wasn't present but that Mr and Mrs Jones, who hadn't felt able to attend the placement meeting, had come. You could have cut the atmosphere with a knife.

The chairperson opened the meeting by introducing himself – Ray Sturgess – and then passed to Kitty, Sharon and Chris, Martin and Janice Jones, and me. The Guardian, health visitor and Jill had been invited but because of the short notice had prior appointments and sent their apologies.

'And Alice's mother?' the chairperson asked. 'Are we expecting her?'

'No,' Mrs Jones said tightly. I could see she was bursting with emotion.

'I tried to invite her,' Kitty said, 'but she screamed at me down the phone.'

Ray, who was also taking the minutes, made a note of those present and then explained he was an independent chairperson unconnected with the social services, and that this was the first review for Alice Jones. He then made the fatal mistake of asking who would like to speak first.

'Me, please,' Mrs Jones said, no longer able to keep a lid on her feelings. Folding her arms on the table, she leant forward and glared at Sharon, who was directly opposite. 'Why are you trying to take Alice away from her mother?' she demanded. 'What has Leah ever done to you? You should be ashamed of yourself! You hussy! And as for you,' she said, now glaring at Chris, 'you're the nastiest, vilest scumbag I've ever come across. I bet you haven't told your new wife what you did to my daughter! And if you think you are having my grand-daughter, you can forget it! Over my dead body!' And I thought it might be if she didn't calm down – she'd gone scarlet and was shaking. When I'd seen Mrs Jones before and after contact, she'd always been so passive and gentle, but now, without Alice present and able to express herself freely, she was giving vent to her anger and frustration. Perspiration glistened on her forehead.

But if I'd been taken aback by Mrs Jones's uncharacteristic outburst, Chris and Sharon's retaliation was even more vitriolic.

'Witch!' Chris shouted across the table. 'You never liked me, you old bag! Like mother like daughter!' It was the most I'd ever heard him say.

'Too right we've never liked you!' Mr Jones yelled back. 'Because of the way you treated our daughter. I knew the first time I clapped eyes on you you were bad news and I was proved right! Leah was eighteen when you got her hooked on drugs and then got her pregnant!

She was fine until she met you. She'd just done her A-levels and was going to university. Then you came into her life. You're vermin! You should be exterminated!'

Ray, chairing, raised his hand for quiet, but Mr Jones and Chris ignored him. 'Your daughter's a bleeding nutter,' Chris shouted.

'If she's unbalanced it's because of the crack cocaine you put her on! You little shit! There was nothing wrong with Leah's mind before you got her on drugs. And she'd recovered once you'd gone and was doing all right with Alice, for four years! But you couldn't let her be, could you? "Here, Leah, one little line won't hurt. Just for old times' sake,"' Mr Jones mimicked. 'But it did hurt. It combined with the tablets the doctor had given her and sent her over the edge. I knew as soon as she phoned me asking for help last August something was wrong. It was you! If I was ten years younger I'd take you outside now and teach you a lesson you wouldn't forget!'

'Stop!' Ray said, loudly enough to be heard. 'Finish. Or I'll call a halt to this meeting now. This is not what a review is about.'

No, I thought, but I was learning an awful lot.

The room fell silent as Mr and Mrs Jones, Chris and Sharon quietly seethed. Mr Jones was now as red in the face as his wife, while Kitty was writing furiously. And while the chairperson was right – the purpose of the review wasn't to use it as a slanging match – Mr Jones had just said something very revealing, if it was true. I wondered if Kitty was sufficiently familiar with Alice's case to understand the significance of what he had said and make the same connection I had done.

She had.

Looking up from her notepad, she fixed her gaze on Chris. 'So you had a relationship with Leah again last August?' Kitty said.

'And he gave her cocaine,' Mr Jones put in, 'which combined with the tablets the doctor had given her and made her very ill.'

'Let Chris speak,' the chairperson said.

'I only saw her once,' Chris admitted reluctantly.

'He's told me about that,' Sharon put in. 'We don't have any secrets.'

'You're naïve, if you believe that,' Mr Jones retaliated, addressing Sharon but talking about Chris. 'He stayed at Leah's flat for the whole of August. He even told Leah he was sorry and wanted them to get back together again so that he could be a father to Alice. I didn't believe him, but Leah was taken in. And what with the cocaine he gave her, building up her hopes and then deserting her again, she was a broken woman. When he left she broke down completely, and the neighbours heard her screaming and called the police. She couldn't cope and it's your fault! Alice came to live with us a week later.'

'I don't know how you sleep at night,' Mrs Jones added.

Chris shrugged. Sharon looked so taken aback that I wondered how much of this she already knew.

The room was quiet again. Kitty and the chairperson were both writing, for if what Mr and Mrs Jones had said about Chris was true it threw a new light on the circumstances leading to Alice being brought into care and also raised big concerns about Chris and his suitability to parent Alice. It certainly sounded plausible and would also explain how Leah had successfully parented Alice for four years before it had all fallen apart last August.

'Is the department aware of all this?' the chairperson asked Kitty.

Kitty shook her head. 'Not as far as I know. I only took over the case three days ago and I'm still getting to grips with it and talking to all the parties.'

The chairperson nodded. 'And where's mum now? Why isn't she here?'

Mrs Jones answered: 'Leah can't be in the same room as him,' she said, pointing to Chris. 'She has lost Alice, the most important person in her life, because of him, and she isn't coping. She can't sleep or eat, and I'm desperately worried about her.'

The chairperson nodded sympathetically and I glanced at Chris and Sharon, who were expressionless. The chairperson then turned to Kitty. 'Can you tell us where the department is with Alice's case?'

Kitty explained the care plan, which was that Alice would remain in foster care (on an Interim Care Order) while Chris and Sharon's parenting assessment was completed. She said that based on a recent psychiatric report the recommendation to the court would be that Leah couldn't parent Alice.

'So you have a psychiatrist's report on Leah?' the chairperson clarified.

'Yes,' Kitty said, but she didn't give any details. With Chris, Sharon and Leah's parents present it would have broken confidentiality.

'And Alice's father and his wife are the only people being assessed to parent Alice?' the chairperson asked.

'Yes,' Kitty said.

'What about us?' Mr Jones asked. 'Why aren't we good enough to look after Alice any more?'

Kitty looked at the chairperson as she spoke. 'It was felt that because of Mr and Mrs Jones's age, they would not be suitable long-term carers for Alice. However, this is one of the issues I shall be looking into and discussing with my manager. If it is felt that Mr and Mrs Jones's age isn't an issue here, then we will start a parenting assessment of them too.'

I heard Mr Jones sigh with frustration, probably feeling that having raised their own children and also having helped look after Alice, it was a bit of a nonsense to 'assess' them as parents. But it is normal practice to assess those wishing to parent a child who is in care, and what Kitty had said was very positive. I hoped Mr and Mrs Jones realized that. Kitty wasn't simply accepting everything that had been passed to her by the previous social workers but was looking into Alice's case afresh, as she had promised to do.

However, Kitty's next statement, while necessary, wasn't so optimistic, and contained very unwelcome news. 'If, when the parenting assessments are complete,' she continued, 'it is felt that neither Mr and Mrs Jones nor Chris and Sharon are suitable, then the department will be looking for an adoptive home for Alice. Alice is young enough to be adopted and she deserves the stability an adoptive family would offer.'

'What!' Mr Jones and Sharon cried, united in their dismay. Chris said nothing while Mrs Jones looked close to tears.

'This is normal procedure,' the chairperson said. 'After all, Alice has to live somewhere until she's an adult.' Then to Kitty: 'What is the most likely outcome for Alice, from what you know of the case at present?'

Concentrating on the chairperson, and carefully avoiding eye contact with Mr and Mrs Jones, Kitty said: 'That Alice lives with her father and his new wife, Sharon.'

Sharon smiled, relieved; Mrs Jones bit her bottom lip to stop herself from crying; and Mr Jones said angrily: 'You'd send my granddaughter to live with a man who is a violent drug dealer! I don't believe I'm hearing this. It's a travesty of justice!' He was white now and his hands, clasped before him on the table, shook uncontrollably.

'There is no proof of that,' Kitty said, addressing the chairperson. 'And Chris's hair-strand test for drugs has come back negative.'

Looking at Mr and Mrs Jones, the chairperson explained that a hair-strand test was a test recognized by the courts, where a strand of hair was tested for drugs, and which could identify substances in a person's body as far back as six months.

'Six months, you say?' Mr Jones demanded of the chairperson. 'When did he have this test?'

'A month ago,' Kitty confirmed to the chair.

Mr Jones raised his eyes in disgust. 'Well, you can't test what's not there. Look at the length of his hair: he had it cut for the test!'

Kitty, the chairperson and I looked at Chris. It was true that his spiked hair had only about a four-to-six-weeks' growth on it. 'They said it was enough to do the test,' Sharon put it in defensively. But that wasn't the issue. If Chris had had his hair cut a couple of weeks before the test and had therefore given the bare minimum sample, it suggested he had something to hide. I remembered that at the placement meeting when the hair-strand test had first been mentioned Chris and Sharon had told Martha they hadn't received the forms for the test, which Martha had thought had been sent out. Had Chris and Sharon purposely delayed the test so that Chris could have his hair cut and let it grow again, drug free? I tried to remember from seeing Chris at contact when he'd last had his hair cut, but it wasn't something I'd paid much attention to.

The chairperson was looking to Kitty for explanation. 'I really don't know,' she said. 'I'm the fourth social worker on this case and my predecessor requested the test. When I'm back in the office I can check in the file and see what sample was given and when.'

'I think you should,' the chairperson said. 'The barrister is sure to raise it in court.' He paused and wrote again. 'And do we know what Alice wants in all this?' he finally asked.

'To live with her mother,' Kitty said. 'Or failing that her grandparents.'

'Yes, she does,' I agreed.

'Perhaps you could tell us about Alice?' the chairperson asked me. 'You are the person who sees Alice the most.'

I started with a résumé of Alice's routine. I said she ate and slept well, attended nursery, and was an intelligent and sociable child who was a delight to look after. 'Alice has clearly had some very good parenting,' I continued, addressing the chairperson. 'She has many happy memories of her mother and grandparents – Mr and Mrs Jones. She has a strong bond with them and loves them deeply. My family is doing all we can to make Alice's stay with us as happy as possible, but Alice deeply misses her mother and grandparents. The sooner everything is sorted out, the better.'

'And contact with Dad?' the chairperson asked. 'How is that going?'

'Alice always has a pleasant time and appreciates the attention,' I said.

'But is there a strong attachment yet?'

Without looking at Sharon and Chris, I shook my head. I couldn't fabricate what wasn't there. Despite Alice seeing her father and Sharon for two hours twice a week, at the end of three months Alice was no closer to her father and Sharon than she had been at the beginning.

The chairperson finished writing and then asked if there was anything else anyone wanted to raise before he closed the meeting.

'Lots,' Mr Jones said, shaking his head sadly, 'but what's the point when we're not being believed?'

'You don't know what she's like!' Sharon pounced, referring to Leah. 'You haven't seen her when she's off her trolley. Chris has, and she's a nutter.'

'Of course Chris has seen her like that!' Mr Jones retaliated. 'He gave her the drugs that made her that way!' He was wagging his finger across the table at Chris, while Mrs Jones was close to tears again. The meeting looked as though it was going to finish as it had begun – with both sides of Alice's family shouting accusations.

'This is not helping,' the chairperson intervened. 'I thank you all for coming and I am closing the meeting.' The room fell quiet as he set a date for the next review, in three months' time. He then suggested Mr and Mrs Jones left first, and Sharon and Chris waited behind until Mr and Mrs Jones had had time to leave the building, to avoid confrontation in reception. It was like dismissing naughty children from the classroom.

As we watched, Mr Jones tenderly helped his wife to her feet and she linked her arm through his. I smiled at them as they passed. They looked so sad and dejected, as though they hadn't a hope in the world. Mr and Mrs Jones left the room and the rest of us waited in awkward silence until the chairperson deemed enough time had elapsed and said that Chris and Sharon could go now. After they'd gone I left with Kitty and the chairperson.

'Leah is very unstable at present,' Kitty confided outside the committee room. 'She phoned me this morning on her way to the doctor. She was threatening suicide, and also said that as she'd nothing left to lose she might as well take Alice again. I've alerted the school. As far as I'm aware, Leah doesn't have your address, Cathy, but obviously if you see her in your street, phone the police.'

'The poor woman must be desperate,' I said. 'I do hope she gets the help she needs.'

The chairperson and Kitty nodded; we said goodbye and went our separate ways. Later, that afternoon, I was to see for myself just how desperate Leah was, for when I went to collect Alice from school Leah was waiting outside.

Chapter Twenty-Three

Hunger strike

Leah was standing, half concealed, behind the large oak tree on the opposite side of the road to the school, as she had been two months previously when she'd wanted to catch a glimpse of Alice dressed up for the Easter parade. Now, as I walked along the pavement towards the tree to cross the road at the crossing, she stepped out from behind its protective cover and straight into my line of vision. All manner of things flashed through my mind at that moment as our eyes met, and my pulse soared with anxiety. There was no sign of the tender, warm openness that I was used to seeing in the photograph Alice had in her room. Taken the previous Christmas, Leah had been cuddling Alice on her lap and they were both laughing. Now her face was set hard, and the wildness and anger in her eyes said she was desperate and out of control. For a second I thought she was going to attack me.

I stopped. Leah was a yard or so in front, blocking my path, and it crossed my mind to dart round her, over the road and into the school, where I could call the police.

But I didn't. Perhaps I saw something behind her eyes that said although she was angry and out of control she was also very scared, and reachable. Without Alice with me I felt I could take a chance.

'Hello, Leah,' I said evenly. 'How are you?'

She started with surprise – that I recognized her?

'I'm Cathy,' I continued in the same even tone. 'I'm so pleased to meet you at last.' I smiled and, closing the gap between us, offered my hand for shaking. She didn't take it; I hadn't really expected her to, but I was hoping that being polite and non-threatening would defuse the situation and that she might respond.

Leah continued to stare at me; then she looked around, her lips moving as though she was trying to think out what to say, but she didn't speak. Although, like Alice, she was an attractive girl, she was now very unkempt and clearly hadn't been looking after herself. Her slender frame looked thin and malnourished, and her long brown hair hung limp and lifeless around her shoulders. She was very pale, and her once-delicate features now looked gaunt, which seemed to deepen and accentuate her large brown eyes. Her gaze flickered back to mine.

'Leah,' I said gently. 'I know how much you miss Alice, but you can't see her here, love. You'll get into trouble.'

She shrugged, despair and dejection replacing her previous anger. 'I've got nothing to lose,' she said, her voice quivering. 'I need Alice. I love her.'

'I know you do, and she loves you, lots. But you are going to have to do what your social worker and solicitor tell you and see Alice at supervised contact for now.

I can't let you see her here. Really I can't.' I glanced towards the school gates, where other mothers were going in to collect their children. I knew if anyone mentioned that Leah was outside or a member of staff saw her, the school secretary would call the police – they couldn't afford to take any chances. 'You must try to cooperate and do as they say,' I said again, although I didn't know if Leah was thinking rationally enough to do so.

'I can't go to contact,' she said, rubbing the back of hand over her forehead in a gesture of despair. 'They want me to see Alice for an hour and then say goodbye. I can't cope with that. I want Alice, I need her. She's my life. I need to look after her. I promise I'll be a good mother.' Tears welled in her eyes. I felt so dreadfully sorry for her.

'You were a good mother,' I said, touching her arm. 'I've told the social worker and your parents that. You brought up Alice beautifully; she is a credit to you. But you're going to have to do as you are told now – co-operate with the social services and see Alice at contact. Trust me, it's the only way forward.'

'But can't I just see her for a few minutes, now, please?' Leah nearly begged. 'I won't cause a problem, I promise. I'll just say hello and give her a kiss and a cuddle. I won't make a fuss.' My heart cramped; at times like this I hated my role as foster carer.

'Leah, it's not my decision, honestly, love. It's your social worker and your solicitor you need to see. I can't help you. Please don't wait here for Alice to come out, because if you approach her I will have to tell your social worker and call the police, and that won't do anyone any good.'

She shrugged despondently as though she'd half guessed as much and clearly thought that in the 'them and us' situation I was one of 'them'. I felt wicked stopping Leah from seeing her daughter, but realistically there was nothing I could do. I dearly hoped she would heed my warning and not approach Alice, for I would have to report her. 'Leah, please try to do as I say,' I said. 'Alice needs to see you too – she misses you dreadfully – but you can't meet her here. Go home, contact your social worker and solicitor, and say you want to see Alice at contact.' It was the only advice I could give her.

As I looked at her a large tear ran down her cheek and she brushed it away with the back of her hand in the same gesture of despair.

'I'm sorry,' I said, touching her arm again. 'Please do as I say, for Alice's sake. Go home or to your parents, but don't wait here.' Another tear fell, and another; then, completely defeated, she turned and walked away.

I watched her go and my heart ached. Although I was relieved she'd taken my advice and gone, and I knew I'd acted correctly and professionally, I felt no less wretched. I waited until she'd disappeared along the pavement and was out of sight before I crossed the road and went into the playground and towards the nursery. I sincerely hoped Leah wouldn't return and wait outside, for if she did I would have no alternative but to call the police. With Alice with me I couldn't do anything else; Leah was desperate and I wasn't convinced she wouldn't try to snatch her daughter again.

In the nursery I greeted Alice, as I always did, with a bright, 'Hi, have you had a good day?' Usually Alice answered and chatted away about all the things she'd done at school. Sometimes she didn't want to talk, and my question was met with a small nod, but that's normal for most children at the end of a tiring day. Now Alice was very quite and pensive, silently slipping her hand into mine. As we walked across the playground towards the main gate, I was watching out for any sign of Leah. Outside, on the pavement, I looked over the road to the tree, and then up and down the street, but it was all clear. Nevertheless I hurried Alice across the road towards the car and was relieved once she was strapped in her seat and I was driving away. I would have to make a note in my log that I had met Leah, but I wouldn't be drawing it to anyone's attention. Alice hadn't seen her mother and no harm had been done, so I felt justified in striking my meeting with Leah from my conscious recollection. And while I wanted nothing more than for Alice to see her mother again, it was essential that any contact took place in the safe confines of the family centre, where it would be supervised and monitored for Alice's well-being.

I didn't know if Alice had picked up my anxiety or had somehow sensed her mother had been close, but she was unusually quiet for the rest of the afternoon; even Adrian couldn't raise a response when he offered her his palm for slapping and said 'Give me five,' which Alice usually loved. Then when I called everyone for dinner Alice sat at the table with her hands in her lap and refused to eat anything. I encouraged and cajoled her to eat but without effect. When I asked her what was the matter she said resolutely, 'If I can't see my mummy I don't want to eat anything ever again.'

And she kept it up for two days.

On the third day, nearly out of my mind with worry, I phoned Jill. 'Alice is on a hunger strike,' I said. 'She hasn't eaten a morsel for three days and says she won't eat unless she can see her mother.'

'Little madam,' Jill said. 'She certainly knows how to put the knife in!' I knew what Jill meant: Alice couldn't have chosen a more effective way to make her point, for, as I'd already found out with Lucy, nothing brings a parent or carer to their knees faster than a child refusing to eat. 'Try not to make an issue of it,' Jill advised. 'Give her the meals as you usually do, and then clear away at the end. Check with the school and see if she's eating her lunches.'

'I have,' I said, 'and she's not, which is why I'm so worried. She can't go for much longer without anything to eat.'

'But she's drinking?'

'Yes.'

'That's more important. You can go for quite a few days without food but not without fluid. Look, Cathy, carry on as you have been doing – prepare her favourite foods, but keep it low key. Serve the meal, give Alice a reasonable length of time to eat it and then clear away. We'll give it another couple of days, and if she still hasn't eaten by the end of the week we'll seek medical advice.'

'Thanks, Jill,' I said. It was at times like this – when I was in the middle of a crisis and too emotionally involved to view the situation dispassionately – that I really appreciated Jill's advice and support.

'I'll phone tomorrow,' she said. 'Take care and try not to worry.'

I did as Jill suggested – made Alice's favourite meals, allowed a reasonable time for her to eat it and then threw it (untouched) in the bin. Two days later, when Alice had gone five days without food, she began eating again, although even then I'm not convinced she would have done so without Lucy's input. Dear Lucy, who had her own eating difficulties, and was aware what it felt like to be in foster care, identified with Alice in a way the rest of us couldn't, and knew what to say. Leaning conspiratorially across the table as though she was letting Alice into a big secret, she whispered, 'I'm not seeing my mum but I still eat. If you don't eat, when it is time to see your mum you won't be strong enough to go, and how sad would that be?'

From the corner of my eye I saw Alice pick up her knife and fork and start to eat. Before long her plate was empty and she was asking for more. I smiled a thanks to Lucy, and motioned for everyone not to say anything. For while we were all relieved that Alice was eating again, I didn't want Alice thinking that refusing to eat resulted in lots of attention and praise, which was a short step to using food refusal as a tool for manipulation. But while Alice had started eating again and would continue to do so, it was as though something had sealed itself in her mind, a resolute, almost morbid acceptance, and it wasn't healthy.

The following morning she announced, quite matter-of-factly, 'I haven't got a mummy any more.'

Chapter Twenty-Four

Rejected

It was a little after 9.30 a.m. on Saturday, and Paula, Alice and I had just finished breakfast. Lucy had spent the night at her friend's and I was going to collect her at 11.00, while Adrian had already left for football practice. Paula was upstairs in the bathroom, brushing her teeth. Alice was helping me clear the breakfast things from the table when she made her announcement. I knew immediately she was feeling rejected.

'Of course you have a mummy,' I reassured her. 'It's just that it isn't possible for you to see her at present. Think of all the happy memories you have of you and your mummy, and have a look at that lovely photograph on the shelf in your bedroom. Mummy is still out there, and she's thinking of you.'

Alice concentrated on handing me the breakfast plate, which looked huge in her tiny hands, before she answered. 'No,' she said almost defiantly. 'I don't have a mummy, not any more.'

'You do, love. She's ill, and we're hoping she'll get better and be well enough to see you soon. I can understand why you're angry with her, but try not to blame her – you'll make yourself unhappy.'

Alice shrugged and changed the subject, and I knew she hadn't accepted what I'd said. I'd looked after children before who, for many reasons, had been unable to see their parents and, feeling rejected, dealt with it by rejecting the parent(s) to the point where they no longer existed. It was an understandable but unhealthy form of denial, and it was often very difficult to persuade the child out of it. It was especially difficult for Alice to accept being separated from her mother, for she was very young and had had a good relationship with her. I could only hope, as with so many losses, that given time, or when Alice began seeing her mother again, the damage done by the separation could be undone, although it would take patience and a lot of reassurance. But feeling that her mother had rejected her was only a short step away from Alice feeling the same rejection from her grandparents, whose contact with her was so limited.

That evening when we phoned her nana and grandpa, Alice was clearly set on punishing them by making them feel sorry for her.

'I haven't done anything all day,' Alice said in a feeble voice when her nana asked her for her news and what she had been doing.

'Nothing?' her nana said. 'You must have done something, Alice.'

'No,' Alice said, scowling. 'I haven't.'

'Tell Nana about how we went to the park, and your new shoes,' I encouraged.

But she didn't. Alice sat beside me on the sofa, her face glum and her lips tightly shut against anything that might have been reassuring for her grandmother to hear, while her nana continued to talk and prompt Alice, trying to elicit some good news. After a while, when the most Alice had said was a grunted 'No' and I could hear Mrs Jones growing anxious, I took the phone from its cradle, cutting off the speaker, and said, 'I'm sorry, Mrs Jones, Alice is feeling rather rejected at present. I've been talking to her and have reassured her you love her very much, but I know she's finding the separation very difficult.'

Mrs Jones was obviously concerned, and very disappointed that Alice didn't want to talk to her, but she was also very understanding. She suggested she put on Grandpa. 'Alice is sure to want to talk to him about the football,' she said. 'Did Alice watch it?'

'Oh yes, and so did Brian the Bear.'

Mrs Jones gave a small laugh. 'Thank you, Cathy. I'll just fetch Martin.'

Before I returned the phone to speaker I said to Alice, 'Your grandpa is coming to the phone. Please make sure you talk to him. It's upsetting for your nana and grandpa if you don't talk to them; they look forward to your phone calls.'

But of course upsetting them, and therefore punishing them for not seeing her more often, was exactly what Alice was doing. When Mr Jones came on the line and began talking about the football, the skill of a winning goal and how pleased Brian the Bear must have been, he was met with the same stony silence and the occasional grunted 'No'.

'Alice, answer your grandpa,' I said, but Alice was resolute in her withdrawal and punishment. Eventually I took the phone from its cradle and apologized to Mr Jones.

'Is she all right?' he asked, very concerned. 'She sounds upset.'

'She's missing you both,' I said. 'But she's had a good day. I'll have another chat with her when we've finished. I think she's blaming you and your wife for not seeing her more often. You have contact next week and I'm sure when she sees you she will be fine, but for now I think it's probably best to end this phone call. I appreciate how upsetting it must be for you to hear her sounding so sad.'

'Yes, it is,' Mr Jones confirmed. 'Can I just say good-night to her?'

'Of course.'

I returned the phone to its cradle. 'Say goodnight to your grandpa,' I said.

'Goodnight, Alice, love,' Grandpa said. 'See you on Wednesday.'

Alice forced a very small and dejected, 'Goodnight,' and that was it – no kisses were sent or caught.

I said goodbye and, severing the line, turned to Alice: 'Look, love, I know you're hurting, but it isn't nice to punish your nana and grandpa by not talking to them. It's not their fault they can't see you more often, and it must be very upsetting for them to listen to you sound-ing so sad. You're not sad most of the time, are you? We've had a nice day.'

'I am sad,' Alice said. 'You don't know. I'm sad inside, but I don't always tell you. I smile and laugh but inside I'm sad.' Her face puckered and I put my arm around her and, drawing her to me, hugged her.

'I do understand, love, honestly I do, but try not to hurt your nana and grandpa. It will just make you unhappy.'

First thing on Monday morning, after I'd taken Alice to nursery, I phoned Kitty. I asked her why Alice's contact with her grandparents had been set so low, and if it was possible to increase it, as Alice was finding the separation more difficult to cope with the longer it went on. Kitty said contact had been set low in preparation for Alice going to live with her father and Sharon, which had been expected to take place within a month of Alice coming to me. She also said it would be inadvisable to increase the contact now, because if Alice went to live with her father (which was still the care plan) then contact with her grandparents would be reduced further – to about once a month, and then three times a year. I knew from looking after other children that this type of reduction in contact was usual, and was designed to encourage the child to bond with the family they were going to live with – that is, their permanent, forever family – and reduce their dependence on any previous family or care giver. All very well in theory, but it wasn't always so easy in practice.

I also asked Kitty if she thought it was at all possible to establish some telephone contact between Alice and her mother if I carefully monitored it, and Kitty said it was something she was already considering. Kitty said she had been trying to meet Leah so that she could assess if Leah was stable enough to have telephone contact and would know what was appropriate conversation if phone contact was started. It wouldn't be appropriate, for example, for Leah to talk endlessly about how unhappy she was, criticize Chris or give Alice false hopes of her being able to live with her again. But to date Kitty hadn't been able to meet Leah, as Leah had failed to keep the three appointments Kitty had set up. Although this wasn't encouraging news, I felt that at least Kitty was on Alice's case, was sensitive to Alice's needs and was doing her best for Alice.

When Alice saw her nana and grandpa at contact the following Wednesday she immediately forgot her anger and ran into their arms. I had thought she would but I was nevertheless relieved and pleased, as were her grandparents. They had a lovely time although, as usual, an hour simply wasn't long enough and all three were very sad at parting.

But while face-to-face contact with her grandparents remained very positive, the telephone contact continued to be variable. Sometimes Alice would chat happily to her nana and grandpa and at other times she refused to speak to them or answered a sombre 'No' to their questions. If Alice had been unresponsive I always spoke to Mr and Mrs Jones and reassured them that Alice was otherwise well and happy. They thanked me and said they understood, although I could hear the great sadness, loss and disappointment in their voices.

But more worrying than Alice refusing to speak to her grandparents on the phone was that Alice remained resolute in her assertion that she didn't have a mummy; she even told her nana and grandpa she didn't at one contact, which made them very upset. By then Alice had completely stopped talking about all the happy memories she had of her mother and indeed never mentioned her. Her mother's photograph, which had sat at the front of the shelf, lost its favoured position and was now in a straight line with the photograph of her grandparents and the one of her father and Sharon – all having equal status at the back of the shelf.

I supposed that in terms of Alice transferring her affection from her mother and grandparents to her father and Sharon (as was intended by the limited contact and in line with the care plan) this 'realignment' could be viewed in a positive light, and might have been had the care plan been continuing as it was supposed to. But, perversely just as Alice's attachment to her mother and grandparents might have been diminishing so that she would be in a better position to transfer her affection to those she was in regular contact with and would likely be going to live with, it was noted by the contact supervisor that 'Sharon's enthusiasm for Alice seems to be wearing thin.'

'What do you mean "wearing thin"?' I asked Kitty when she told me over the phone. 'Alice isn't a new toy where the novelty wears off.'

'No, but that's what the supervisor has noted. I suppose you can't really blame Sharon, as it's all been going on for so long. Sharon had expected Alice to go and live with them months ago, and we're still a way from that. Their parenting assessment isn't complete yet, and I'm still waiting for the results of some other enquires I've made. I take it Alice hasn't said anything to you about Sharon losing interest?'

'No, but she has never talked much about her.'

'I'm going to meet Chris and Sharon next week and see what's going on. I'm also still trying to find out exactly what happened last August. Mr and Mrs Jones are adamant that Chris reappeared in Leah's life and was responsible for getting her into drugs, which led to her breakdown. They claim he assaulted her. Chris denies it and says he saw Leah only once, and that was in the street. I wonder if it's worth asking Alice what she remembers of last summer? She's smart, and at her age she should have some recollection of a year ago. Do you think you could bring up the subject? Don't push it if she seems reluctant or can't remember.'

'I'll try,' I said. 'Although I'm not sure how productive it will be. As you know, Alice refuses to talk about her mother now, even about the happy times.'

'Try approaching it from another angle,' Kitty said, thinking aloud. 'Ask Alice if she remembers seeing her dad last summer. If she does, see if you can find out when, where and how often. I would ask her, but I've only been in her life a short while, and she trusts you.'

'I'll do my best,' I said.

'Thanks, Cathy. If Alice says anything that is relevant, can you write it down and send me a copy, please?'

'Yes, of course.'

I didn't hold out much hope of Alice telling me anything if it was connected with her mother. Alice was dealing with her pain and loss by burying all memory of her mother and the years she had lived with her. I didn't see why mentioning her father would make a difference. But as it turned out, Alice was not only able to remember seeing her father the previous summer, but willing to tell me of the traumatic events that were to change the course of her life.

Chapter Twenty-Five

'Icing Sugar'

It was the following Sunday, late morning, when I spotted a golden opportunity to introduce the subject of the past, and the memories we carry from it. Alice had wanted to look at some of my photograph albums, as she did from time to time. These albums contained pictures of my family and also the children we'd looked after, some of them going back years. Alice and I were in the sitting room with the French windows open on another gloriously warm sunny day. I was sitting beside her on the floor as she turned the pages of the album and asked questions about the children in the photographs.

'You've got lots and lots of pictures,' she said, closing one album and opening the next.

'Yes. I like photographs.'

'Why?' she asked.

'It reminds me of all the good times we've had. Sometimes memories can fade, so it's nice to have something to remind us. That's why I take lots of photographs of you – so that when you leave we will

both have something to remember each other by.'
Alice didn't say anything but studied the present page
of photographs, which had been taken in the summer
two years previously. Adrian had been twelve, Paula
eight, and Lucy hadn't arrived yet. In Lucy's place was
a five-year-old boy who had stayed with us for three
months. Adrian was kicking a ball to him while Paula
could be seen in the background on the swings.

As Alice looked at the photographs I casually said:
'These photographs were taken one summer. I like
summer. Do you remember last summer – before you
went to live with your nana and grandpa?'

'Yes,' she said with a small nod.

'I thought you might, because you have a very good
memory. Do you remember seeing your dad last
summer? Before you started seeing him at the family
centre for contact?'

'Yes,' she said again, still looking at the photographs.

I was surprised, because Alice had never mentioned
it. I paused, wondering how best to proceed, and then
decided a direct and honest approach would work best
with Alice. 'Alice, this could be important, so I want
you to think hard. Kitty has asked me if you can tell
me what you remember of seeing your dad last
summer.'

'We met him outside our flat,' Alice said without hesitation.

'Who's "we"?'

'Mummy and me.'

'What, you mean in the street outside the flat, where
you lived with your mummy?'

Alice nodded. This confirmed what Chris had said at the review – that he'd met Leah in the street once, although he hadn't mentioned Alice being there.

'Were you surprised to see him?' I asked. 'Or did Mummy tell you that you were going to meet him?'

'I was surprised. I didn't know him. He said he was my daddy, and Mummy said he was.'

'And was Mummy surprised to see him, do you remember?'

'Yes.'

'So what did you do? Did you talk to him or just carry on going with Mummy? Do you remember?'

'He came into our flat,' Alice said, again without hesitation.

'Your mummy asked him to come in?'

'I think so.'

'And were you happy for him to come to your flat?' She shrugged and turned another page in the album. 'So what happened when Daddy came in? Did Mummy make him a drink? Did he play with you? Don't worry if you can't remember.'

'He stayed, for a long time,' Alice said.

'What, for the whole day?'

'No, lots of days and nights. Mummy was happy to begin with, and I liked it for a bit. It was like a proper family with a mummy and daddy. Then he made Mummy upset and angry and she shouted a lot.'

'That was very sad, and it can be frightening when adults shout. Did Mummy shout at you?'

'No, she shouted at Daddy. And he made Mummy cry,' Alice added. I wondered if this could have been the screaming and shouting the neighbours had heard last August and had reported to the police – unaware that Chris was in the house, they'd assumed it was Alice Leah had been shouting at.

'Alice, what did Daddy do to make Mummy shout and cry? Do you know?' I sensed I might not want to hear the answer, and I was right.

'He kicked Mummy in the head and the tummy. It hurt her so much she screamed and cried.'

I looked at Alice carefully. She had stopped turning the pages of the album and was now staring at it as though staring through it, as she concentrated on what she was remembering.

'It was very naughty of him to hurt Mummy,' I said. 'It's wrong for people to hurt each other, and certainly mummies and daddies should look after each other. Alice, why haven't you told me all this before?'

'He' – she meant her father – 'said I mustn't tell. And Mummy said it would make it bad for her if I told.'

'When was this said to you? Last summer?'

Alice nodded. Then her brow creased. 'Sometimes he used his head and banged it in Mummy's face. He made her nose bleed and it was all swollen. One day I saw Mummy on the floor and Daddy was kicking her. I went to help her and he kicked me too. Daddy said he didn't mean it – I got in the way. But I didn't like him hurting my mummy. I wanted to help her.'

I was appalled. This was the man Alice was seeing regularly at contact and with whom she was supposed to be going to live! 'Daddies shouldn't do hurtful things and certainly not kick and head-butt,' I said. 'It's very, very wrong.'

'That's what Nana and Grandpa said.'

'You told them?'

'They saw what he did. The last time, when Mummy was on the floor, there was lots of blood and she couldn't get up. After Daddy had gone, I helped Mummy crawl to the phone so she could phone Grandpa. She told him she had been hurt and Grandpa and Nana came in the car and took us to their house. They made Mummy better and said Daddy was an evil man.' Alice paused and, still deep in thought, said reflectively: 'Daddy was horrible to me and my mummy at our flat, but he's nice to me now.' Well, yes, I thought, he would be in supervised contact and in front of Sharon; he couldn't be anything else but nice! My anger flared.

I was shocked by what Alice had told me, and greatly saddened that a young child had had to witness such horrendous domestic violence. But on another level I was pleased Alice had witnessed it, and had been able to tell me, for it supported what Mr and Mrs Jones had been claiming all along, and also put Chris in an entirely new (and worrying) light. Once Kitty was aware of what Alice had said, doubtless further investigation would be carried out into Chris's background and suitability to parent Alice, which must now surely be called into question.

However, as if what Alice had already witnessed wasn't bad enough, there was more to follow, which made me wonder why Mr and Mrs Jones's claims had been so easily dismissed, and why Chris hadn't been investigated sooner, before it was decided that Alice should go and live with him.

'Alice, you did very well remembering all that,' I said, giving her a hug. 'Is there anything else you want to tell me or is that it?'

'He stayed lots of nights,' Alice said again, returning her gaze to the photographs. 'And he was horrible to my mummy. Sometimes he pulled her hair out and made her scream. Sometimes he teased her and made her beg.'

'How do you mean, "teased her and made her beg"? Can you explain?'

Alice was looking at the photograph of Adrian and Paula having a water fight in the garden, their enjoyment a far cry from what Alice was now remembering. 'Daddy had something Mummy wanted and he wouldn't give it to her. He teased her with it,' Alice said.

'What sort of something?'

'I don't know. It was like icing sugar in a small plastic bag. He held it in his hand above Mummy's head, and when she tried to grab it, he moved it and laughed. That's teasing, isn't it?'

'It certainly sounds like it.'

'The only way she could get the bag was to beg. She had to kneel down in front of him and pretend she was a dog. He made her run round his legs and bark. Then she had to kiss his feet and he gave her the bag of icing sugar.'

'Then what happened after he'd given Mummy the bag?' I asked, trying to keep my voice even.

'Mummy went into the bathroom and when she came out she was happy again, for a little while. Daddy put some of the icing sugar on some paper in a little line and sniffed it like he had a cold.'

I nodded. There was no doubt in my mind that the 'icing sugar' was an illegal drug, probably cocaine – which was either snorted, or sometimes diluted in water and injected. At the review Mr Jones had said that Chris had introduced Leah to drugs and used his words – 'one little line won't hurt, just for old times' sake'. A line of cocaine is exactly what it says – a thin line of cocaine powder, which can be snorted. What Alice had just told me seemed to substantiate Mr Jones's claim that Chris had got Leah on drugs. It was shocking that Alice had had to witness all this, but thank goodness she had.

'Well done for telling me all this,' I said again. 'It must have been very upsetting for you to watch.' She nodded and I gave her another hug. 'Is there anything else you can remember so I can tell Kitty?' Alice shook her head. 'One last question, Alice: did you see your dad after you left the flat and went to live with your nana and grandpa?'

'I didn't see him, but he came to Nana's house and wanted to see Mummy. Nana wouldn't let him in. He pushed Grandpa and tried to force his way in. Nana called the police.'

'But you didn't see him?'

'No.'

'All right, love, well done. Let's talk about something nice now. You see these photographs,' I said pointing to the next page in the album. Alice nodded. 'They were taken while we were on holiday. When school finishes in July we shall all go on holiday to the seaside.' Alice smiled.

While Alice pored over the photographs of sea and sand and happy children paddling, I grabbed my folder and began writing up my log notes while what she had told me was still fresh in my mind. As I wrote, I used the words Alice had used as much as possible – a verbatim account gives credence to the disclosures a child makes. But I knew that while I believed what Alice had told me, it would doubtless be hotly denied by Chris (and Sharon), and would still have to be proved. How could it be proved? I'd no idea, but one thing that had occurred to me was that if Chris had gone to Mr and Mrs Jones's house looking for trouble, and Mrs Jones had called the police as Alice said, then surely the police would have a record of that 999 call. I knew it wasn't much in terms of evidence, but it was a starting point that would surely uphold what Alice had told me and what Mr and Mrs Jones were saying, and would, I hoped, lead to the truth of what had happened last summer when Chris had reappeared in Leah's life.

Later that afternoon, while Paula played with Alice in the garden, I typed up my log notes, printed out a copy and put it in an envelope addressed to Kitty. I would post it when we went out later, and I would also phone her on Monday and update her. The doubts I'd previously entertained about Chris parenting Alice (due to his lack of enthusiasm and commitment) were compounded and I felt very protective towards Alice. For while I knew that contact was strictly supervised and Alice was safe there, I also recognized how confusing and upsetting it must be for Alice to be seeing her (abusive) father. She was now in regular contact, and being encouraged to form an attachment to a man whom she'd witnessed violently and sadistically assaulting her mother, while her mother – the victim, whose only crime was not being strong enough to stand up to Chris and say no to the drugs he'd offered – had been banished from Alice's life. What a conflicting and warped message this must be sending to Alice, I thought! How confusing and frightening! And if he had behaved as Alice had described, what was stopping him from behaving similarly in future when Alice went to live with him? I feared for Alice's safety and wanted desperately to protect her.

Chapter Twenty-Six

Happy sand

Kitty wasn't in the office when I phoned on Monday; she was in court on another child protection case, which was expected to last most of the week. I left a message with her colleague, saying I had spoken to Alice as Kitty had asked, and I had put a copy of my log notes in the post. I guessed Kitty would receive my telephone message and log notes when she returned to the office later in the week, and phone me.

In the meantime the week ran as usual for us. The following day was Tuesday and Alice was due to see her father and Sharon again. I wasn't looking forward to meeting Chris after what Alice had told me. I knew I would have to wear my most professional, neutral face and put my own feelings to one side.

Chris and Sharon always arrived early at the family centre which, according to the contact supervisor, was a sign of their commitment to parenting Alice. They waited in reception where they could see us as soon as we walked in. Sharon used to rush over to greet Alice, while Chris remained sitting in his chair, waiting for

Sharon to take Alice to him. But in recent weeks Sharon and Chris had remained seated and I had taken Alice over to them to say hello. I always waited with Alice until the contact supervisor arrived before I said goodbye and came away, and they went to whichever room they were using for the contact. Chris and Sharon had never missed contact, unlike some parents, and their reliability was taken as another sign of their commitment to parenting Alice.

On Tuesday afternoon, true to form, they were already sitting in reception. Alice and I went over, and I said hello. As usual Sharon spoke before Chris and said: 'Hi, Alice,' and then, 'Say hello to your dad,' which Alice dutifully did. Having observed the way they'd greeted Alice in previous weeks, with Sharon always taking the initiative, I had put Chris's lack of enthusiasm down to simply that – ambivalence towards Alice, or possibly (and more kindly) an awkwardness from not really knowing Alice or how to behave as a father, although it hadn't improved with time. Similarly I'd attributed Alice's reticence towards her father to not having had a relationship with him in the past. But knowing what I now knew I realized that Alice's reserve – her guardedness – could be due to fear. I wondered if it continued in the contact room and, if so, if the supervisor had noticed and included it in her reports. Part of the contact supervisor's role is to observe and note how family members interact with each other. The standard of the reports and the training and experience of contact supervisors varies greatly, from excellent to not good, but this supervisor had noted

Sharon's enthusiasm waning towards Alice, so I thought there was a good chance she'd noticed Alice's reaction to her father.

Having said a polite hello to Sharon and Chris, as usual I said that Alice was well, and told them any news she had. In the early weeks Sharon had been eager to hear all snippets of information about her 'future daughter' but now, as in recent weeks, they both looked at me blankly and nodded, uninspired.

'Thank you for telling us,' Sharon managed when I'd finished, while Chris nodded with as much enthusiasm as a wet lettuce leaf. The contact supervisor appeared, so I said goodbye to Alice, and then watched the four of them go down the corridor towards the contact room, with the supervisor chatting brightly to Alice, and Chris and Sharon following in silence at the rear.

Alice never spoke about contact afterwards and, other than asking her if she'd had a nice time, which was usually met with a shrug, I didn't press her. I would be told anything I needed to know by Kitty, who received a copy of the contact supervisor's reports each week. Alice had contact again on Thursday, and Sharon seemed to make a bit more effort and gave Alice a hug when we went in. Chris remained as impassive as ever and waited until Sharon told Alice to say hello before he said hi.

On Friday Kitty phoned and immediately apologized for not phoning sooner, as she'd been in court all week. She'd read the copy of my log notes I'd sent her and was shocked by what Alice had witnessed last summer at her mother's. Kitty believed what Alice had said, as I had done, for it tied in with what Mr and Mrs Jones were claiming, and it was also unlikely that a child of Alice's age could have invented a story with that degree of detail. However, Kitty quickly pointed out that Chris was vehemently denying Alice's allegations, and they would be difficult to prove.

'When I spoke to Chris this morning,' Kitty said, 'he said Leah must have told Alice to say that.'

'When? Alice hasn't seen her mother in nearly four months. And she isn't a child who can easily be manipulated, not as some children can, or else Sharon would have had her calling her Mummy by now. Furthermore Alice isn't feeling very loyal to her mother at present. She's still angry with her for not seeing her, and doesn't speak of her mother, so she's hardly going to lie for her.'

'I know,' Kitty said, 'but the problem is there aren't any independent witnesses. I've contacted the police and asked them to check their records for the calls the neighbours made about Leah shouting. I want to see exactly when those calls were made and what the neighbours reported hearing. I've also asked them for details of the 999 call Mrs Jones made when Chris went to her house. Mrs Jones can't remember the exact date the incident happened, so it's going to take a while. When I spoke to Chris he admitted he went to Mr and Mrs Jones's house, but he says it was only to see Alice and he came away quietly when they wouldn't let him in. He denies pushing Mr Jones. Mrs Jones says Chris arrived at their house very angry, demanding to see Leah and cause trouble, and didn't ask for Alice.'

'That is more or less what Alice said.'

Kitty sighed. 'It's a dreadful mess. My feeling is that a more thorough investigation should have taken place when the social services were first involved, before it was decided that Alice should live with her father, but don't quote me on that.'

I gave a tight laugh. 'No, I won't quote you, but I'm pleased to hear you say it.'

'I shall be observing contact as soon as I can,' Kitty continued, 'so will you explain to Alice that I'll be in the contact room sometimes? I've also asked a psychologist I've used in the past to make an assessment of Alice in relation to her father and Sharon, and her grandparents. Her name is Brenda Taylor and she'll be observing contact too, but not at the same time as me. Brenda is very nice and I've found in the past she can spot things in the way a child relates to their parents that the contact supervisor has missed.'

'That sounds very positive,' I said. 'I'll explain it all to Alice. Thanks for all you're doing.'

'It's the least little Alice deserves,' Kitty said with another sigh. 'But you know, Cathy, it may be that in the end the judge decides Alice should go to live with her father. If hitting an ex-partner was a bar to parenting there would be an awful lot of kids without fathers. Chris's and Sharon's parenting assessment has been positive so far and, apart from Sharon's enthusiasm waning a bit, which I suppose is understandable given all the delays, the contact supervisor's notes are positive. I'll see what the police come up with, but as you know there are two sides to every story. Who's to say Leah didn't provoke Chris?' Which of course was perfectly possible.

The next five weeks until the end of the summer term flew by, and before I knew it Alice was saying goodbye to her friends at nursery and I was saying, 'See you in September' to the parents, which seemed increasingly likely. A place was being kept open for Alice in the first year of the infant school, although the head teacher was aware of the uncertainty surrounding Alice's future. If Alice did go to live with her father and Sharon, she would go to a different school, closer to where they lived on the other side of the county.

  Kitty, and Brenda, the child psychologist, attended contact and observed Alice with Chris and Sharon, and also with her grandparents. Brenda was indeed very pleasant and sat, as Kitty had done, unobtrusively at the back of the room and made notes, while Alice played. But whereas Alice continued as normal, uninhibited by the presence of an extra adult in the room, Mrs Jones confided in me during the following telephone contact that she found it most intrusive and felt very self-conscious at being monitored and having everything she said and did written down. Of an older generation and having looked after Alice she couldn't see why a contact supervisor was necessary, let alone the added intrusion of the social worker and psychologist. I reassured Mrs Jones this was normal practice and that while the supervisor would always be in contact until the final court hearing when the judge made a decision on Alice's future, Kitty and

Brenda's presence was only temporary – half a dozen sessions at the most. But I could understand the indignation she and Mr Jones felt, and I again wondered how my grandparents would have coped in their position.

We went on holiday the first week in August and had a wonderful time. Alice had seen the sea before – her mother and grandparents had taken her on day trips to the coast – but she hadn't actually stayed at the seaside. I rented a three-bedroom bungalow overlooking a small Pembrokeshire bay in Wales. Lucy and Paula shared a bedroom, as did Alice and I, while Adrian had a room to himself. Alice was a little unsettled to begin with and woke the first two nights, wondering why she wasn't in her 'own bed' and where all her things were – not fully understanding that we would be going home again at the end of the week. After that she slept well, helped, I think by exhaustion from having spent all day on the beach and eating late in the evening. Interestingly, halfway through the week, Alice suddenly began talking about her mother again – of happy thoughts and memories as she used to. It was as though being away had helped heal her feelings of anger and rejection.

'I wish my mummy could come on holiday with us,' she said more than once as we made sandcastles or paddled in the sea. 'My mummy would like a holiday. It would make her happy.'

'Perhaps Mummy will be able to have a holiday another year,' I suggested.

Alice nodded thoughtfully. 'I'll take my mummy on holiday. When I'm grown up I'll bring her here on holiday and we can make sandcastles.'

I smiled. 'That's a nice idea, love, although there are lots of different beaches you can go to. It doesn't have to be this one.'

'I'll bring her here,' Alice said decisively. 'This sand has made me happy and it will make my mummy happy too.' Which I thought was a lovely sentiment, and how popular this beach would become if its therapeutic qualities became known.

The only 'negative' aspect to our holiday was Lucy's eating. Having seen her make so much improvement in recent months – Lucy had been eating small regular meals and encouraging Alice to eat – I now saw a dramatic decline in Lucy's eating, and in her swimming costume I noticed how slim she was. She didn't have the skeletal frame of some anorexics, who cover up their starved bodies with layers of baggy clothing, but she didn't have an ounce of fat on her. I knew she was still underweight for her height and needed to put on at least a stone in weight.

Since we'd been on holiday Lucy had been eating a slice of toast for breakfast, one small sandwich for lunch, which we usually had on the beach, had refused all ice creams and candies, and had eaten very little of the evening meal, which we usually had at a restaurant. I'd half anticipated that dining out might cause Lucy a problem as she panicked at the sight of a full plate of food and the expectation to eat, but I'd assumed she could perhaps just have a starter and pudding, which she did a few times but left more than she ate. I also caught her examining her stomach and patting it as if it had suddenly ballooned.

I was tempted to say something but, in keeping with my usual policy at home, I decided against drawing attention to the problem, which would probably have made Lucy self-conscious and was unlikely to improve her eating. My amateur psychology and reading on eating disorders had told me that, away from home and all that was familiar, Lucy felt a loss of control – similar to that she'd experienced when she'd first come into care. As a result she was exerting control in the one area where she had absolute control and for which she was totally responsible: her food intake and body weight. I hoped that once we returned home she would start eating again and resume the progress she had made.

On the last day of our holiday we left the beach early to go present shopping. The children wanted to buy their close friends little mementos of our holiday; I wanted to buy my parents something; and Alice should likewise take something back for members of her family. We spent over an hour in the gift shop, with other families doing similarly, and finally had a small souvenir for everyone, including Alice's grandparents, Alice's mother (which we'd send via her grandparents) and, after much persuasion, a box of candy for Alice's father and Sharon. I felt it would have been impolite not to give Chris and Sharon something, especially if they found out that we'd bought gifts for Alice's mother and grandparents.

As it turned out, Alice didn't get the chance to give the box of candy to her father and Sharon, for on our return home the second letter I opened was from Kitty, advising me that contact with Alice's father had been stopped.

Chapter Twenty-Seven
The Letter

The letter from Alice's social worker also said that contact with Alice's grandparents remained unchanged – an hour every two weeks, and telephone contact each Saturday. Kitty didn't give a reason for the suspension of contact with Alice's father but asked me if I would tell Alice, and said that she would phone me on Monday – presumably to explain.

It was a little after 3.00 p.m. and we'd just arrived home. I was standing in the kitchen opening the mail as I waited for the kettle to boil so I could make a cup of tea. The children were upstairs, familiarizing themselves with their bedrooms after our week away; we'd had a lovely holiday but everyone was pleased to be home again. I wondered if Alice's grandparents were aware that contact with Chris had been suspended and, if so, if they knew the reason. I couldn't think of any reason myself. Alice's allegations against her father hadn't yet been proved and even if they had that wouldn't have been grounds enough to stop contact. Contact is set by the judge at one of the first hearings in childcare proceedings and I knew from previous experience that the arrangements were only altered before the final court hearing in very exceptional circumstances. We were due to phone Alice's grandparents at 6.00 p.m. and I was sure Mrs Jones would say something if she knew; failing that I would have to wait until Monday to find out what was going on when Kitty phoned.

After I'd finished opening the mail, which was largely bills and circulars, and I'd had a cup of tea, Adrian, Lucy and Paula helped me unload the suitcases from the car and heave them upstairs. I took Alice's case into her room and began taking out the essentials of Brian the Bear, wash bag, etc.; the rest of the unpacking could wait until later or even tomorrow. Alice was busy peering into her toy boxes, happy to be reunited with her possessions, while I considered what to say to her about not seeing her father.

Children can become very upset if contact is cancelled – even if it is just one session that is missed. The routine of contact and the expectation of seeing a parent (or whoever the main care giver was before the child came into care) quickly becomes part of a looked-after child's life, and generally children still love their parents and want to see them, even though their parents may have fallen short in their parenting. Only in the worst cases of (sexual) abuse do children not want to see their parents. If contact is cancelled, I usually have to let the child down gently and explain that mummy (or whoever they were due to see) unfortunately can't make it, but they send their love and will see them next time. However, given Alice's lack of a relationship with her father and ambivalence towards Sharon, I didn't think Alice was going to be too disappointed.

I propped Brian the Bear in his usual place at the bed head, and then said matter-of-factly: 'Alice, I've just opened a letter from Kitty, your social worker. She says you won't be seeing your dad or Sharon for the time being, but you will still be seeing your nana and grandpa.'

As quick as a flash and making a reasonable, albeit wrong, deduction, Alice said brightly: 'Does that mean I can go and live with Nana and Grandpa again?'

'No, love, I'm afraid not. You will still see them at contact, but you will continue to live with me for now.'

Alice's face fell as she paused from rummaging in her toy box and looked at me, most concerned. 'Cathy, if I'm not going to live with my dad and Sharon where am I going to live?'

Chris and Sharon weren't supposed to have told Alice that she was going to live with them – a young child isn't told the care plan until the judge has approved it at the final court hearing and it's definite. But in the early days when Sharon had been unable to contain her enthusiasm she'd often said to Alice 'When you come to live with us/when you're my daughter' etc.

I had to answer Alice's question, but I was acutely aware that what I could say would sound dreadfully unsettling. 'Alice, love, we don't know where you will be living for certain yet, but for now you are staying with me. Once everything is sorted out and the judge has made his decision, Kitty will tell us who you will live with permanently. In the meantime I'm very pleased you are living with us, and so are Adrian, Lucy and Paula.' I smiled and hoped the positive outweighed the negative.

Alice appeared to accept this and returned to the toy box. I noticed she hadn't asked why contact with her father had been stopped, which is what most children would have done. I realized the reason she hadn't asked when she said: 'It's because my dad was horrible to my mummy. I'm glad I told you. I won't have to see my dad any more, and I won't have to live with him and Sharon.'

My heart sank as I realized the finality with which Alice was viewing any possibility of her going to live with her father. Her assumption that it wouldn't happen now simply wasn't so. 'We don't know that yet, love,' I said again. 'The judge hasn't decided what is best for you, but I know Kitty will tell us soon as she has any news.'

'Fine,' Alice said, 'but I'm not going to live with him.'

Any question of Mr and Mrs Jones not knowing that contact had been suspended came to an end when we phoned that evening. As usual I dialled their phone number and when Mrs Jones answered I said a brief hello and then put the phone on speaker so that Alice could talk to them. If Mrs Jones wanted to speak to me, which she often did, she did so after she and Mr Jones had spoken to Alice, when I'd taken the phone off speaker and Alice was out of the room.

'Hello, Alice,' Mrs Jones said brightly. 'Have you had a wonderful holiday?'

'Yes,' Alice said. 'And I'm not seeing my dad any more.'

I heard the silence on the other end of the line and had no way of knowing if this had come as news to Mrs Jones. 'I've received a letter from the social worker,' I said. 'Perhaps we can speak later, if you wish?'

'Yes, thank you, Cathy,' Mrs Jones said. Then, addressing Alice, she tried to steer the conversation back to the holiday: 'Tell me all about your holiday, Alice. Thank you for the postcard. The beach looked lovely. Did you go in the sea?'

'I'm not seeing my dad ever again,' Alice said. 'I don't have to see him now, and I'm not going to live with him and Sharon.'

'Alice,' I said, aware Mrs Jones could hear me over the speaker phone, 'I've already explained that we don't know where you will be living yet. Please talk to Nana and tell her about your holiday. She's waiting to hear all about it.'

But any thoughts of our holiday had been steam-rollered for Alice by the most recent news of contact. 'Cathy had a letter and I'm not seeing my dad,' Alice continued, unfazed. 'Cathy says I can't live with you, and I know I can't live with my mummy, so where am I going to live, Nana? I don't think anyone wants me any more.'

And while this might have been a little play for sympathy on Alice's part – though she'd been fine before the phone call – nonetheless my heart went out to her, and also to Mrs Jones, who had just heard her beloved granddaughter say she thought no one wanted her. 'I'm sorry, Mrs Jones,' I said. 'That's not what I said to Alice. I've tried to explain the situation, and reassure her as best I can. I'll have another chat with her later. She knows how much you love her, and I've explained it's not your decision where she lives.'

'Thank you,' Mrs Jones said gratefully. 'It must be very difficult for Alice to understand. I don't know what to say to reassure her. I thought she'd be happy, having just come back from holiday.'

'She is, really, and she had a very good time. We all did. If Alice isn't going to tell you about her holiday then I think I should.'

This was the prompt Alice needed to get her off the subject of contact and recover her previous enthusiasm for our holiday. She began telling her nana all about the sea, sand and ice creams, and included a detailed description of the 'surprise' present she'd brought back for them. Twenty minutes later, sounding a lot happier, Mrs Jones began winding up. At the end of each phone call they sent their kisses of love down the phone. It was their little ritual and despite having been party to it for the best part of five months, it never failed to move me.

'Be ready to catch my kiss, then,' Mrs Jones said to Alice.

Alice moved to the edge of the sofa and cupped her little hands in front of her, towards the phone. 'I'm ready,' she called. We then heard Nana's kiss and Alice waited expectantly as it flew down the phone, finally landing in Alice's outstretched hands. 'I've caught it, Nana,' she cried, closing her hands around the kiss; then, carefully drawing it to her face, she released it on to her cheek. 'I've got your kiss, Nana. I'll send mine now.' Alice leaned closer to the phone and, taking a deep breath, blew her kiss down the line.

'I've caught it,' Mrs Jones said. 'Thank you for the kiss, Alice. See you on Wednesday. I'll put Grandpa on. Night, love.'

A moment later Mr Jones came on the phone: 'How's my girl, then?' he said. 'Did you take Brian the Bear on holiday with you?'

'I'm not seeing my dad any more,' Alice said. Oh, no, not again! I thought. But Mr Jones, probably having heard the conversation his wife had had with Alice, said firmly: 'We're not talking about that now, Alice. Cathy will explain later and answer your questions. For now I want you to tell me about your holiday. Did Brian go with you?'

'Yes,' said Alice. Then she chatted for a good quarter of an hour, happily reliving our week away, before Mr Jones said goodnight and that he would see her on Wednesday. They too exchanged kisses down the phone before saying a final goodnight.

I saw Alice out of the room and into Paula's care; then I returned to the sitting room and closed the door. Sitting on the sofa I picked up the receiver, cutting off the loudspeaker. Mrs Jones was already waiting on the other end.

'I'm sorry you had to hear all that from Alice,' I said, still uncertain how much Mrs Jones knew of the suspension of contact. 'There was a letter from Kitty waiting for me when I got home. It said contact with Chris and Sharon had been suspended, but didn't give a reason. Kitty asked me to tell Alice, but I could only tell Alice what I knew. I think she's read more into it.'

There was a short pause before Mrs Jones said: 'Chris can't go to contact because he is being held in police custody. He was arrested on Thursday for breaking into Leah's flat and badly assaulting her.'

Chapter Twenty-Eight
Judge's Decision

'Perhaps they'll believe us now,' Mrs Jones said tightly. 'We tried to tell them that he was no good but they wouldn't listen. This is the last thing poor Leah needs on top of everything else!'

'I'm so sorry,' I said. 'How is Leah now?'

'Very poorly. She's bruised all over and her left eye is swollen shut. She's got stitches in her hand where she tried to defend herself, and she's badly shaken up. The police have taken a statement from her and she's included all the times Chris assaulted her last summer, some of which even I didn't know about. Chris has told the police he went to Leah's flat to talk to her and she invited him in. At two in the morning and through a broken window? Fortunately the neighbours heard the glass smashing and called the police. When the police arrived they heard screams and broke down the front door to get in. He had Leah pinned to the floor and it took two of them to get him off. I think he would have killed her.'

I listened in silence, appalled and horrified at what I was hearing. I felt for Leah and I was also shocked at the apparent extent of Chris's violence.

'Leah is staying with us until she's properly well,' Mrs Jones continued. 'Her doctor has prescribed a mild sedative for now, and he's talked her into seeing a counsellor for therapy when she feels up to it. The poor lass has been to hell and back, but maybe some good will come out of all this in the end. That man' – she meant Chris – 'has finally shown his true colours and I hope social services are taking note. I want him locked up and the key thrown away, not only for what he's done to Leah but for tearing our family apart.'

'I'm sorry,' I said lamely as Mrs Jones finished. 'Please send Leah my best wishes for a speedy recovery.'

'Thank you, I will.'

I knew that when Kitty phoned on Monday she would confirm or qualify exactly what had happened at Leah's flat. It wasn't that I doubted what Mrs Jones had told me – far from it, for she'd always appeared very honest and open – but past experience had taught me that when it came to family loyalties and protecting loved ones, situations could become grossly exaggerated, as feelings ran high, although I didn't think that was so here. 'I won't be telling Alice any of what you have told me,' I said. 'It would make her very anxious and upset.'

'No, which is why I didn't say anything to her earlier. But what reason will you give Alice for her not seeing her father?'

'I'll ask Kitty what she wants Alice to be told, when she phones. Alice hasn't asked why she isn't seeing her father, and Kitty may want to talk to Alice herself and explain.'

Mrs Jones gave a small humph. 'I would rather it was you who talked to Alice. I don't trust that lot not to make something up. Truth hasn't been their closest bedfellow in the past.'

Despite Kitty being an excellent social worker, Mrs (and Mr) Jones still viewed the social services as the enemy, which was understandable given what had happened in the past, and even more understandable now if Mrs Jones's account of Chris attacking Leah was correct. For if it was true, then it would substantiate what Mr and Mrs Jones had been claiming all along: that Chris was violent and abusive. It would call into doubt his honesty and suitability to parent Alice, and would also raise questions as to the competency of the social services when they had decided Alice should live with him.

There was little I could say to Mrs Jones other than reassuring her that Alice was fine, and that she was looking forward to seeing them at contact on Wednesday.

Sunday was taken up with unpacking, a week's laundry and generally getting straight after our holiday. The children were happy to amuse themselves – mainly in the garden, as it was another lovely sunny day. Alice didn't mention her father again or that she wasn't seeing him, apparently accepting the suspension of contact as a fait accompli – almost as if she'd known all along that good sense would prevail and his crimes would be found out. At dinner that evening I was pleased to see that Lucy ate most of what was on her plate – not a vast amount, but what she ate she enjoyed unreservedly and she even had a small helping of pudding. I breathed a sigh of relief, as too, I imagined, did Adrian and Paula, who were aware that Lucy didn't always eat as much as she should and didn't have weight to lose.

When I woke on Monday it was with a heightened sense of expectation, for I anticipated that the contents of Kitty's phone call would be highly significant in deciding Alice's future. That morning I found myself running through all sorts of scenarios in my head: from Alice going to live with her mother, who had made a miraculous recovery, to Alice being returned to her grandparents, who had been assessed as suitable and not too old to look after Alice, to Alice staying with me. And with this last one I pictured Alice as part of our family in a year's time, five years' time and forever, but I do this with almost all the children I look after. Goodness knows what size house I'd need if it ever became more than a fantasy!

As it was, when Kitty phoned that Monday afternoon the scenarios she described were very different from any of those of my speculation. They were also very, very worrying.

Having confirmed what Mrs Jones had told me – that Chris had broken into Leah's flat and badly assaulted her – Kitty said: 'Chris is out of police custody and on bail, and Sharon is very angry that contact has been suspended. Their solicitor phoned me this morning and he is taking the department back to court this week to ask that contact be reinstated immediately. As he pointed out, Chris hasn't been found guilty and it is not for the social services to prejudge him.'

'But Chris has been charged with a very bad assault,' I said, incredulous.

'Yes, and breaking and entering, but his case won't appear in court for weeks, possibly months, and in this country you are innocent until proved guilty. Sharon has told their solicitor that if they don't see Alice during any of this time their relationship with Alice will suffer, which is true.'

I paused, struggling to understand the logic of what I was being told. 'Chris has never really had a relationship with Alice, and I thought Sharon's enthusiasm for parenting Alice was wearing thin. That's what the contact supervisor said.'

'It seems Sharon's enthusiasm has resurfaced since Chris was arrested, and it is their right to see Alice. I shall argue against it, but it is possible the judge will decide that contact should continue while Chris is out on bail. It is supervised, after all.'

I steeled myself to ask the next question, dreading, yet half anticipating, what the answer would be. 'But you wouldn't still consider sending Alice to live with Chris and Sharon? Not when he's shown how violent he can be?'

I heard Kitty's silence and knew she too was struggling with her reply. 'Chris won't automatically be ruled out to parent Alice at this stage. He hasn't been convicted of anything, and it is possible there is another side to all this.'

'Like what!' I demanded rudely, my voice rising. 'What possible explanation could there be for him breaking into Leah's flat and badly assaulting her? He's got a violent streak in him. Alice witnessed it last summer, and it's not going to disappear. How long will it be before he hits Sharon, or even Alice? It would be ridiculous to consider sending Alice to live with him now.' I stopped, aware I had probably said far too much, but if the social services weren't going to protect Alice, then who was left but me? Although it wasn't really poor Kitty who was to blame but legislation, policy and procedure.

'I appreciate what you're saying,' Kitty said. 'Believe me, and, off the record, I agree. I wouldn't put my child in his care. But if Chris goes to court, admits to the charges and asks to go on an anger management course, it is quite possible he will get off without a custodial sentence. In which case Chris and Sharon could still be deemed suitable to parent Alice. He is her father, after all.'

I inwardly sighed. 'And if he is given a custodial sentence? I hope you wouldn't be thinking of Alice starting prison visiting?' I knew from Kitty's silence what her answer would be.

'If Chris applies for contact I can't rule it out,' she said. 'You know it's felt that children should keep in touch with their natural parents wherever possible. If Chris's barrister can make a case that shows Chris's relationship with his daughter would suffer as a result of their separation, then Alice could be visiting him in prison. I'd be against it, as Alice doesn't have a long relationship with her father and she is quite young, but it would be for the judge to decide.' Kitty paused. 'Anyway, Cathy, I just wanted to let you know what the position is. I'll phone again as soon as I have any more news. In the meantime could you tell Alice that she won't be seeing her father tomorrow but she might on Thursday. Sorry to have to heap all this on you when you've just returned from holiday. I haven't even asked if you had a nice time?'

All thoughts and therapeutic value of our holiday had disappeared with what I'd just been told and the effect I knew it would have on Alice. 'It was good,' I said with as much enthusiasm as I could muster. 'Alice enjoyed it. I don't know how she's going to take all this. Since I told her she wouldn't be seeing her father she has seemed quite relieved. She's also taken it as a sign she won't be going to live with him, although I've told her we don't know that yet.'

'When I see Alice I'll try to explain,' Kitty said, 'but in the meantime can you prepare her for every eventuality?'

'I'll try,' I said.

'I won't go!' Alice said bluntly when I told her there was a possibility she would be seeing her father on Thursday. 'I saw Nana and Grandpa yesterday. I love them, and I'm not seeing him.'

I didn't say anything further; I'd done as Kitty had asked and had told Alice, but I saw no point in making an issue of it now, when there was a chance the judge might not make the order to reinstate contact. If the judge did decide Alice should see her father, then I would speak to Alice when I knew for certain, but I quietly hoped this wouldn't be necessary, for where was the logic in forcing Alice into a relationship with her father, now that he had shown his violent nature, when Alice hadn't had a relationship with him in the past, and didn't want one?

Chapter Twenty-Nine

A Milestone Missed

'I'm not going,' Alice said again on Thursday morning when I told her she would be seeing her father that afternoon. It was 11.30 a.m. and Kitty had phoned five minutes before, having just come out of court. She said the judge had reinstated contact and I should take Alice to the family centre to see her father at 1.30 p.m. Kitty apologized and I could tell she felt pretty deflated by the decision.

'I'm afraid we have to go,' I said gently to Alice. 'You remember I explained how a man called a judge decided what was best for you? Well, he has decided it is best for you to see your father. I have to take you – otherwise I will get into trouble.'

Alice looked at me, her usual wide-eyed innocent expression now tight and emotionless. 'All right, then, I'll go, because I don't want you getting into trouble.'

'Good girl. And we must remember to take the candy we brought back from holiday to give to your father and Sharon.'

Alice shrugged and returned to her crayoning.

Sometimes foster carers have to put their own feelings and opinions to one side, and just get on with what they have been asked to do, and this was one such time. I didn't believe it was in Alice's best interest to force her into seeing her father, but then I didn't have all the information that had been available to the judge and on which he had based his decision. On Thursday at 1.00 p.m. Lucy and Paula came with me in the car to take Alice to the family centre while Adrian stayed at home. When we'd been to the centre the day before for Alice's contact with her grandparents, she'd been overjoyed and had rushed up the path to the centre, eager to give her nana and grandpa the small gift from our holiday. But now as I once more walked up the path Alice kept close by me, holding my hand, with the box of candy for Chris and Sharon tucked unenthusiastically under her other arm. I'd left Lucy and Paula in the car; it wasn't really appropriate for them to come into the centre, but they liked to accompany Alice in the car. I pressed the security button on the grid mounted on the wall, gave my name and the door clicked open.

Alice didn't say anything as we went in and she hadn't said much in the car either. Chris and Sharon were already in reception and came over, Sharon first, her previous enthusiasm apparently restored, only it was directed at me: 'Have you heard what that cow has done to us now?' Sharon cried, referring to Leah. 'She's made up a pack of lies and had Chris arrested! If I see her I'll scratch her eyes out and—'

'Sharon,' I interrupted, raising my voice over hers. 'This isn't the time or place. Not in front of Alice, please.'

Sharon stopped and bent to Alice, who was expressionless. 'Hi, precious!' she cooed. 'Don't you worry about Mummy Sharon.' Then, seeing the candy: 'Ah! Are those for me! How sweet of you!'

Alice dutifully handed over the box of candy; Sharon hugged and kissed her but Alice remained stiff and unresponsive. The contact supervisor appeared and, having said goodbye, I watched them walk away. Alice, upright and emotionless, went down the corridor between Sharon and Chris as though being escorted away by two security guards. I returned to the car and as I got in I let out a small sigh.

'Alice says she hates her father,' Paula said, as I started the engine. 'So why does she have to see him?'

'Because at her age no one listens to what you want,' Lucy said. 'You're just a kid. When you get to my age they have to listen because they can't force you.' Lucy saw her mother no more than twice a year, and never saw her father or the many aunts she had sometimes stayed with. And what Lucy said held some truth: at twelve Lucy's wishes had been taken into account when contact had been decided, while Alice's wishes clearly hadn't.

When I collected Alice at the end of contact she seemed a bit brighter, possibly relieved.

'Everything all right?' I asked as we walked down the path, away from the centre and towards the car.

Alice nodded.

'Did Dad and Sharon like their candy?' I asked.

Alice nodded again. 'Sharon ate most if it. She's such a pig. But she did play with me. Dad didn't say anything to me.'

'Perhaps he's preoccupied,' I said generously. 'You know – thinking of other things.'

'That's what Sharon said. I think it was to do with my mummy, but he wasn't allowed to say.' The contact supervisor would have stopped Chris or Sharon talking about Leah – one of the supervisor's roles is to monitor conversation and tell the adults what isn't acceptable.

Contact with Chris and Sharon, having been re-established, continued twice a week throughout the rest of the summer holidays; Alice continued to see her grandparents once a fortnight. Alice always looked forward to seeing her nana and grandpa, and accepted the contact with her father and Sharon with resigna-tion. The Guardian ad Litem visited in the last week in August and spent an hour with Alice and me, but didn't really have any more news beyond what I already knew from Kitty and Jill, who kept me regularly updated. I knew that the police were still investigating the case against Chris to decide if there was enough evidence to proceed with a prosecution, and a trial date hadn't yet been set. I also knew that the care proceedings (to some extent) rested on the outcome of the criminal proceed-ings – in terms of the advisability of Alice going to live with her father – so no date had been set for the final court hearing in the childcare proceedings, when the judge would decide where Alice would live.

When Kitty made her next four-weekly visit, two days after the Guardian had visited, she told me that the psychologist, Brenda Taylor, had filed her report. This report had been based on her observations of Alice at contact – both with her grandparents and with Chris and Sharon. Kitty summed up the conclusion to Barbara's report: Alice has a warm and loving relation-ship with her grandparents but is very cautious and wary around her father.

'Hardly surprising, as Alice witnessed him beating up her mother last summer,' I said.

'Exactly,' Kitty said, feeling, I sensed, that while Brenda's report was necessary for the court it didn't really say more than was obvious.

Kitty also said the psychologist had written that Alice often mentioned her mother during contact with her grandparents and still appeared to have a strong bond with her mother despite the lengthy separation, but she hadn't been able to assess this first hand because there was no contact between Alice and her mother at pres-ent.

Jill paid her monthly visit on the last day of August and I updated her about the psychologist's report; the rest she knew from Kitty.

September came, and I bought Alice's school uniform, new shoes, book bag and PE kit. I took photographs of her, looking very smart on her first day at school.

The first day at school is a milestone for any child and their parents and while I glowed with pride I was very sorry that Leah couldn't be there to see Alice's first day. I half hoped she might appear from behind the tree outside the school, but she didn't. I would have extra copies of the photographs of Alice in her school uniform printed – for Leah, Alice's grandparents and of course Chris and Sharon – but I felt this was small recompense for Leah not actually being there to see Alice. Again my heart went out to her for what she was missing of her daughter's life.

All the new children starting school went in for mornings only the first week to give them time to adjust; then from the second week they went all day: 8.55 a.m. to 3.15 p.m. And whereas when Alice had been at nursery I had collected her early on the days she had contact, now she was at school the social worker, rightly, felt that Alice shouldn't miss school, and so contact was rescheduled to start at 4.00 p.m. So two afternoons one week and three afternoons the next I collected Alice from school and took her straight to the family centre; then I returned at 6.00 p.m. to bring her home.

Alice was so exhausted on the nights she saw Chris and Sharon that she was often too tired to eat her dinner and just wanted to go to bed. I raised this with Kitty, who suggested that contact with her father and Sharon could be shortened to one hour during termtime (contact with her grandparents had only ever been one hour), which meant Alice would be home at 5.30 instead of 6.30 – as when she saw her grandparents. This seemed a good idea, for Alice's sake. However, when Kitty asked Chris, whose permission she would need to change the contact, as it had been set under a court order, he first agreed and then changed his mind after speaking to Sharon. Sharon was vehemently opposed to any reduction in contact, even though Kitty explained how exhausting it was for Alice, having just started school. It wasn't worth the time and cost for Kitty to take such a relatively small matter back to court and ask the judge to amend the contact order. So contact remained as it was, with Alice being too tired to eat her dinner and wanting to go straight to bed on returning from seeing her father and Sharon.

At the end of September, when Alice had been with me for six months, her next review was due, and I received a standard letter inviting me to attend. My thoughts went to Alice's first review, when Leah hadn't felt able to attend and there had been heated exchanges between Mr and Mrs Jones and Chris and Sharon. Although an invitation would have been sent to Leah, I doubted she would attend this review either. So it came as no surprise to me when, two weeks later, I walked into the committee room – the same one we had used for the last review – to find that Leah wasn't present. What did surprise me, though, was that Chris wasn't present either.

Chapter Thirty

Torn Apart

Sharon was at the review and her hostility was immediately obvious. Even before we'd introduced ourselves she was glaring at Mr and Mrs Jones. 'Chris can't come,' she said, accusingly. 'He's got an emergency meeting with his solicitor. The police are going to prosecute him, and all because of your bloody daughter!'

'So there is justice in the world,' Mr Jones said.

'Thank goodness,' Mrs Jones said quietly, with obvious relief.

The fact that the police had enough evidence to go ahead and prosecute Chris was clearly news to Mr and Mrs Jones, as it was to me and apparently everyone else seated around the table. The chairperson, Ray Sturgess (the same chairperson who had sat at Alice's previous review), was looking to Kitty for explanation, but she was shaking her head, not knowing. 'There's probably an email waiting for me,' Kitty said. 'I haven't had a chance to check my inbox yet this morning. I was aware the police were investigating Chris to see if they had a strong enough case to take to court. It seems they have.'

'And the charges?' Ray asked.

'Lies, made up by their daughter,' Sharon put in, jabbing a finger across the table toward Mr and Mrs Jones.

'Grievous bodily harm and breaking and entering,' Kitty clarified.

'He put our daughter in hospital,' Mrs Jones said. 'He nearly killed her.'

Ray, who was also taking minutes, wrote on his notepad, and then looked up. 'I think we had better introduce ourselves and I'll open this meeting properly before we go any further. I'm Ray Sturgess, external chairperson.' We then went round the table introducing ourselves, as is usual at the start of any meeting, even though we'd all met before. Next to Ray was Kitty; then Mr and Mrs Jones, Jill and me; then Sharon, who was sitting directly opposite Alice's grandparents. Ray said the Guardian had sent her apology for absence as she was in court with another case. Kitty said the school hadn't been invited, as Alice had only been in reception a few weeks.

'And Mum?' Ray asked. 'Is Leah expected?'

'No,' Mrs Jones said. 'She's not up to it. She suffered a setback after Chris attacked her.'

'He didn't touch her,' Sharon said. 'She's lying.'

Ray raised his hand for silence, perhaps feeling that this meeting was likely to continue where the last one had left off – in a slanging match. 'Tell me about the alleged attack,' Ray said, looking at Mrs Jones. The chairperson's only contact with the social services is at the child's review, so he wouldn't have known what had happened in the interim.

In a subdued and very sad voice Mrs Jones recounted how, a month previously, Chris had broken into Leah's flat at 2.00 a.m. and badly assaulted her. 'He would have killed her if the neighbours hadn't called the police,' she said again. 'Leah is staying with us for now, too scared to go out or return to her own flat.'

Ray wrote. 'And these are the charges Chris is seeing a solicitor about now?' he asked, looking up and round the table.

'I assume so,' Kitty said.

'Yes,' Sharon said. 'And they're a pack of lies.'

'That will be for the court to decide,' Ray said, surprisingly sternly, and then, looking at Kitty: 'Do these criminal proceedings against Chris change the care plan for Alice? At the last review the plan was for Alice to live with her father and Sharon; has that changed?'

'Not at present,' Kitty said. I heard Mr Jones's sharp intake of breath. 'The childcare proceedings are on hold and we are waiting for the outcome of the criminal proceedings,' Kitty said. Jill made a note.

'I assume Alice is still living with you, Cathy?' Ray said, looking at me. I nodded. 'Perhaps you could give us an update now, and tell us how Alice has been getting on since her last review.'

'Yes, of course.' I smiled as I said that Alice had been doing very well, considering all that was going on, and that she was a delight to look after. I said she'd enjoyed our summer holiday and had now settled into school, where she had made many friends. I mentioned she was tired after contact, and that she still had a strong bond with her mother and became sad when she spoke of her, as she missed her greatly.

'And the bond with her father and Sharon?' Ray asked. 'Has the high level of contact encouraged that bond?'

I paused. 'Not obviously,' I said carefully, without looking at Sharon. 'It appears to have remained the same as it was at the last review. Alice isn't upset before she goes to contact with her father and Sharon, but she never asks after her father or talks about him as she does her mother.' I felt Sharon's eyes on me but I had to say it as it was.

Ray nodded, and then said to Kitty: 'Will you reduce Alice's contact with her father and Sharon now there is a chance she might not be going to live with them?'

'No,' Sharon said. Ray ignored her.

'Not at present,' Kitty confirmed. 'My manager has advised me we should wait until the outcome of the criminal proceedings. Otherwise we could be seen to be prejudging the case.'

'And if Chris is found guilty?' Ray asked, pausing and looking up from writing. 'Where will Alice live then?'

Kitty paused, and toyed with the pen on the table in front of her before answering. 'We are carrying out a parenting assessment of Mr and Mrs Jones, which will shortly be complete. If it is decided that Alice cannot live with her father and Sharon, and that Mr and Mrs Jones's ages prohibit them from being the best choice for long-term care for Alice, then Alice will be placed for adoption.'

'And what is the most likely outcome?' Ray asked.

'Adoption,' Kitty said.

Although at the last review Mr and Mrs Jones had been made aware that adoption was a possibility, it had been remote – one of a number of possible outcomes for Alice, not the 'most likely'. Now the chances of Alice being adopted had stepped that much closer and there was absolute silence round the table. I didn't dare look up for fear of meeting Mr and Mrs Jones's gaze. My heart went out to them. I knew how uncomfortable Kitty must be feeling, having had to say this, and I felt uncomfortable too. I also felt guilty for being part of an 'establishment' that could be responsible for removing Alice from her grandparents for good.

After a few moments Mrs Jones spoke, her voice slight and shaky. 'Why should Alice be adopted? She already has us and a mummy.'

'But not a mummy who can look after her,' Ray said gently.

'We can look after her,' Mr Jones said, almost pleading. 'Please don't send our little Alice to a stranger. We're not too old to look after her, and when we are Leah will be well enough to look after Alice again. I'm sure of it.'

I swallowed hard as Ray answered, giving as much reassurance as he was able: 'Nothing has been decided yet, Mr Jones,' he said, 'and if your assessment is positive adoption might not be necessary.' Then, looking at Kitty: 'Is the department doing parallel planning?'

'Yes,' Kitty said. 'A family-finding meeting has been set up for two weeks' time to set the process in motion.'

I glanced sideways at Jill, aware of the significance of this, while Ray explained it to Mr and Mrs Jones, undoing the slight hope he had previously given them that Alice might not be adopted. 'Parallel planning allows the social services to explore more than one avenue at the same time,' Ray said. 'While you are being assessed the social services will start looking for a suitable adoptive family for Alice. It can take many months to find such a family, but it means that by the time of the final court hearing, if the judge decides adoption is the best option for Alice, then a family is already waiting for her. Alice shouldn't be kept in foster care any longer than is necessary.'

'But if Alice is adopted will we lose her forever?' Mrs Jones said, her voice quavering with emotion. Mr Jones stared blankly ahead, clearly struggling to come to terms with what he was hearing.

'Will Alice's grandparents be able to keep in contact with Alice if she is adopted?' Ray asked Kitty.

Kitty very slightly shook her head and concentrated on Ray as she spoke. 'It is felt that letterbox contact only is appropriate in cases of adoption. This means that Mr and Mrs Jones will be able to write and send cards to Alice, but there will be no face-to-face contact.'

Ray gave a small nod and I thought raised his eyebrows – in surprise or shock? – before he minuted what Kitty had said. Mr Jones sat very still while Mrs Jones took a tissue from her pocket and pressed it to her eyes. We were all silent again, Kitty, Jill and myself concentrating on the table in front of us. Again I thought of my own parents and I wondered how they would have coped hearing that the only contact they could have with their grandchildren was 'through a letterbox'.

After a moment Sharon, who had fallen silent while this was explained, cleared her throat and purposefully leant forward on to the table as she spoke.

'What about me?' she said. We all looked at her. 'If Chris goes to prison, and Mr and Mrs Jones are too old, I could adopt Alice. I can't have children and I'd make a good mother. Alice loves me and I'll look after her.' For a minute I felt very sorry for Sharon: she appeared so vulnerable and desperate in her bid to have Alice, and not being able to have children in itself was very sad; but my sympathy vanished with her next comment: 'I'll be a better mother than your Leah,' she said, looking at Mr and Mrs Jones. 'She's a waste of space and the sooner Alice forgets her the better.'

'No! She must never have Alice,' Mr Jones cried. 'Never! It's not right.'

'You will need to discuss any application you are thinking of making with Kitty,' Ray said diplomatically to Sharon. Then, turning to Mr and Mrs Jones: 'It's highly unlikely this would be considered the best option for Alice,' he reassured them.

'I'll see you about my application after the meeting,' unperturbed Sharon said to Kitty. 'I've been thinking that I might leave Chris if he goes to prison, but that won't matter. Alice never knew him, so it will just be me and her.'

I looked at Jill, and then at Ray and Kitty, as we all recognized the significance of Sharon's almost throwaway comment. Unwittingly her remark about leaving Chris and him not knowing Alice had just undermined everything on which her and Chris's application to have Alice had been based. Perhaps Sharon realized this too, for she quickly added: 'Or we can stay together if you like.'

There was little more to be discussed at the review. Ray confirmed that Alice would be staying with me until a decision was made at the final court hearing; then he set a date for the next review in six months' time. 'Another review might not be necessary if Alice is no longer in foster care,' he explained to Mr and Mrs Jones, 'but it is usual to set a date for the next review.'

Mr and Mrs Jones nodded, silent and clearly in despair, yet despite their own desolation as Ray wound up the meeting Mr Jones said: 'On behalf of my wife and myself I would just like to say how much we appreciate all Cathy is doing for Alice. We are very grateful to her for looking after our granddaughter so well. She treats Alice like one of her own children. From our hearts we thank you, love.'

I swallowed hard. 'Alice is a pleasure to look after,' I said, humbled by their courage and dignity. 'I pray things work out for the best. I find this all so very sad.' Jill and Kitty nodded. Then Ray closed the meeting.

Sharon remained seated as the rest of us stood, presumably holding back to speak to Kitty about her application to adopt Alice. Mr and Mrs Jones said goodbye and left first, followed by Ray. I was on my way out with Jill when Kitty came over, and said quietly, 'The family-finding meeting is scheduled for 10 October.

Can you make it, Cathy? It's important you're there, as you know Alice better than anyone.'

'I'll make sure I'm there,' I said.

'Alice will be easy to place for adoption, if that is the decision,' Jill said, glancing across at Sharon, who was busy on her mobile phone.

I nodded. 'But losing Alice will finish her grand-parents. They won't cope.'

'I know,' Kitty said. 'But adoption might be our only option. Leah can't parent Alice, and age may well count against Mr and Mrs Jones in the end.' She sighed. 'In all my years of social work this is probably one of the saddest cases I've ever come across. Drugs have a lot to answer for. If this hardworking and decent family can be torn apart, so can any family.'

Chapter Thirty-One
Don't You Want Me?

The following day was Tuesday and Alice was due to see her father and Sharon. I obviously hadn't said anything to Alice about her father being prosecuted, and I hoped Chris and Sharon would have enough good sense not to say anything either. Unusually, they were late arriving at the family centre, so Alice and I waited in reception. When they arrived, fifteen minutes after the scheduled time, they looked sombre and, as they signed the register, they just about managed a nod in our direction. Chris had never been one for open displays of affection and had always left greeting Alice to Sharon, but now Sharon showed no more enthusiasm than Chris as they came over and we waited for the contact supervisor to appear.

Once the supervisor had arrived, Alice exchanged my hand for hers and kissed me goodbye. As usual I watched them go; Alice and the supervisor went first with the supervisor asking Alice about her day at school, while Chris and Sharon followed in silence. I guessed Sharon, usually the one to do all the talking, was preoccupied with Chris's prosecution; or maybe Kitty had told Sharon that an application by her to adopt Alice was unlikely to succeed; or possibly it had become obvious to Sharon that while she and Chris were still being considered to have Alice long term, their position had become seriously compromised by the criminal proceedings against Chris. I wondered if Sharon ever doubted Chris's integrity now there was enough evidence for a police prosecution. She didn't appear to.

At the end of contact Alice told me that Sharon hadn't wanted to play with her, and her father had had a headache, so they had watched television. At the end of the next contact, on Thursday, as I was driving us home Alice told me that Sharon had said she thought two hours after school was too tiring for Alice and she would speak to the social worker about reducing contact. Sure enough, the following afternoon Kitty phoned to say that Sharon and Chris had agreed to reduce their contact to one hour, in line with the grand-parents', as they recognized Alice was exhausted after a full day at school. While I was relieved and pleased that Sharon had been able to do the correct thing, I wondered if she was losing interest in Alice as she had before. Chris had never shown that much interest in Alice and appeared to do as Sharon told him. But what-ever the reason, the upshot was that by reducing their contact to one hour, Alice wasn't too tired to eat her dinner and had time to play before going to bed, which was much better for her.

* * *

Two weeks later, on 10 October, Alice went into school blissfully unaware of the family-finding meeting I was about to attend, which was the first step to Alice being adopted. Alice no longer asked where she would live permanently, not because she didn't have the maturity or intelligence to contemplate her future – she did – but because she had convinced herself that when her mother was well enough she would return to live with her. 'Happily ever after, like in the books,' she said.

When Alice said this or made similar comments about her future I tried to steer her to the idea there were other possible outcomes, so it wouldn't come as such a shock when the judge made his decision. I had accepted it was impossible for Alice to return to her mother and that the social services wouldn't leave Alice in care indefinitely on the off chance her mother might one day recover. Trying to prepare Alice, I showed her photographs of, and talked about, some of the other children I'd fostered who had gone to 'live happily ever after' with new forever families – i.e. had been adopted. But while Alice nodded politely and liked looking at the photographs, I knew that what I was saying fell on deaf ears. 'I'm pleased I won't need a new family,' she said. 'I've got my own family,' meaning her mother and grandparents.

Part of my role as a foster carer is to prepare children for the future and I was concerned that if Alice didn't adjust, and was adopted, she would have problems bonding with her new family because of the strong bond she still had with her natural family. It was all so dreadfully sad, and not for the first time since I'd begun fostering I wished I had a big magic wand to turn back the clock and make everything OK.

At the family-finding meeting I raised these concerns, and Kitty, Jill and Faith (from the family-finding team) appreciated what I was saying.

'I'll have to do some work with Alice to prepare her for moving on,' Kitty said. 'Once we know the outcome of the criminal proceedings, and are advertising for an adoptive family, I'll speak to Alice. And perhaps you could try talking to her again,' Kitty said to me. 'She trusts you and I like the way you used the examples of the other children you've fostered who were adopted. That sounds very positive.'

Faith nodded.

'I'll do my best,' I said. 'But Alice firmly believes she will be returning to live with her mother at some point, so strong is their bond.'

'Which is surprising when you think how frightened Alice must have been when her mother snatched her and took her up to the quarry that night,' Jill said. 'You'd have thought Alice would have lost faith in her mother's ability to keep her safe. Alice must be angry with her.'

'I don't think she is,' I said. 'Alice never appears to be angry or feels let down by her mother. Clearly she didn't see the danger in being at the quarry at night. I think she views her mother taking her as a sign of her love and loyalty, which in a way it was.'

Jill nodded.

'I'll talk more to Alice about all of this when I begin preparing her for moving on,' Kitty said. 'If necessary I'll make a referral to a therapist. We don't want a failed adoption on our hands.' I inwardly cringed at the very thought – Alice going to an adoptive home and then having to leave if it didn't work out. This does happen to some children, and it's a rejection from which they take a long time to recover.

Faith then asked me to describe Alice's character, her routine, likes and dislikes, in fact anything that should be taken into account when matching her to a suitable adoptive family. A lump immediately rose in my throat as I began describing Alice, the little angel who'd come to us in the dead of night and had become so much a part of our lives.

'She's a beautiful child,' I said. 'Small for her age, petite, but very intelligent. She has a naturally happy disposition and brightens up any room – you can't stay sad around Alice very long. She sleeps from seven p.m. until seven a.m. and eats well: she enjoys a wide range of food and is willing to try anything new. She loves all types of games, especially role playing – shops, schools, etc., and she likes dressing up as a nurse. She says she wants to be a doctor when she grows up so she can make her mummy, and all the mummies like her, well again.' I stopped and felt tears well in my eyes. 'Can you add anything?' I asked Jill, my voice unsteady.

Jill, who knew Alice from all her visits, added to my description, as did Kitty, while Faith took notes. Faith hadn't met Alice but would do so in the months to come, as she was responsible for drawing up a profile of Alice and the type of adoptive family she would be looking for – i.e. one that would best match Alice. It was decided that in order to meet Alice's cultural needs, the family should be white, British and preferably Christian, as Alice and her mother had been christened and Alice's grandparents went to church. Given that Alice had enjoyed having older siblings in the family in the form of Adrian, Lucy and Paula, it was felt that her adoptive family could have older siblings but not a baby or toddler, as Alice was going to need time and attention in order to settle in.

'I can see Alice going to a childless couple in their early thirties,' Faith said thoughtfully, looking up from her notes. 'I have a number of childless professional couples on my books who have already been approved to adopt. Some of them have been waiting for years for a young child. There is a shortage of healthy white children who need adoptive homes. Alice would be ideal.'

While it sounded as though Alice was a commodity that could be packaged and shipped to new owners, I recognized that if she was going to be adopted then a good match was imperative. A childless couple in their thirties, desperately wanting but unable to have children of their own, seemed ideal, and they would appreciate what a special gift Alice was. Doubtless they would love and cherish Alice as her mother and grandparents did. Whether or not Alice could ever return that love only time would tell.

Once Faith had clarified the legal position with Kitty and also the time frame, she drew the meeting to a close. Faith said another family-finding meeting would be arranged once the criminal proceedings were out of the way. In the meantime she would type up her notes – the profile of Alice and the type of family she would be looking for. Faith asked me if I could find some recent photographs of Alice and bring them to the next meeting so that she had them on file to show would-be adopters.

On the drive home I tried to picture the – as yet unidentified – childless couple waiting to start a family, who would be lucky enough to have Alice if she went on to be adopted, which was looking increasingly likely. I knew their gain would be our loss, but the loss my family and I would feel when Alice eventually left us would be nothing compared to the loss Alice's mother and grandparents would suffer if Alice was adopted. As a foster carer I have to prepare myself for children leaving, painful though it is, but not so with Alice's mother and grandparents, who had naturally assumed Alice would be with them forever.

That afternoon when I took Alice to the family centre for contact with her grandparents I felt underhand and deceitful for having attended the family-finding meeting where, unbeknown to Mr and Mrs Jones, I had been 'plotting' with Kitty, Jill and Faith to take away their granddaughter. I couldn't look Mrs Jones in the eye for the guilt I felt, and to make matters worse she gave me another pot of her home-made chutney. 'I know you like it as much as Alice,' she said, smiling. 'So I've stepped up production.'

I thanked her and silently prayed that the strength and courage that had seen them through so much would stay with them and see them through what was to come.

Regardless of my own feelings I still had to do my job as a foster carer, so the following weekend I took the opportunity to talk to Alice about the future as I'd tried to in the past, and as Kitty had asked me to continue to do. Alice was looking at one of the many framed photographs I had on the walls in the sitting room, and I told her the boy in the picture was called Oliver, and he had stayed with me for a year. When she asked where he was now I said he'd been found a new mummy and daddy – a forever family who loved him very much and with whom he was very happy. Alice seemed quite interested and began asking questions: Where does he live? Does he have any brothers or sisters, or pets? Does he go on holiday with his family? And so on. I told Alice what I knew of Oliver's family and then added: 'It's possible that one day you might be found a new mummy and daddy who will love you as Oliver's do, and you will be very happy.'

Alice turned from the photograph and looked at me as though I had just spoken the unspeakable. 'You mustn't say that,' she said, her little face creasing. 'I don't want a new mummy. I want my old mummy. She's the best mummy in the world.'

'But Alice, pet,' I said gently. 'Your mummy can't look after you as mummies are supposed to. You don't want to stay in foster care forever, and keep having to go to the family centre for contact, do you? You want a normal family life with parents who can look after you and play with you, and will love you more than anyone else in the world.'

Alice continued to stare at me. 'I want to stay with you, until my mummy is better. Then I can go home. Don't you want me to stay with you, Cathy? I thought you liked me.'

'Oh, of course I like you, pet,' I said, putting my arms around her and drawing her to me. 'I like you very, very much, and you will stay with me until everything is sorted out. But you have to understand that where you live permanently isn't my decision. The judge will decide what is best for you. And I think he will want you to have a proper mummy and daddy who will love you forever and be your very own family.'

Alice continued to stare at me; then her eyes slowly filled and her little face looked sadder than I had ever seen it before. A large tear escaped and ran down her cheek; then another and another. I drew her to the sofa and on to my lap, where I cuddled her closely as she sobbed openly. Alice had been so brave for seven months, holding it all together in the unshakable belief that her mummy would recover and she could eventually return to live with her. Now she was finally starting to listen to what I was saying, and having to accept there might be a different outcome and she wouldn't be returning to her mother, and it hurt. It hurt Alice, and it hurt me, for there was nothing I could do but reassure her, and hope that eventually, given time, she would come to terms with it.

Chapter Thirty-Two

Love from Mummy

Despite everything that was going on, the week leading up to 2 November was a light-hearted and joyous one. Not only was Christmas on the horizon – the shops were already displaying Christmas cards and novelties – but 2 November would be Alice's fifth birthday, and she was getting very excited.

'I'm going to be a big, big girl,' she said, strutting around the house with her back straight and head held high, making herself as tall as possible. 'Soon I'll be as big as you,' she said, measuring herself up to Adrian who, 80 centimetres taller, looked like a giant beside her. 'I've got long legs,' she said, 'and on my birthday I'm going to be bigger than all the other four-year-olds in the whole wide world.' Quite clearly this wasn't so – Alice was very petite and one of the smallest in her class – but we didn't disillusion her.

'Five is a very big girl,' I said, and Adrian, Lucy and Paula agreed.

'My friend Tammy doesn't have to go to bed until nine o'clock now she is five,' Alice said, testing the water for an extension on her bedtime.

'Really?' I said, unconvinced. 'I bet she's tired the next day at school.'

'No, she's not,' Alice said quickly. 'And Shaun is allowed to stay up till midnight watching television with his dad now he's five.'

'If that is so,' Lucy put in dryly, 'someone should tell the social services. Sleep deprivation is a form of abuse.'

I laughed. 'Very well put,' I said.

'Cathy,' Alice said, finally getting to the point. 'When I am five what time will I have to go to bed?'

'Well, let me see,' I said, thinking out loud. 'You're four now and you go to bed at seven o'clock. Is that right?' Alice nodded. 'So when you are five I think six o'clock would be a good time. What do you think, Lucy?'

'Yes,' Lucy said, stifling a smile. 'Definitely.'

Alice looked at me, horrified, before she realized we were joking. 'You're teasing me,' she said with an old-fashioned smile. 'And you, Lucy!'

I went over and kissed her cheek. 'OK, seriously, love, I think seven o'clock on a school night is late enough for a big person of five. But we could make your bedtime seven thirty at weekends – on a Friday and a Saturday when you don't have to be up early in the morning.'

Alice smiled, pleased. 'But when I tell my friends I'll say now I'm five I go to bed at seven thirty, and forget the bit about weekends. Emily still has to go to bed at six and she's been five for ages.'

'I think I've been duped!' I said, and Lucy agreed.

* * *

On the Wednesday before her birthday Alice had contact with her grandparents and they took her birthday presents to the family centre so that she could open them while they were together. Her grandparents also gave Alice a little party – just the three of them, with the supervisor joining in. The family centre accommodates families wanting to celebrate birthdays and can provide plates, cutlery, cups, glasses, microwave oven, etc. Mrs Jones had taken in party food and a small iced birthday cake with five candles. When I went into the contact room to collect Alice at the end she was very flushed and excited, and eager to show me her presents and tell me of the games they'd played. Mr and Mrs Jones were clearly pleased that Alice had enjoyed herself, but I could see it had been a bittersweet event for them. This year they had been forced to celebrate Alice's birthday in the confines of one hour at the family centre, under supervision, unlike previous years when presumably the family had all been together at home.

'Leah has promised to send Alice a present and card,' Mrs Jones said quietly to me as Mr Jones helped Alice into her coat. 'I offered to put her name on our present and card but she wants to do something of her own.'

'That'll be lovely,' I smiled. 'How is Leah now?'

'Making progress. It's good she feels up to organizing a present and card. She wouldn't have done that a month ago. Having Chris prosecuted has helped.'

'Oh?' I asked, uncertain what she meant.

'Leah felt everyone was against her, but now the police are prosecuting him she feels someone believes her and is on her side.' Mrs Jones shrugged. 'We've always believed her and have been on her side, but that hasn't been enough to help her.'

I nodded, and then turned towards Alice, who had finished kissing Grandpa goodbye and was on her way over to us.

'Now, have I put in all her presents?' Mrs Jones said, checking the large carrier bag before passing it to me. 'I hope you don't mind, Cathy, I'm taking the rest of the cake home with me. Leah is coming later and we'll have a slice with her as a little celebration.'

'No, of course I don't mind,' I said. 'I've bought a cake for Alice's actual birthday on Sunday. I hope you have a nice evening.' But I thought how sad it was that the closest Leah would get to celebrating her daughter's birthday this year was with a slice from the remaining birthday cake.

The following day, Thursday, Alice had contact with her father and Sharon and they also took in a birthday present, which Alice unwrapped. There was no party food or cake, but it was a nice present – a child's first computer, which taught letter sounds, word and number recognition, and had small puzzles to do. At the end of contact Sharon, always ready to undermine Leah, asked me in front of Alice if her mother had bought her anything for her birthday. The contact supervisor was still present and motioned for Sharon not to continue.

But Sharon didn't have to say anything further, for Alice, having heard Sharon, naturally asked: 'Will my mummy remember my birthday?'

'I should think so, love,' I said. Then I redirected Alice to say goodbye.

Outside, in the car, Alice asked again: 'Cathy, do you think my mummy will buy me a present and card?'

'I hope so.' I couldn't say yes, for clearly I didn't know for definite. Mrs Jones had said Leah was going to arrange to send something but I hadn't heard anything from Kitty to this effect. Leah didn't have our address, so I assumed the present and card would come to us via the social worker, which is what had happened in the past with other children I'd fostered who hadn't seen their parents on their birthdays. But Leah was leaving it a bit late, for the next day was Friday – the last possible day for a present and/or card to be given to the social services in time for Alice's actual birthday on Sunday. That night as I tucked Alice into bed she looked sad.

'Are you OK?' I asked, adjusting the duvet under her chin. I was sitting on the edge of the bed, as I did every night after reading a story – making sure Alice was all right, that there was nothing worrying her and that she was ready to go to sleep. I've found – with my own children and those I've fostered – that this time, this little space between daytime ending and night-time beginning, is when children are most relaxed, and more likely to share a worry or release a secret. It is also a good time for me to talk to a child, as they are often more receptive.

'I hope my mummy remembers it's my birthday,' Alice said pensively. 'She doesn't have to buy me a present or send me a card, but I would like her to write a little note. It could say "Happy Birthday, love from Mummy". It will make me so very happy.'

'Alice, love,' I said, stroking her cheek. 'I know your mummy won't forget your birthday. Not this year, not ever. I know wherever your mummy is on your birthday she will remember and be thinking of you. But what I don't know is if mummy will be able to send you anything. It is very difficult for her right now. But if she doesn't send a card or present, I want you to know mummy hasn't forgotten you, but is thinking of you on your birthday; it will make you both feel that little bit closer. Like the kisses you send down the phone to Nana and Grandpa – they bring you closer, don't they?'

Alice thought for a moment; then she gave a little nod and a smile crossed her face. 'If I think of my mummy now perhaps it will help her write a card.' She screwed her eyes closed in concentration, willing her mother to write her a birthday card. 'I think she's writing it,' Alice said. 'I think she's writing: "Happy Birthday to my darling Alice. Love from Mummy". Yes, I'm sure she is.'

Alice was right: her wish was granted, although the wording in the card wasn't quite the same. The following day, after I'd taken Alice to school, Kitty phoned from her mobile. 'I need to ask you a favour,' she said, against the sound of a train on the track. 'Two favours, actually.'

'Yes?'

'Leah has dropped off a present and card for Alice at the offices. They're in reception. I won't have time to collect them and bring them to you today. I'm visiting a child who had just been placed out of the area. Could you collect the present and card so Alice has them for her birthday?'

'Yes, of course. I'll go as soon as we've finished.'

'Thanks. And secondly could you have a little look at the present before you give it to Alice to make sure it's suitable? I'll leave it to your judgement, Cathy, and also how much of the card you read out. I don't want Alice upset, so if mum is pouring out her heart could you edit it out when you read it, please? Fortunately Alice can't read yet.'

'Yes, of course, I understand. I'm just so pleased Leah has sent Alice something. It will mean the world to her.'

'Yes, although it was Leah's partner, Mike, who took the present and card into reception while Leah waited outside,' Kitty said, mildly critical. 'Leah still thinks the department is out to get her, so she won't come into the building.'

'It's understandable, given everything that's happened,' I said, instinctively rallying to Leah's defence. 'And it's nice that Leah has Mike's support. Chris has Sharon's.'

'Agreed. Well, thanks for your help, Cathy. Have a great day on Sunday. I've put a card from me in the post for Alice.'

While Sharon's presence and support of Chris was viewed in a positive light, Mike's similar support of Leah had been interpreted as something lacking in Leah. I'd noted similar before and I wondered if a negative comment had been made by one of the first social workers involved in Alice's case, before Alice came to me, and the attitude had persisted. I was sure if it had been Sharon taking a gift for Alice into reception at the social services while Chris waited outside it wouldn't have been commented on.

We had a fantastic day on Sunday – Alice's birthday and also the day of her party. I had invited six of Alice's friends from school and Alice wore a new cream dress and matching slipper-shoes. She looked and behaved liked an angel. It had been some years since I'd had an opportunity to provide a full-scale children's birthday party, with jelly and ice cream, games, pass the parcel, and party bags to take home at the end. My children understandably considered themselves too old for all that, and the children we'd looked after recently, being that bit older too, had preferred bowling, football and themed parties; Paula had had a sleepover.

But suddenly age and maturity were forgotten when it came to joining in and having fun at Alice's party. Lucy's sophistication vanished as she competed with the little ones in trying to keep a balloon in the air without using her hands. We all laughed when Adrian, following Alice's instructions, got down on his hands and knees so she could reach to blindfold him for a game of 'pin the tail on the donkey', while Paula, aged ten, was a little child again and joined in unreservedly with everything.

By the time the parents arrived to collect their children at 6.00 p.m. and we called our goodbyes from the doorstep we were all pleasantly exhausted. I knew Alice had had a lovely party and had liked her presents –

from us and her friends, but the present and card that was most treasured were of course those from her mother. The present, opened that morning, was a china doll in beautiful hand-knitted clothes, which Alice had tucked into her bed; and the large card with sparkling letters stood in place of honour on the mantelpiece in the sitting room. When Alice had opened the card that morning, following Kitty's advice and my own intuition, I had read only some of the words: 'To my beautiful daughter. Have a wonderful birthday. I'll be thinking of you. All my love Mummy xxxxx'.

Once everyone had gone, we'd cleared up and Alice was in bed, I returned to the sitting room, where I took down the card and looked at it again. On the front in large glittering letters was 'To My Darling Daughter' with a glittering picture of a fairytale princess. I carefully opened the card and began re-reading the lines written on the left-hand flap of the card – those I hadn't read aloud to Alice that morning. The words were very moving and I knew they would have been upsetting for Alice, but there was something else, something that had been niggling at me all day, but which I'd put on hold so I could concentrate on Alice's birthday and party.

'My dear Alice,' Leah wrote, 'I'm so very sorry I can't be with you on your birthday. Please try and forgive me. I will be thinking of you as I think of you every minute of every day. I know I haven't been a good mother and now I am being punished by losing you. I have no one to blame but myself. I should have been stronger, I should have said no. I did so well for four years and we were happy, but then I stupidly put him before you and now

I have lost you for good. I know you won't make the same mistakes I did. You are a bright girl and I have been such a fool. If only I could turn back the clock and have another chance, but I can't. If we don't see each other again please try and find it within your heart to forgive me. I didn't mean to cause you pain. I love you more than life itself. Take care my precious one. All my love Mummy xxxxx'

I read the last few lines again and then looked up and stared across the room with the card still open in my hand. What I didn't like, and what had been bothering me all day, was the ring of finality at the end: the way Leah seemed to be saying goodbye for good – 'If we don't see each other again'. And while I recognized that the words could have been referring to the way Leah had lost Alice into care, or would lose her permanently through adoption, increasingly I was feeling that there could be another, more sinister interpretation, and that given Leah's desperation she could be thinking of ending her life.

Alice had phoned her grandparents the evening before and wasn't due to phone them again until the following Saturday; she wouldn't be seeing them until the week after. I remained seated on the sofa with a growing need to reassure myself and make sure Leah was all right. I didn't want to leave it until Kitty was in the office the following day. Realizing I was probably over-reacting and about to make a complete fool of myself, but at the same time feeling that if I didn't say anything and something dreadful happened I'd never forgive myself, at nearly 9.00 p.m. I phoned Alice's grandparents.

'Is Alice all right?' Mrs Jones immediately asked, anxious on hearing my voice.

'Yes, she's fine. She's had a lovely birthday and is now asleep.'

'Thank God. I thought for a moment something was wrong.'

'No, Alice is fine. I'm sorry to phone you like this but I just wanted to make sure Leah was all right. I know it's probably nothing, but Leah wrote some words in Alice's birthday card that made me think she might be considering doing something silly – desperate.'

There was silence before Mrs Jones spoke and in that silence I knew I had been right to be worried. 'Leah tried to commit suicide last night,' Mrs Jones said. 'Thankfully Mike came home and found her in time.'

Chapter Thirty-Three

Expecting an Ogre

'I should have realized Alice's birthday was more than Leah could cope with,' Mrs Jones continued in a subdued voice. 'Leah was doing so well, and now this. She had returned to her flat and Mike had moved in. He's blaming himself for not spotting the warning signs.'

'I'm so sorry,' I said. 'Where is Leah now?'

'At home, with Mike. They pumped out her stomach at the hospital and she returned home early this morning. Mike is taking time off work to look after her. His manager at the garage is being very understanding. Mike is badly shaken up too. He got in late last night, after working the evening shift, and found Leah on the sofa with a bottle of tablets beside her. She left a note saying that life wasn't worth living without Alice. The poor girl misses her daughter so much – she desperately needs to see her.'

'And Alice needs to see her mother,' I said. 'Even though she can't live with her, they should be seeing each other, at contact.'

'I know,' Mrs Jones said quietly.

I hesitated, aware that having been reassured Leah was safe, I should now say goodnight and that I would phone with Alice as usual the following Saturday, but I didn't.

'Janice,' I said, using her first name. 'I think you and I have worked very well together since Alice came into care. I hope you trust me enough to know I always have Alice's best interest at heart.'

'Oh yes, of course, Cathy. Martin and I can't thank you enough.'

'There is no need to thank me – Alice is a treasure to look after – but I would like to speak plainly to you, if I may. How much of what I say you pass on to Leah is obviously up to you, but I think the present situation, with Alice not seeing her mother, has gone on far too long. It is very bad for both of them.'

'Well, yes,' Mrs Jones said hesitantly. 'Go ahead.'

'I appreciate that when Alice first came into care Leah wasn't well enough to see her daughter, but from what I understand from Kitty now, Leah has improved in recent months, apart from the setback last night.'

'Yes, she has,' Mrs Jones confirmed.

'I think the reason Leah won't engage with Kitty and talk to her about the possibility of contact being set up is now more to do with Leah's anger, and her fears, rather than her present mental health.'

Mrs Jones was quiet for a moment. 'What do you mean, exactly?'

'Did you know that Kitty phoned Leah three times last month, inviting her to go to her office to discuss setting up contact so she can see Alice?'

'No, I didn't. When was this?'

'I don't know the exact dates. But I do know that each time Kitty phoned Leah, Leah became so angry that Kitty eventually had to end the call. Leah wouldn't listen to what Kitty was saying but shouted down the phone that she would never agree to supervised contact, and then called Kitty a lot of names, which didn't help. I think Leah's anger and fear are getting in the way of her seeing Alice. She is angry with herself for Alice going into care, and it is stopping her from moving forward. In the birthday card she sent to Alice she says she should have been stronger and blames herself for losing Alice. Leah needs to stop blaming herself, and accusing Kitty, and concentrate on trying to see Alice. I know Leah isn't well enough to look after Alice and might never be, but I think if she could let go of her pain and anger and stop wallowing in her own misery, she might be well enough to start seeing Alice again at contact. She has the support of Mike, and I know Kitty suggested that Mike accompany Leah to any meetings.'

'Did she?' Mrs Jones asked, surprised.

'Yes, but Leah wouldn't listen and screamed that Kitty had taken Alice from her. Kitty is one of the best social workers I have come across and she is doing all she can to help Leah, so that mother and daughter can see each other. Janice, if you have any influence over Leah I think you need to talk to her and tell her it is essential she put her own hurt and anger to one side for the sake of her daughter, before it's too late.

Mrs Jones was quiet on the other end of the phone and I wondered if I had said too much and she'd taken offence. No one likes to be told what to do, particularly when it comes from some know-it-all trying to give a mother unasked-for advice about her daughter. I would have been most put out if I'd been in the same situation, although I hope I would have been able to swallow my pride and listen to what I was being told. 'Anyway,' I said after a moment. 'I've said what I wanted to. Please take my advice in the spirit in which it is given. I only want what is best for Alice. I'm relieved Leah is safe and being looked after; please give her my best wishes. I'll phone you again, as usual, with Alice next Saturday.'

'Goodnight,' Mrs Jones said quietly. The line went dead.

Before I went to bed that night I wrote up my log notes, including Alice's party and the unscheduled phone call I'd made to Mrs Jones. Although I thought it was unlikely, I couldn't be sure that Mrs Jones wouldn't report me to the social services for phoning her and making a nuisance of myself. If a complaint was made by Mrs Jones (and I seemed to be attracting complaints since I'd been looking after Alice), I could produce my log notes and justify my action in the context of my concerns for Leah. Detailed log notes are not only for the child's and social services' benefit but can also be used as evidence to support what a foster carer is saying.

The following day, Monday, we fell into our school routine, with Alice still chattering happily about her birthday and party, and the wonderful time she'd had. She wanted to take her birthday cards into school to show her class, as they were allowed to do, and

I gathered up the cards from the mantelpiece in the sitting room, all except the one from her mother, which Alice said was 'private' and only for her.

Jill phoned just after lunch and for a moment I thought Mrs Jones had reported me but Jill asked how Alice's party had gone and also wanted to update me. She said she'd spoken to Kitty that morning, who'd told her of Leah's attempted suicide and also that the criminal proceedings against Chris hadn't yet been given a court date, so the childcare proceedings were still on hold.

'Kitty phoned the CPS,' Jill said, referring to the Crown Prosecution Service, 'and they have promised to set a date for the case against Chris soon. It's unfair to keep Alice in foster care indefinitely without a decision on her future. Alice will certainly be with you for this Christmas, and possibly the following Christmas too at this rate!' And while I wouldn't have minded one little bit if Alice had been with me for all the following Christmases, I too recognized it was unfair to keep her in care and she should be settled with her forever family as soon as possible.

The week continued as usual: Alice went to school, played with the toys she'd had for her birthday in the evenings and saw her father and Sharon for an hour on Tuesday and Thursday. I heard nothing more about my unscheduled phone call to Mrs Jones, so I assumed it hadn't been reported and Mrs Jones had taken my advice in the spirit in which I'd given it. Then on Friday, as I was looking forward to a reasonably relaxing weekend after all the excitement of the previous one, with Alice's birthday and party, a little miracle happened, for which I was truly grateful.

It was just after 11.00 a.m. and I'd not been in long from shopping – stocking up the fridge for the weekend – when the phone rang. Leaving the unpacked carrier bags in the kitchen, I answered the phone in the sitting room. It was Kitty and as usual she asked after my family and me before coming to the reason for her phone call.

'A step forward,' Kitty began, her tone optimistic. 'I've finally had a meeting with Leah and Mike. Yesterday afternoon they came into the office and as a result I'm setting up contact for Alice to see her mother this Monday.'

'Alice is seeing her mother on Monday!' I repeated, unable to believe my ears. 'Fantastic. Absolutely fantastic.'

'Yes, it is, but I don't want you to tell Alice yet, not until Monday, when Leah has arrived at the family centre and I know she is able to go through with the contact. Cathy, this is what I would like you to do. On Monday collect Alice from school as usual in the afternoon. Then start a slow drive to the family centre. I will phone you when mum arrives, and at that point pull over and tell Alice she is seeing her mother. But when you tell Alice, please make sure she understands she is only seeing her mother and it certainly doesn't mean she will be living with her.'

'Yes, I will.'

'If Leah doesn't arrive at the family centre I will phone you and you'll have to think of an excuse as to why you haven't gone straight home with Alice after school. I don't want you to say anything to Alice. I don't want her hopes raised and then dashed. I'm really not sure if Leah will be able to go through with it, but if she does, and contact is good, then we will continue every Monday.'

'Fantastic!' I said again.

'I've asked Leah to meet me just before the start of contact so that I can make sure she is in a fit state to see Alice. If she's too upset, I'll have to cancel it. Mike will be bringing Leah to the family centre, but he understands he won't be part of the contact, not for the first few sessions at least. These will be between Alice and her mother, so they can get to know each other again after all this time. Although of course if Alice is going to be adopted,' Kitty added, 'the contact will be stopped, but at this stage Leah is entitled to see her daughter, and Alice should be seeing her mother.'

'Yes,' I replied, thoughtfully. 'In some ways this has come too late.'

'We'll see,' Kitty said. 'I liked Leah. I was expecting an ogre but she's actually very pleasant. She can talk sensibly, although she can become agitated very quickly. It's something I've warned her to be careful of at contact. Leah understands that contact will be supervised by one of the staff at the family centre, and I too will be there for the first session. I've explained that the supervisor and I will intervene if we feel it isn't going well or it is too much for Alice to cope with. I know it puts Leah under pressure but I'm safeguarding Alice.'

Kitty paused as though she was considering whether to tell me something.

'Cathy,' she continued after a moment, 'Leah said something at the meeting which made me wonder about the true level of violence Chris inflicted on her. She said if there was no chance of her looking after Alice again, and her parents were considered too old, then she would rather Alice was adopted than go to Chris, although she understands this would mean she would never see Alice again. Leah said she was sure it was only a matter of time before Chris's violence resurfaced and he hit Sharon, and possibly Alice. I've found a note on the file where Leah had said something similar to the social worker who was first involved in the case, but that social worker felt Leah was being vindictive towards Chris. Given what has happened since – with him breaking into her flat and assaulting her – and what Alice has told us of last summer, I think Leah and her parents have been telling the truth. I'm pleased Alice didn't go straight to Chris and Sharon's as was first intended, when his behaviour wasn't an issue.'

'It has always been an issue for the grandparents,' I said cautiously.

'I know. Mr and Mrs Jones should have been listened to more closely. They played a big part in Alice's life but their views seem to have been dismissed.' Kitty paused again, perhaps reflecting on how Alice's case could have been handled differently at the beginning, for it did seem that not enough time had been spent listening to, and taking into account, what Leah and her parents had been saying instead of 'fast-tracking' Alice to Chris and Sharon, who I suppose offered the best (and easiest) solution at the time. 'Anyway,' Kitty said, 'fingers

crossed that it all goes well on Monday. Thank goodness Mrs Jones was able to make Leah see sense. Leah
told me her mother gave her a good talking to and it
seems to have worked.'

'Thank goodness,' I agreed.

Chapter Thirty-Four

Don't Make Me Go!

Although I was acutely aware that if Alice was adopted, seeing her mother would quickly come to an end, it didn't dampen my enthusiasm for Alice seeing her on Monday. It would have been very negative and harmful for both of them if their last memory of each other had been as fugitives, hiding at the quarry, with Alice being taken to the police station in the dead of night. At least now, if everything went according to plan, mother and daughter would have the chance to spend some time together each week before eventually having to say goodbye (if Alice was adopted), painful though that would be. Parting forever was in the future – months, possibly a year ahead; for now I was elated that Alice and Leah would finally be seeing each other again after a separation of eight months.

It was 3.25 p.m. as, hand in hand, Alice and I left the school playground and walked along the pavement, towards the car. Alice was telling me what she'd had for school dinner: fish fingers, mashed potatoes and peas, followed by sticky-toffee pudding and custard;

her dinner often seemed to be the highlight of the school day. According to Kitty's instructions I should now take a slow drive in the direction of the family centre, twenty minutes away, during which time Kitty would phone to advise me if contact was going ahead, when I would tell Alice. I took my time settling Alice into the car and adjusting her seatbelt before I climbed into the driver's seat and closed the door. It was now 3.31. I started the engine and slowly pulled out. As I did I said a silent prayer that Leah would find the strength to go to the family centre, meet Kitty and then wait for Alice to arrive.

The route to the family centre is the same as that from school to home for the first ten minutes, and then the two routes divide. I knew that Alice, intelligent and alert, would spot straightaway when we turned off and were no longer following the route home. I'd already decided that if Kitty hadn't phoned by then I would have to tell Alice a little fib and say we were going to the retail park for something I needed to buy. Likewise if Kitty phoned to say contact wasn't going ahead I would use the same excuse for not having gone straight home, and then stop off at the retail park. I'd no idea what I was going to buy, but doubtless I would think of something.

Sure enough at 3.43 as I turned off the route home, Alice's little voice came from the rear of the car: 'Cathy, this isn't the right way. It's Monday, and I don't have contact on Monday.'

'It is Monday …' I said slowly and was preparing to tell her we were going to the retail park when, with perfect timing, my phone started ringing from its perch on the dashboard. Leaving the sentence unfinished, I pulled over and answered the phone.

It was Kitty. 'We're going ahead,' she said. My heart lurched. 'Leah is here. We've had a chat and although she's quite emotional, I'm sure she'll be fine to see Alice.'

'Thank God,' I said, and I meant it. 'I'll tell Alice now.'

'Yes, but please make sure she understands it's only a meeting and she isn't going home with mum.'

'I will. Thanks. See you soon.' I cut the phone, switched off the engine and turned in my seat to face Alice.

'That was Kitty,' I said, with a small smile. 'We're going to the family centre to see your mother. Just for an hour, like you see your Dad and Sharon, and Nana and Grandpa. Then I will come and collect you.'

Alice stared at me, her eyes growing rounder and larger by the second, as her lips parted in wonder. 'Mummy?' she asked quietly, not daring to believe. 'I'm going to see my mummy?'

'Yes, love, just for an hour. Then I'll come and collect you,' I emphasized.

'Mummy?' she asked again in the same, small, incredulous voice. 'Why am I seeing my mummy?'

Reaching over the seat I took her hand and patted it reassuringly. I would have liked to have had time to prepare Alice for seeing her mother, but that hadn't been possible, so I would talk to her more in the evening. 'Mummy is well enough to see you for a little while now,' I said. 'She is looking forward to seeing you again.'

Alice nodded; then she turned her head and looked out of her side window. She didn't smile, she didn't say anything; she just sat staring out, completely over-whelmed. I turned to the front, started the engine and rejoined the traffic.

'All right, love?' I asked after a moment. Alice nodded.

After a few minutes her little voice came from the back. 'Are we going to see my mummy?' she asked, still not fully believing.

'Yes, love, at the family centre. We'll be there soon.'

She was silent again. For the rest of the journey she stared out of the side window, overawed and doubtless at a loss to know what she should be thinking, feeling or saying. Even when I pulled up and parked outside the family centre, she still didn't say anything. I got out and opened the rear door; then I waited as Alice slowly climbed out. I could see her reticence, sense her anxiety at meeting her mother again after all this time and having parted in such traumatic circumstances. It was understandable. Eight months is a long time, especially in a child's life.

'Is Mummy better?' Alice asked as we walked hand in hand up the path to the security door.

'She's getting better,' I said. 'Kitty and a contact super-visor will be there to help Mummy if she needs it. But from what Kitty told me Mummy is doing very well.'

I pressed the security buzzer. As we waited for the door to release Alice said: 'I love my mummy. I hope she still loves me.'

'She does, pet. I'm sure of it.'

We went in and my heart thumped with a mixture of anticipation and anxiety, which were compounded by finding the reception empty.

'Where is she?' Alice asked, gripping my hand tighter as panic set in. 'Where's my mummy? She's not here.'

'I'll find out,' I said. I tapped on the sliding-glass partition to the office and fervently hoped that Leah was still here and hadn't been overcome and fled since Kitty had phoned. One of the family centre workers slid open the window. 'Alice is here to see her mother,' I said. 'Kitty should be here somewhere with Leah.'

She consulted a chart on her desk. 'They're in Red Room,' she said. I breathed a sigh of relief. 'Are you all right to take Alice through or shall I go with you?'

'I'll take her,' I said. 'Thanks.' With Alice gripping my hand even tighter we went along the corridor, through the double doors and over to the door with pictures of red roses and marked 'Red Room'.

The door was closed and through the glass panel in the door I could see Kitty and the contact supervisor sitting on the sofa facing the door. On the other sofa, facing away from me, was another woman, Leah, her slight frame and ponytail suggesting someone younger than the twenty-three I knew her to be. Alice wasn't tall enough to see through the glass panel, so she didn't see Kitty wave for us to go in; nor did she see her mother leap from the sofa and turn to the door, her expression an indescribable mixture of expectation, pain and joy. I opened the door and Leah dropped to her knees so that she was Alice's height, and spread her arms wide, ready to hug her daughter.

'Mummy?' Alice said quietly, not leaving my side. 'Where have you been?'

'I'm here, love. I'm sorry. I'm here now, Alice. Please forgive me.' I looked at her and could have wept.

On hearing her mother's voice Alice let go of my hand and rushed into her mother's waiting arms. Leah buried her head in her daughter's shoulder and cried openly. Alice hugged her mother as though she would never let go. I looked at Kitty and the contact supervisor, who were both dewy eyed, and I felt my own eyes mist.

'I'll say hello to Leah at the end,' I mouthed to Kitty. She nodded, and I came out, leaving Alice where she should have been a long time ago: in the arms of her mother.

I drove home, sombre and deep in thought. When I went in I found Lucy and Paula waiting expectantly in the hall, having heard my car draw up. I'd told them all that morning I might not be coming straight home after collecting Alice from school, as there was a chance she would be seeing her mother; now the girls were waiting for any news.

'Well?' Lucy asked. 'Did contact go ahead?'

I nodded.

'You don't seem very happy about it,' Paula said.

I shrugged and took off my coat and shoes.

'Don't you like Alice's mother?' Lucy asked.

'I didn't speak to her, but I'm sure she's lovely. It's not that.' I sighed and looked at the girls. 'I really can't see where all this is going to lead. It's good that Alice is seeing her mother, but she can't live with her. Alice's grandparents are likely to be considered too old to look after her long term. Alice's father has the prosecution hanging over him, and if I'm honest I've never felt living with him and Sharon was right for Alice. There are no other relatives who can look after Alice, so the most likely outcome is that she will be adopted, but in my heart of hearts I can't believe that is right for her either. The bond Alice has with her mother and grand-parents is so strong I can't see how she would ever love her adoptive parents. And if she doesn't, the adoption will fail. I really can't see what is best for Alice,' I ended despondently as I had begun.

I went down the hall towards the kitchen, to make a quick cup of tea before I had to return to the family centre. Lucy and Paula followed, and then hovered, watching me carefully as I filled the kettle and set it to boil. 'I know it's not my decision,' I continued, 'but obviously we want what is best for Alice. We want her to be happy. I was asked my opinion at the family-finding meeting and I told them Alice had a strong bond with her mother and grandparents. I'll say it again at the next family-finding meeting, which will be after the prosecution. It's all I can do.'

The girls were quiet, understanding the dilemma. With the vast majority of the children we'd looked after, the decision as to where they eventually lived – with parents, relatives, long-term foster carers or adop-tive parents – seemed right, but not here. Now, there seemed no ideal solution.

'I feel sorry for Alice,' Paula said at last. 'It's not like her family were horrible to her.'

'No,' Lucy agreed. 'They were very kind to her but she can't live with them.'

I looked at Lucy and Paula, whose faces I had made glum by sharing my concerns. 'Don't you two worry about it,' I said with a brave smile. 'I'm sure it will all turn out for the best in the end.' Although for the life of me I couldn't see how it would.

After a quick cup of tea I returned to the family centre to collect Alice, my thoughts now concentrating on meeting Leah and comforting Alice after she'd had to leave her mother. I waited in reception until it was exactly five o'clock; then I went to Red Room and knocked on the door before going in. Kitty and the contact supervisor were more or less as I'd left them – on the sofa facing the door – while Alice now sat beside her mother on the other sofa, listening to a story. They all looked up as I entered and Alice's face puckered, aware what my arrival meant. I felt like a wicked witch coming to take her away.

'It's time to go now,' Kitty said gently.

I smiled at Leah as I crossed to shake her hand. 'I'm very pleased to see you.'

Leah returned my smile and, keeping one arm around Alice and the book open on her lap, shook my hand. 'I can't thank you enough for looking after Alice,' she said in a small gentle voice. 'You've been so kind to us.'

My heart went out to her. 'Alice is a pleasure to look after,' I said. 'She's a lovely child, and a real credit to you.'

I realized immediately it was the wrong thing to say. In Leah's fragile and sensitive state my well-intentioned comment touched a raw nerve. Leah's face crumpled and she began to cry. Taking her arm from around Alice, she rummaged in her handbag for a tissue.

Kitty stood and came over. 'Time to go now, Alice,' she said again. 'Say goodbye to Mummy.'

I knew saying goodbye was going to be painful but I also knew, as did Kitty and the contact supervisor, that prolonging it was only going to make it worse. Alice remained where she was, seated on the sofa and now holding on to her mother's arm. 'Say goodbye, Alice. Good girl,' Kitty said as Leah wiped her eyes.

Alice shook her head. 'No,' she said, and began to cry.

Leah turned to her daughter and, lightly placing her hands on her shoulders, turned to her so she could look into her eyes. 'We have to say goodbye now, love,' she said, being incredibly brave, 'but we'll see each other again next week.'

Alice shook her head and clung tighter to her mother's arm. 'No,' she cried. 'I want to stay with you. Don't make me go, Mummy. Please don't make me go.'

Leah started crying again as she tried to open Alice's fingers from around her arm. 'Come on, love, give me a kiss, and say goodbye,' she said. Alice wouldn't. Leah kissed her daughter's forehead. 'Please, Alice, you have to go.'

'No!' Alice shrieked.

'Come on, Alice,' Kitty encouraged, going closer. 'Say goodbye to your mummy.'

'No!' Alice shrieked again and clung on to her mother all the more.

Crying openly now, Leah looked up at Kitty and pleaded: 'Just take her, please. I can't bear to see her like this.'

Kitty leant forward and, opening Alice's fingers from around her mother's arm, quickly lifted Alice from the sofa and put her into my arms.

'Goodbye, Alice,' Leah called through tears. 'See you next week. Be a good girl.'

Alice shrieked. 'No! I want to stay!'

I carried Alice from the room, down the corridor and out of the family centre with her sobbing and thrashing her arms and legs. It was just as well Alice was slight, but even so I struggled to hold her and not drop her. I managed to open the rear door of the car and lift her into her seat. 'I hate you,' she shouted at me through her tears. 'I don't want to go home with you. I want my mummy.'

'I know you do, love. I understand.'

I climbed into the back of the car and sat next to Alice, where I held her and tried to reassure her, as she sobbed that she wanted her mummy and hated me. After about ten minutes she was calm enough for me to wipe her face with a tissue and then fasten her seatbelt, ready for the drive home. Alice didn't speak during the twenty-minute journey and I didn't say anything either – I recognized she needed time to come to terms with seeing her mother and having to say goodbye.

By the time we arrived home Alice didn't look quite so sad. As I opened the car door and helped her out, she said quietly: 'I love my mummy.'

'I know you do, pet. And she loves you very much. I know how difficult this is, but now you are seeing your mother each week it should start to get a bit easier.'

Alice nodded and slipping her hand into mine gave it a squeeze, and I knew I had been forgiven for taking her away.

Lucy and Paula, as before, were waiting in the hall. 'I've seen my mummy,' Alice announced proudly, although still a little subdued, as we entered.

Lucy and Paula both clapped and gave little whoops of joy, which made Alice laugh. I helped her out of her coat and she began telling Lucy and Paula all about her mummy: how her hair was longer than it had been when she'd last seen her, how kind she was and the games they'd played at contact. The phone rang and I answered it in the hall. It was Kitty, asking if Alice was all right now.

'She's fine,' I said. 'We've just got in.'

'Good. I promised I'd phone Leah after I'd spoken to you to put her mind at rest. She was so upset after Alice had left. I told her how well she had done.'

'She did very well,' I said. 'Please tell Leah Alice soon settled in the car and is all right now. She's going to have some dinner soon. She sends her love and is looking forward to seeing her next week.'

'Thanks, Cathy. I'll tell Leah.' Kitty paused and I heard her take a long breath. 'You know, Cathy, although Leah has had a lot of problems, underneath she's a lovely person. Despite losing her daughter, she isn't bitter and only wants what's best for Alice. The trouble is I'm not sure I know what *is* best for Alice. I've had sleepless nights over this. I can't for the life of me see a way forward, and in some respects I question the decision to bring Alice into care in the first place.'

'I completely understand,' I said.

Chapter Thirty-Five

Very Disappointed

Kitty wasn't the only one who was expressing doubts about the decision to bring Alice into care. The following day, Carole, the Guardian ad Litem, telephoned to make an appointment to visit Alice, and at the same time asked me for an update. Since Carole had visited Alice six months previously, when Alice had been with me for two months, apart from a phone call when she'd asked me to update her, we hadn't seen her. I now told her that Alice had settled into school, was eating and sleeping well, and had finally seen her mother the evening before, which she already knew from Kitty.

'And how is Alice today?' Carole asked.

'Counting the days until next Monday when she can see her mother again.'

Carole sighed. 'Oh dear. I had doubts about this case right at the beginning and I'm not at all happy with the way it's going. Alice has been kept without a decision on her future for far too long. Remind me when she came to you.'

'Beginning of March.'

'And it's now mid-November, so that's over eight months. She was supposed to have been with you for four weeks, then settled with her father and Sharon.' She sighed again.

'Are you're still considering Alice going to live with Chris and Sharon?' I asked.

'The social services are.' From which I took it that Carole didn't necessarily agree – Guardians work independently of the social services and don't always uphold the social services' decisions. 'Cathy,' she said after a moment. 'You're an experienced foster carer. How would you have handled this case? I'd be interested to hear your view.'

I'd never been asked that before by a Guardian. But put on the spot I went over the worries I'd harboured since Alice had first arrived. 'Alice was being well looked after by her grandparents,' I began. 'I know there were concerns about Leah having access to Alice while she was at her grandparents, but personally I trust Mr and Mrs Jones's judgement. They wouldn't have put Alice in danger and I'm sure they would have supervised Alice when Leah was there. Based on what I know of the case, if it had been my decision, I would have left Alice with her grandparents with monitoring and support. It would have given Leah the time she needed to seek help and hopefully recover. I'm sure losing Alice by having her taken into care – with the prospect of her going to live with Chris – has set back Leah's recovery. Also a more thorough investigation of Chris could have been carried out at that time, while Alice was with her grandparents.'

'Chris was investigated,' Carole put in a little defensively. 'And based on what the department knew at the time, it was felt that going to her father was the best option for Alice's long-term care. And might still be. I don't think the social services would have had the resources to investigate further.' How many times had I heard that! – lack of resources, i.e. not enough money being responsible for a less-than-perfect job?

'At least having Alice in foster care for all this time has allowed a more thorough investigation to take place,' I said.

'Yes, by default,' Carole admitted. She paused again, presumably thinking about what I'd said. 'Anyway, I'll see you next week. Will you tell Alice I'm coming and remind her who I am? It's a while since I've seen her.'

'Yes, I will.'

'Carole is the Guardian ad Litem. You've met her a couple of times before,' I said to Alice the following Wednesday as we waited for Carole to arrive. Alice saw her grandparents on alternate Wednesdays and this was one of the Wednesdays when she didn't see them, so we'd come home straight from school. 'Carole speaks to all your family,' I explained. 'Your mum, dad, nana and grandpa, and you and me, and then she tells the judge what she believes is best for you.'

'I know what is best for me,' Alice said. 'I want to live with my mummy.'

'You can tell Carole that,' I said, 'but, Alice, we've already talked about why it isn't possible for you to live with your mummy.' As usual when I said this or something similar Alice returned to her play or changed the subject.

When Carole arrived ten minutes later, Alice told her what was best for her, even before Carole had taken off her coat! 'You must tell the judge I want to live with my mummy, not Dad and Sharon,' Alice said defiantly.

'I see,' Carole said with a small smile. 'Shall we go and sit down first? Then we can have a chat.'

I showed Carole through to the sitting room, made her a cup of coffee and then left her alone with Alice, which was usual when the Guardian visited, just as it was when the social worker visited, so that they had a chance to talk in private.

Half an hour later Alice came into the kitchen to fetch me. 'Carole wants to see you now. Can I watch television?'

'Yes. Pop upstairs and ask Paula or Lucy to switch it on for you.'

Alice raced upstairs on all fours as I went into the sitting room.

'Alice is very articulate for a child of her age,' Carole said ruefully. 'She certainly knows her own mind, although of course she doesn't know what is best for her. She really doesn't understand why she can't live with her mother.'

'I have tried to explain,' I said.

'I'm sure you have, but she's not taking it in. She's in denial, which is understandable but is going to need addressing in therapy. Look, I won't keep you further,' Carole said, making a move to go. 'You updated me on the phone last week. The only new development is that I've found out it will be at least six months before Chris's case goes to the criminal court.'

I looked at her in dismay. 'I thought it was being hurried through?'

'Apparently not: there is a long list of prosecutions waiting to go to court. I'm not prepared to keep Alice waiting indefinitely for a decision on her future. I know she's happy with you, but this was only ever going to be a short-term measure. I'm meeting with the social services the week after next to review Alice's case. If the care plan is wrong, and Alice isn't going to live with her father and Sharon, then they need to be putting it right very quickly.'

'But how?' I asked. 'Adoption?'

'Possibly. I'm not sure yet. I'm exploring all avenues.'

Although I was pleased Carole was being proactive and questioning Alice's case, I couldn't see what other 'avenues' there were to explore, as all options for Alice's long-term care seemed to have been considered. Sometimes care plans, drawn up early in childcare proceedings, need slightly adjusting as time passes and situations change. But to admit a care plan was entirely wrong is unusual, and putting it right in Alice's case wasn't going to be easy. None of the options available seemed right for Alice and, not for the first time, I considered offering to keep Alice permanently – either as a long-term foster placement or by adopting her. But I wasn't sure this was right for Alice either; and if I made the offer now, might it confuse and slow down the process even further? If Alice was going to be adopted, shouldn't it really be to a younger, childless couple who had been denied the wondrous gift of parenthood? I already had two natural children and had been privileged to foster many, many more; wasn't it greedy of me to want Alice? The whole situation was becoming very confused and in the meantime, while Carole and Kitty were re-examining Alice's case, Alice was in limbo, unsure of whom she should be bonding with, or where she would eventually live.

Alice's next contact with her mother the following Monday was less traumatic, although Leah and Alice still parted in tears, and I again felt like the wicked witch as I carried Alice away sobbing from her mother. That week Alice had contact as usual with her father and Sharon on Tuesday and Thursday, as well as the fortnightly contact with her grandparents on Wednesday. So for four afternoons I collected Alice, already tired from a day at school, and took her to the family centre, and then returned to collect her an hour later. By Friday she was so exhausted she fell asleep on the sofa at 6.00 p.m.

By the first week in December I was using all my spare time to go Christmas shopping. Apart from buying presents for my family and friends, and filling four sacks (Adrian, Lucy and Paula didn't feel they were too old to hang up their sacks on Christmas Eve), I also took Alice shopping to buy presents for her grandparents, mum, dad and Sharon, and also Leah's partner, Mike. Paula helped Alice write her Christmas cards.

On the second Saturday in December, in the evening, when Alice had finished speaking to her nana and grandpa on the phone, Mrs Jones asked to speak to me, as she often did. I sent Alice off to find Adrian, Lucy or Paula, and I closed the sitting-room door so I couldn't be overheard. Mrs Jones often simply wanted some reassurance – to know Alice was eating well, or warm enough, and how she was getting on at school, etc. – but I didn't like talking about Alice in front of her, even if it was positive, which was why I always spoke so Alice couldn't hear. Now what Mrs Jones told me certainly wasn't for Alice's ears.

'Did you know Chris hit Sharon last week?' Mrs Jones said as soon as I picked up the phone.

'No,' I said shocked. 'I didn't. I'm sorry. Was she badly hurt?'

'No. More shaken than anything. She turned up at Leah's flat at nine o'clock on Thursday evening in a right state.'

'Sharon went to Leah's?' I asked, incredulous.

'Yes. I'd have sent her packing. But Leah has a heart of gold and felt sorry for her, and asked her in.' I couldn't believe it – here was Sharon, who didn't have a good word to say about Leah and wanted her child, seeking refuge in Leah's flat!

'Good grief!' I said. 'So where is Sharon now?'

'Once Sharon had stopped crying, she phoned Chris on her mobile from Leah's flat, apologized to him and then asked him to collect her in the car. She said she had provoked him into hitting her. I doubt it, but that's up to her.'

'And did Leah speak to Chris?'

'No. She stayed in her flat while Sharon went out to the car.'

'Does Kitty know all this?' I asked.

'Yes, I told her. I wasn't sure Leah would. And the other piece of news, which is better news, is that our parenting assessment has been completed satisfactorily.'

'Good,' I said hesitantly, and hoped Mrs Jones hadn't read too much into this. A positive parenting assessment simply means that those being assessed have demonstrated an acceptable level of parenting skills and are therefore eligible to be considered for the child. It does not give them automatic right to the child. 'When we see the Guardian next week we shall be asking to have Alice returned to us,' Mrs Jones continued brightly, and I feared they were going to be very disappointed. But it wasn't for me to explain: the social worker or Guardian should have done so already, and possibly had. In the same optimistic tone Mrs Jones then said she was thinking of buying Alice a bike for Christmas and what did I think.

'That's a lovely idea,' I said. 'We've got a bike here Alice uses, but having one of her own would be so much nicer. What a fantastic present. She'll love it.'

'Good. Martin and I will get it next week. We've a park near by which will be ideal for Alice learning to ride. I can't wait to see her face when she unwraps it on Christmas morning.' And my heart sank as I realized Mrs Jones was expecting Alice home for Christmas.

Chapter Thirty-Six
A New Year's Wish

I telephoned the Guardian on Monday and left a message on her voicemail saying that I thought Mrs Jones could have misinterpreted the purpose of the parenting assessment and now believed Alice would be returned to her; could she explain when she saw her? Carole didn't return my call, but I assumed she must have spoken to Mrs Jones and explained, for the following Saturday when we phoned Alice's grandparents, Mrs Jones talked to Alice about the 'wonderful Christmas' she would have at 'Cathy's'. She didn't ask to speak to me on this occasion, but she must have been very disappointed to have had her hopes raised and then dashed. I felt sorry for her, and yet again marvelled at her courage as she put aside her own feelings to be so brave and positive for Alice.

The week before Christmas was very busy. Apart from finishing the preparations for Christmas, friends dropped by, and Alice had extra contact at the family centre as it was Christmas. She saw her mother on Monday for an extended contact of two hours, when they exchanged gifts: Alice proudly presented her mother with a wrapped box of perfume we had chosen together and Leah handed me a large carrier bag of presents and asked me quietly if I could put them beside Alice's bed so that she would wake up and find them on Christmas morning, which is what she would have done if Alice had been with her. 'Of course,' I said. 'I'll put them with the "Father Christmas" presents from us.'

I knew that saying goodbye at this contact – the last before Christmas – was going to be particularly difficult, and when I returned to collect Alice, mother and daughter were already in tears. Eventually the contact supervisor gently lifted Alice from her mother's arms and put her into mine, and I left the room to the sound of Alice crying and her mother calling 'Merry Christmas' through her tears.

'Merry Christmas,' I returned, although without Alice I doubted it would be very merry for Leah or Mr and Mrs Jones.

On Wednesday Alice had an extended two-hour contact with her grandparents and she once more proudly presented them with wrapped gifts. Mrs Jones told Alice they would put the presents away until Christmas, while Mr Jones said to me he had the 'you know what' (Alice's bike) in the boot of the car and he would transfer it to my car at the end of contact. Mrs Jones had taken in some party food and a Christmas cracker each, and the three of them, plus the supervisor, had a little Christmas celebration with lemonade, sausage rolls and mince pies. Sadly this was the closest

Alice's grandparents would come to celebrating Christmas with Alice this year and yet again I marvelled at their courage to be able to go through with it.

At the end of contact Mr and Mrs Jones and the contact supervisor came with me into the car park, where I put Alice in her car seat and closed the car door so she couldn't see. Mr Jones opened the boot of his car and I did the same with mine. He carried over the gaily wrapped bicycle, which was to be given to Alice on Christmas morning, and laid it carefully in the boot. 'Hopefully we'll see Alice ride it one day,' Mrs Jones said sadly. 'Have a good Christmas, Cathy, and thanks for everything.'

'And you.' We hugged, and as they waved goodbye to Alice I saw that Mrs Jones was finally in tears.

On Thursday, contact with Alice's father remained at one hour; I assumed this was because they'd already seen Alice as usual for an hour on Tuesday. They didn't mention Chris's assault on Sharon – I hadn't expected them to. Sharon bore no obvious bruises or marks; indeed they now seemed even more lovey-dovey, making a big show of holding hands and talking attentively to each other. I'd had to persuade Alice to buy her father and Sharon a present, and then persuade her further to wrap the gifts and take them into contact. Unlike when Alice had seen her grandparents and mother, Alice had been allowed to open her Christmas presents during contact with Chris and Sharon. When I collected her I immediately spotted the new doll's pram which Alice was doing her best to ignore.

'Don't you like the present?' Sharon said as we said goodbye and came away with me wheeling the pram. 'I spent a long time choosing it.'

'I think she's just a bit overwhelmed,' I said, excusing her. 'You know how exciting the build-up to Christmas can be. It's been quite a week.' Sharon seemed to accept this, although I knew Alice's coldness towards the gift was because it had come from Sharon, whom she still resented; had it come from her mother her reaction would have been very different.

On the Friday morning Jill and Kitty both popped in with a gift for Alice, and a Christmas card for us all. Jill also had a gift for me from the fostering agency, and we had a box of chocolates ready under the tree for each of them. Kitty was so touched and appreciative at being given a present that I guessed she didn't often receive gifts or thanks – such is the nature of her job.

By Friday afternoon I had more or less finished the shopping, the presents were wrapped and there was no more contact until after Christmas. On Saturday Adrian and Paula went out with their father for the day and returned with their presents from him, which went under the tree. Unsurprisingly there wasn't one for me.

That evening Lucy's mother phoned, for the first time in three months, to wish Lucy a merry Christmas. Lucy hadn't seen her mother for five months because her mother was now living 'abroad', although no one was quite sure where exactly. Lucy had never known her father and had never had a proper relationship with her mother. In effect we were the only real family she'd ever had. This was one of the reasons why she'd bonded with us so quickly, and occasionally called me Mum. Lucy was on the phone to her mother for only a few minutes as her mother was dashing off somewhere. Lucy seemed to take this rejection, as she had all the other rejections from her mother, in her stride; the only outward sign that she was hurting was her attitude to food and the cynical comments she sometimes made.

Christmas is always a difficult time for children in care. Everywhere you look there are pictures of adoring parents smiling at their perfect children to a backdrop of family harmony and domestic bliss. It is a stark reminder to children who are fostered that their own lives haven't matched up to the ideal, and indeed they can't even be with their families at Christmas. While foster carers do their best to give the children they look after a fantastic time at Christmas we are also painfully aware of the many conflicting emotions looked-after children must experience. More than once, in the build-up to Christmas, I'd found Alice in her bedroom quietly studying the photograph of her mother, taken the Christmas before when they had all been together.

'I know Christmas will be a bit different this year,' I said. 'But I'll make sure you have a lovely time with games, presents and lots to eat.'

'Thanks, Cathy,' Alice said wistfully. 'But I'd give up all that if could just have my mummy.'

Yet like all young children Alice got caught up in the joy of Christmas and was awake early on Christmas morning, very excited at finding Father Christmas had been and she was surrounded by presents. I took lots of photographs as she tore off the wrapping paper and her little face lit up; and she was temporarily able to forget her loss as the magic of Christmas took over. Her mother had given her some beautifully illustrated story books, a huge compendium of paints, crayons and puzzles, a Barbie doll all dressed up for an evening out and some very pretty clothes. Alice loved them all, and also the Father Christmas presents I'd bought – a dolls' house with furniture and little doll people. Adrian, Lucy and Paula were awake early too and I went into their bedrooms as they delved into their sacks and unwrapped their presents. I took plenty of photographs of them too, much to the consternation of Lucy, who said I should have waited until she'd put on her make-up! Downstairs there were more presents under the tree, including the bike from Alice's nana and grandpa which, despite being well wrapped, was easily identifiable. 'A bike of my own!' Alice gasped as soon as she saw it.

As we'd done in previous years, my parents, my brother and his wife and their three-year-old son came to us on Christmas Day; then on Boxing Day we continued the festivities at my brother's house, where we had a chance to meet again with my sister-in-law's family. There were thirty of us in all, including ten children, aged eighteen months to Adrian at fourteen. My sister-in-law produced a wonderful buffet and organized games where we won prizes off the Christmas tree. As I finally drove us home at 10.00 p.m. I was the only one in the car still awake.

The next day was Tuesday and contact resumed. Because Alice hadn't seen her mother on Monday –

Boxing Day – it was rescheduled for an hour on Tuesday morning; then she saw her father and Sharon for an hour in the afternoon. She wasn't due to see her grandparents this Wednesday, and she saw her father and Sharon for an hour again, as usual, on Thursday. So what with contact, visiting friends and playing with Christmas gifts, the week between Christmas and New Year slipped by. Poor Adrian even had some homework to do!

On New Year's Eve we were invited next door to my neighbour, Sue, as we had been in previous years. There were twenty of us with our children – all living in the road and knowing each other. It was a lovely atmosphere and we could have a drink and see in the New Year without the worry of finding a babysitter or driving home. As midnight approached everyone squeezed into the sitting room and, with the television on, we counted down to midnight. As midnight struck on Big Ben we cheered, kissed each other and sang a chorus of 'Auld Lang Syne'. By 1.00 a.m. we were saying goodbye, wishing each other a happy New Year and steering very tired children home to their beds.

Alice was so tired she was nearly asleep on her feet, and Adrian carried her down Sue's front path and then up ours. Alice didn't wake as Adrian carried her upstairs and laid her on her bed. While he, Lucy and Paula got ready for bed I changed Alice into her pyjamas and tucked her in with Brian the Bear. She didn't wake. Before I left I stood for a moment, gazing down at her little face – so similar to her mother's and so peaceful in sleep. I wondered what the coming year would bring for her. I worried about Alice, more than I cared to admit. I feared for her future. If the wrong decision was made it could be disastrous, and I thought if I was to be granted one New Year wish it should be that everything turned out right for Alice, although how that could possibly happen I'd no idea.

Chapter Thirty-Seven
Ten Days

'We're going to reduce Alice's contact with her father and Sharon,' Kitty said. 'I had a meeting with the Guardian a week before Christmas and we have decided it's appropriate now.'

'I see,' I said, taken aback. It was Tuesday and I had just returned from taking Alice to school – it was the first day of the new term. I was in the hall with my coat still on. 'Will she have contact with her father as usual tonight?'

'No. From now on she will see her father for an hour every two weeks on a Thursday. Alice had contact with him last week, so there will be none this week. Contact with her mother will remain unchanged – every Monday. Contact with the grandparents will be increased from fortnightly to weekly – every Wednesday.'

'I see,' I said again, aware these changes were highly significant and hadn't been made lightly, but without knowing the reason behind them. 'Alice will be very pleased she is seeing her nana and grandpa more often,' I said.

'Yes. Cathy, as you know the Guardian and I have had doubts about the care plan for a while now. But the social services couldn't simply take the decision to alter it and reduce contact with Alice's father without very good reason. Now the Guardian has raised concerns we have a better chance of altering it. I have rewritten the care plan, reduced contact in line with it, and am taking Alice's case back to court next week.'

'So that Alice can be adopted?' I asked, which seemed the most likely explanation for the reduction in contact with her father, but didn't explain the increase in contact with her grandparents.

'No. Not for adoption at this stage.' Kitty paused, and as I waited my heart set up a queer little rhythm in expectation of what I might hear. 'If the judge agrees,' Kitty continued, 'we are hoping to return Alice to live with her grandparents temporarily.'

'Oh! Returned? Temporarily. When?'

'Probably within the month – after a period of transition.'

'Oh,' I said again, trying to sort out my thoughts.

'If the judge agrees to the new care plan, we will return Alice to live with her grandparents to allow Leah time to complete her recovery. If Leah doesn't recover fully within a year then we will place Alice for adoption. Alice will remain on a care order while she is with her grandparents and we will monitor the situation carefully. Leah will continue to have supervised contact with Alice at the family centre and she knows she must keep to the arrangement and not try to see Alice at the grandparents'. I am meeting Mr and Mrs

Jones, and Leah and her partner Mike, tomorrow morning to make sure they understand these contact arrangements, so there can be no misunderstanding as there appears to have been last time, which led to Alice coming into care. Obviously don't say anything to Alice until it is definite. I'm in court a week on Thursday, so we should have a decision then.'

I was quiet for a moment as all manner of thoughts and feelings flashed through my mind. The good news was that Alice could be returning to live with her grandparents, where she belonged; the bad news was she might be removed again if Leah didn't make a full recovery within the year. 'Kitty, can I ask why you have taken this decision now?'

Kitty paused before answering. 'I have read all the case notes in depth and my feeling is that a different social worker might have made a different decision and not brought Alice into care, but continued to monitor the situation instead. Although Mr and Mrs Jones are considered too old to give Alice long-term care, they are more than capable of giving Alice short-term care. Having said that, there were concerns that Mrs Jones was allowing Leah unsupervised contact with Alice. I think she now has a better understanding of why we make the decisions we do. Also, more evidence has come to light in respect of Chris – his violence and past record – and to be honest his and Sharon's marriage is very shaky. Sharon has phoned me a number of times and said she's seriously considering leaving Chris.'

'And Chris and Sharon are aware of the changes you are asking for?'

'Yes, although their barrister has advised them they still have a good chance of Alice going to live with them. He will be in court next Thursday to challenge our decision.'

'So Alice could still go to them?'

'It's possible.'

'And Mr and Mrs Jones understand this – that nothing is definite?'

'I hope so. I have explained the process to them in depth, although Mrs Jones is sure the judge will "see sense", as she puts it, and return Alice to them. I have warned her. I have also warned Leah that nothing is definite, and also that she mustn't say anything to Alice at contact on Monday.'

'Thanks, Kitty. It would be dreadful if Alice had her hopes built up only to have them dashed. And thanks for all you have done for Alice. You have been so thorough. I just hope the judge makes the right decision.'

'So do I,' Kitty said flatly. 'So do I.'

I replaced the handset and finally took off my coat and hung it in the cupboard under the stairs. Deep in thought, I walked slowly down the hall and into the sitting room, where I sat on the sofa by the French windows and gazed out on to the wintery garden. Only a few nests of lilac crocuses suggested there was life in the barren soil, and the overhanging leafless branches were a stark reminder spring was still a long way off. It has been said that social workers are damned if they do and damned if they don't, and this was certainly true of Alice's case. When Kitty went to court next week if the judge decided to return Alice to live with her grandparents then presumably the decision to take Alice into care in the first place had been wrong. But conversely if Alice hadn't been taken into care and something had happened to her, the finger of blame would have pointed directly at the social services. Alice was known to the social services, and was being visited by a social worker, who would have been castigated for not having seen the warning signs and acting sooner.

Yet while I sympathized with the difficult decisions social workers have to make on a daily basis, I was troubled by the often frequent changes of social workers – as in Alice's case – which meant there was little continuity. Had one social worker been involved right from the beginning, he or she would have been able get to know Alice's family and would have been in a better position to judge the situation and whether or not Alice was at risk. I had seen so many cases where, for reasons I'd never understood, multiple social workers had been involved. Alice had had four social workers in three months and perhaps that had contributed to the 'quick fix' solution of deciding to send Alice to live with her father. Kitty had taken time to investigate and research Alice's case, and as a result had drawn up a new care plan that the judge would, I hoped, approve. But even if the right decision was now made and Alice was returned to her grandparents, it was temporary and dependent on Leah's full recovery within a year. Once again I worried for Alice's future and the emotional damage Alice had suffered as a result of being separated from her loved ones.

* * *

There were ten days until the Thursday, when Kitty would be in court, but it seemed more like ten years, so slowly did the time pass. When I saw Alice's grand-parents at contact on Wednesday Mrs Jones handed me another jar of her home-made chutney 'Just in case it's needed,' Mrs Jones said bravely, meaning she hoped Alice would be with her by the time our present jar was empty.

'It would be nice if I was eating this one alone,' I smiled, and Mrs Jones nodded.

Leah also put on a very brave face when I saw her at contact the following Monday. Indeed, she seemed to be coping very well with the additional pressure of knowing Kitty was going back to court and that so much rested on the judge's decision. The only outward sign of her anxiety was a certain nervous restlessness and biting her fingernails, which I hadn't seen her do before, and she quietly admitted to me she couldn't settle to anything at home.

In line with the new care plan there was no contact with Alice's father on Tuesday. When I took Alice to the family centre to see her grandparents on Wednes-day, it was the eve of the court hearing, and only Mr Jones was present. 'Nana isn't feeling too well,' Mr Jones explained to Alice and me. 'She's having a lie-down so she'll be well in the morning.' I understood the reference to the morning but obviously Alice, unaware of the impending court case, didn't. I could imagine the dreadful stress the care proceedings were causing Alice's grandparents; little wonder Mrs Jones was ill. I asked Mr Jones to pass on my best wishes for a speedy recovery and Alice sent her love.

On Thursday morning I took Alice to school as usual, stopped off at the supermarket and then came home. Kitty had told me that Alice's case was in court at 9.30 a.m. and had been allotted half a day, so I was expecting to hear something early afternoon. Alice was due to see her father and Sharon for contact at 4.00 p.m. and I envisaged it being a pretty difficult meeting. I hoped Kitty would phone me in plenty of time, as it would be very awkward if I went into contact without knowing the judge's decision.

She did.

At 2.30 the phone rang and I pounced on it, nearly knocking it to the floor. Kitty was calling from her mobile. 'Cathy, I've just left court and, with a few provisos, the judge has agreed to our care plan. Alice will be returned to her grandparents while Leah has time to recover.'

'Thank God,' I said. 'Fantastic. Well done. I'm so very pleased.'

'Thanks. The judge made a few changes: contact with dad will be reinstated to once a week for the time being, and reviewed in three months. The judge also decided that no transition period was needed and that Alice should be returned to her grandparents as soon as possible. He was critical of the social services' decision to take Alice into care and said there was no reason not to return her straightaway. Is this Saturday all right?'

I took a breath, shocked by the suddenness of it all, but pleased for Alice. 'Yes. Shall I tell Alice or do you want to?'

'Could you tell her, please? Then I will see her tomorrow after school and explain in more detail. I don't think Chris will cause trouble, but I have notified the family centre of the outcome. He didn't seem too fussed about the decision in court. It was Sharon who was upset, but then she has always been the one who wanted Alice.'

'Yes,' I said reflectively. 'I hope she'll have a chance to have her own child one day.' But while I empathized with Sharon, I wasn't letting it stand in the way of my sheer joy for Alice, who was going home to her dear nana and grandpa, albeit temporarily. 'I'll tell Alice when I collect her from school, then.'

'Yes please.'

'And thanks again, Kitty. I think it's true to say this wouldn't have happened without you.'

Chapter Thirty-Eight
You can say NO

I had just enough time to make a quick telephone call to my parents to tell them the good news before I left to collect Alice from school. 'I've just heard: Alice is going home to her grandparents,' I said as my mother answered. 'This Saturday!'

'That's fantastic, but you'll miss her so much. We all will.' Alice had found a very special place in my parents' hearts just as she had in ours.

I could hear my father in the background, asking my mother what was 'fantastic', and she repeated what I'd said, and then passed the phone to him.

'I'm very pleased,' he said. 'But if you want my opinion Alice should never have been taken away in the first place. Those poor grandparents.' Although my parents had never met Mr and Mrs Jones they had identified with their plight and felt their loss personally.

'We won't have time to visit you before Alice leaves,' I said. 'So we'll phone tomorrow evening, and you'll be able to say goodbye then.'

'Thanks, love,' my father said, a little subdued, and told my mother what I'd said. It's as difficult for grand-parents in a family who fosters as it is for the family itself, as they welcome new 'grandchildren' into their homes and lives and then have to say goodbye.

Adrian, Lucy and Paula were aware that Alice's case was in court today and that, as it was Thursday, I would be taking Alice straight from school to the family centre. I left a note telling them what they would be wanting to know: 'Good news! Alice is returning to live with her grandparents – on Saturday! Will tell you more when I see you at 4.30. Love Mum xxx'.

It was now 2.50, time to put on my coat and leave the house to collect Alice from school at 3.15. I must have had a silly grin on my face when I arrived, for as I went into reception the class teacher said: 'You look happy. Won the lottery?'

'Nearly,' I said. 'I've just had some very positive news. I'm sure Alice will tell you tomorrow.' And perhaps her teacher guessed for her eyes widened with delight and she nodded knowingly.

'I'll look forward to hearing your news,' she said, smil-ing at Alice.

Outside, as Alice slipped her hand into mine and we crossed the playground, I said. 'Alice, love, you know I've talked to you about the judge – the wise man who decides where you live?' She nodded. 'Well, Kitty saw him today, in court, and he has decided you will live with your nana and grandpa again, for the time being, while Mummy gets better. He wants you to go home as soon as possible – this Saturday.' I looked at Alice.

Her little face was expressionless, overawed, as she struggled with the enormity of what I was telling her. 'So I will pack up all your things,' I continued, spelling it out. 'And on Saturday you will go and live with Nana and Grandpa again, just as you did before you came to me.'

'On Saturday,' she repeated, still not fully comprehending. 'I watch the football on Saturday afternoons with Brian the Bear and you.'

'Yes, I know, love, we have done for all these months, but this Saturday and for many Saturdays to follow you will be watching the football with Brian the Bear at your nana and grandpa's house. Just as you did before you came to me.'

Alice looked up at me and her eyes widened. 'But Nana doesn't watch the football. Only Grandpa and me, and Brian the Bear sits on the sofa between us.'

'That's right, love, and all that will happen again – this Saturday. Just as it used to.'

I opened the car door, helped Alice into her seat and fastened her belt. Closing her door I climbed into the driver's seat and started the engine. As I drove I continued to talk to Alice, occasionally glancing in the interior mirror to make sure she was all right. 'Kitty is coming to see us tomorrow after school to explain more,' I said. 'But the judge has decided you will live with your nana and grandpa, as you used to, and you will see your mummy at the family centre, as you have been doing. You will also see your dad and Sharon once a week at the family centre. I expect next week your grandpa will take you.'

In the interior mirror I saw Alice nod as she slowly took it all in. A minute later my phone began ringing from its holder on the dashboard and I pulled over to answer it. It was Kitty. 'Have you told Alice?' she asked. My heart sank as I thought she was going to tell me she'd made a mistake and Alice wouldn't be returning home, for I too was struggling to believe it.

'Yes. We're in the car now, on our way to contact.'

'Sorry, but you're going to have to turn round and go home. Sharon has telephoned and neither she nor Chris will be going to contact tonight.'

'Oh, I see,' I said.

'They have decided to separate and need time to get things sorted out. Can you tell Alice? I'll leave the explanation up to you.'

'Yes, yes, of course.'

'Thanks. I'll see you tomorrow after school.'

Swivelling round in my seat to face Alice, I told her that unfortunately her father and Sharon couldn't make contact tonight but they sent their love, which seemed enough of an explanation and satisfied Alice. 'That's all right,' she said amicably.

I turned the car round and drove home, with Alice now asking questions about the move to her nana and grandpa, having finally started to take it all in: 'What time will we be going?' 'Will all my things fit in the car?' 'Will I still see you?' 'Will you look after another child?' etc. By the time we arrived home Alice had come to terms with what was happening and was ecstatic. Eager to share her news with Adrian, Lucy and Paula, she dashed up the front garden path. But as I

opened the front door a welcoming party appeared in
the hall: Adrian, Lucy and Paula, with my parents! who
were just taking off their coats.

'We came straight over,' Mum said. 'We couldn't let
little Alice go without saying a proper goodbye.'

Alice rushed straight into my mother's arms. 'I'll miss
you, Gran,' she said, giving her a big kiss and squeezing
her tightly. I saw my mother's eyes immediately mist.

We went into the sitting room and, once settled, everyone wanted to know what had happened to allow Alice
to return to her grandparents and how it had happened
so quickly. Smiling at Alice, who was sitting on my
mother's lap, I explained that after further investigation, and having discussed Alice's case with the
Guardian, Kitty had revised the care plan and the judge
had agreed that it was best for Alice to live with her
grandparents. I wasn't sure how much Kitty was going
to tell Alice of the long-term plan of Alice eventually
returning to live with her mother, as it relied on Leah
making a full recovery, so I didn't say anything about
that. My parents were happy for Alice, as we were,
although of course we were all going to miss her dreadfully.

I made my parents a cup of tea and then my father
suggested we order a take-away by way of a small celebration, so the evening turned into an impromptu
leaving party for Alice. Alice stayed up long past her
normal bedtime as we sat around the table and ate a
Chinese take-away, washed down with lemonade and
followed by Neapolitan ice cream. We then played
some of Alice's favourite games and by 8.45 Alice was

yawning and rubbing her eyes. My parents said they would make a move and go now. My father gave Alice a hug and my mother hugged and kissed her.

'I'm afraid we haven't had a chance to buy you a leaving present,' Mum said. 'So we are giving you a little something you can spend when you're living with your nana and grandpa.' My mother produced a card from her handbag. Alice opened it and a £10 note fell out.

'Thank you,' I said. 'That's very generous.' Then to Alice: 'Shall I read what it says in the card?'

Alice nodded and I pointed to the words as I read what my mother had written: 'Dear Alice, thank you for being part of our lives. You are very special and will be greatly missed. Please say hello to your nana and grandpa from us. All our love and best wishes for a healthy and happy future.' Both my parents had signed it with kisses.

'Thank you,' Alice said, and gave them another kiss each.

We all went down the hall and I helped Mum and Dad into their coats. Then Adrian, Lucy and Paula said: 'Goodbye, Gran, Grandpa,' and Lucy added: 'Is it all right if I call you Gran and Grandpa now? I'd like to. I've never had grandparents of my own.'

Mum, who was already close to tears at having to say goodbye to Alice, now took a tissue from her pocket to wipe her eyes. 'Yes, of course, love,' she said to Lucy. 'We'd be honoured.' She hugged and kissed Lucy, then Adrian and Paula, while Lucy kissed my father's cheek, as Paula had done, and Adrian gave him a 'man hug'.

It was a cold but dry night and we followed my parents down the path and then stood on the pavement and waved until they were out of sight. It was unlikely that my parents would see Alice again, although I would obviously pass on any news I had about Alice in the future.

Returning indoors, Lucy paused and looked at Paula. 'So if I'm calling your grandparents Gran and Grandpa,' she said, 'is it OK if I call you sister? You feel like a proper sister to me.'

I was touched by Lucy's request but I looked to Paula for her reaction; so too did Adrian. For while I recognized that Lucy had fitted easily into our family, was particularly close to Paula and was loved by us all, I wondered if Paula would resent her request and didn't actually want a sister. I should have known my daughter better!

'Sure,' Paula said with a smile. 'You've felt like my big sister for ages.'

'Oh no!' Adrian cried in mock displeasure. 'Not two sisters! How will I cope!'

I took Alice up to bed and tucked her in; she was nearly asleep by the time I said goodnight and came out. As I passed Lucy's room she called out: 'Cathy? Have you got a moment? There's something I need to ask you.'

Lucy had left her bedroom door open – a sure sign there was something on her mind and she needed to talk. I went in and found her already in her pyjamas and propped up in bed. Lucy often got into bed early and then read a magazine, listened to music or sometimes even did her homework in bed, although I didn't encourage this. Having never had a proper bed or bedroom room of her own before coming into care, she really appreciated the comfort and security her own space offered. I perched on the bed and she looked at me seriously.

'Cathy, it was nice of your parents to let me call them Gran and Grandpa.'

'They were touched you wanted to,' I said.

'And it's nice Paula wants me as a proper sister.'

'Yes,' I agreed. 'You two get along very well.' I waited, for I knew this wasn't the real reason Lucy had called me into her room – to tell me she was pleased she had grandparents and a sister to call her own. I sensed there was something much bigger, heartfelt, that she needed to share with me but was finding difficult. I wasn't wrong.

'Cathy,' she continued hesitantly after a moment, toying with the edge of the duvet. 'I want to ask you something, and you can say no if you like. I'll understand. I promise I won't be hurt or disappointed – well, I will be, but I'll try not to be.'

'Yes?' I prompted, wondering what on earth it could be she was finding so difficult to ask. Lucy didn't normally have this much trouble talking to me.

'Well, it's this,' she said, still looking very serious and fiddling with the duvet. 'You know I think of all of you as my proper family?' I nodded. 'And you know I sometimes call you Mum?' I nodded again. 'Well, this feels like my home to me – my proper home – and I don't ever want to have to leave it. I've been reading some books in the school library, doing some research, about adoption, and I was wondering, well, if you could adopt me? Then I wouldn't have to leave and could be part of your family forever. I promise I won't be any trouble, and I could help you with the washing up. You can say no if you want … I'm sorry, Cathy, I didn't mean to make you cry.'

I put my arms around her and held her close, and for a few minutes that was all I could do: I was too choked-up to speak. Finally, drawing slightly away, I wiped my eyes. While I knew what my answer was, I also knew I had to be practical.

'Lucy, love,' I said. 'I already look upon you as a daughter, and I hope you will be with me forever. I would be very happy to adopt you, but you realize it's not my decision.'

'I know, it's the judge's,' Lucy said.

I nodded. 'Look, love, I'll speak to your social worker tomorrow and see what she says. You still have some contact with your mother and her views will be taken into account. It may be she won't want you to be adopted.' Lucy's face clouded. 'I can ask, love, but if it doesn't happen we don't need a piece of paper to say we're mother and daughter, do we?'

She smiled sadly. 'I guess not, but it would make me very happy and feel more secure.'

'I know, love, I understand, and I'll try my best.'

Chapter Thirty-Nine
Adoption

As one foster daughter was preparing to leave, another was preparing to stay – forever. That same evening as I said goodnight to Paula, and then Adrian, I told them what Lucy had just said about wanting to be adopted and asked what they thought, for clearly it had to be a whole-family decision. They were both happy with the idea, feeling that Lucy was already like their sibling and they'd assumed she would be staying for good. So the following morning, after I'd taken Alice to school and before I began her packing, I telephoned Lucy's social worker and told her that Lucy had asked if I could adopt her.

She was sympathetic and said she would support my application, but added the same warning I had given to Lucy: that her mother could (and probably would) object. Parents of children in care often accept that their child has to be looked after but fiercely oppose adoption, when they would lose all legal rights to the child. Lucy's social worker also said Lucy's mother had no fixed address, so it was going to be difficult and would take time to trace her, and then set up a meeting to try to get her permission to begin the lengthy process of adoption.

'And you can't free Lucy for adoption without her mother's consent?' I asked. 'She's never been a proper mother to her.'

'Not really, not at Lucy's age. It would be too costly and time consuming for the department; I'd never get the funding. It would be different if Lucy was younger: the department would consider the cost of pursuing an adoption a good investment, as it would take Lucy out of foster care, but not with a teenager. If we can't find mum or she won't give her permission, I assume Lucy can still stay with you as a long-term foster placement?'

'Yes, of course.'

'Leave it with me and I'll see what I can do, but warn Lucy she may be disappointed.'

'I already have.'

We said goodbye, then I went down the hall and opened the door to the cupboard under the stairs. Switching on the light, I reached in and pulled out two suitcases – the suitcases Alice's grandmother had asked me to keep so I had them ready if Alice was ever returned to her. It was a hope that had seemed completely unrealistic at the time as Alice had been going to live with her father and Sharon within the month. Now, as I wiped off the thin layer of dust, I was about to complete Mrs Jones's request: ten months later and against all the odds, Alice was returning to live with her.

It was just after eleven o'clock when I started the packing and it took over two hours. Apart from all the clothes Alice's nana had sent and the many I'd bought, Alice had had a birthday and Christmas since she'd been with us, so there were boxes and boxes of toys. Kitty had offered to take some of Alice's possessions in her car to the grandparents, after she'd seen us that evening. At the time I'd thought that wouldn't be necessary – that everything would go in one car – but I now realized this had been wildly optimistic. Apart from the two suitcases, boxes and bags covered all available floor space in Alice's bedroom and more bags were lined up on the landing, ready to be taken downstairs. Alice's bike – her Christmas present from her nana and grandpa – was in the shed and I would bring that in later. I smiled reflectively as I thought of Mr and Mrs Jones at the family centre just before Christmas, when we'd secretly transferred the bike from their car boot to mine and, with litte hope of Alice ever returning to them, Mrs Jones had said sadly: 'Hopefully we'll see Alice ride it one day.' Now, very soon, they would.

While I'd been busy packing, I hadn't really had time to dwell on the gap Alice's departure would leave in my family, but as I checked under the bed for any stray objects, and then stood and surveyed the room, I got a sudden flash of what it would be like tomorrow, after Alice had gone. I felt very sad and empty. I'd taken down all her posters, so the walls were bare, and her shelves were empty of her books, photographs and knick-knacks. Likewise now that I'd packed her clothes, her drawers and wardrobe were empty and had a hollow sound. All that remained were Alice's pyjamas, folded under her pillow, a change of clothes for tomorrow on her chair, and Brian the Bear in his usual place at the bedhead – I would pack him first thing in the morning. Brian and I had become well acquainted during all the Saturday afternoon football matches, when he either jumped up and down as a goal was scored or covered his eyes with his paws in shame as a goal was missed. Tomorrow Brian too would be back where he belonged – sitting on the sofa between Alice and her grandpa as Mrs Jones doubtless fussed over them. I came out and closed Alice's bedroom door, aware that the next few days were going to be very difficult for all of us.

When I collected Alice from school that afternoon, Alice's teacher gave me a bunch of spring flowers with a card thanking me for all I'd done, which was very thoughtful and entirely unexpected. This was my last trip to the school, for on Monday Alice's grandpa would take and collect Alice, just as he had been doing nearly a year before when Alice had attended nursery. I thanked Alice's teacher and teaching assistant for the flowers and also thanked them for all they'd done. Between us we had kept the school/home continuity running smoothly without any major upheaval to Alice. As Alice and I left I had the chance to say goodbye to a couple of mothers I'd got to know – mothers of Alice's friends – but there were other mothers I'd chatted to in the playground, whom I didn't see, so I missed the chance to say goodbye. Sadly, they would simply arrive at school on Monday morning to find me gone.

Kitty came as promised at four o'clock and was met by a very excited Alice. Once settled in the sitting room, Kitty confirmed what I had already told Alice: that she would be returning to live with her nana and grandpa the following day, and would see her mother and father every week at the family centre. Kitty also explained to Alice that she wouldn't be seeing Sharon any more, as she and her father had separated and were no longer living together. Alice, having never warmed to Sharon and resenting her mothering role, accepted this news without comment, although I felt sorry for Sharon. Sharon had been married for only just over a year and was now separated, and during that time she'd had her hopes of motherhood built and then dashed. I hoped things worked out for her and, wherever she was, she found happiness. Kitty finished by saying that Alice's grandparents would come and collect Alice the following morning at about eleven o'clock. Then Kitty asked Alice if she had any questions.

'Will you take some of my things in your car?' Alice said. 'Cathy said you would. There is too much for one car.'

Kitty smiled. 'Yes, of course. Don't you worry: nothing will be left behind. Is there anything else you want to ask me?'

'Can I still see Cathy, Adrian, Lucy and Paula?'

I knew this was more difficult for Kitty to answer, for although we would be allowed to phone Alice and see her once or twice after the move, like most of the children who left us we had to withdraw from their lives to allow them to bond with their forever families, or in

Alice's case re-bond with her grandparents and ulti-mately (we hoped) her mother.

'Cathy will phone you in two weeks,' Kitty said gently – two weeks is now the accepted time for this phone call. 'Then she will arrange to visit you.'

'Can Adrian, Lucy and Paula come too?' Lucy asked.

'Yes, of course, if they're free.'

'They will be,' I confirmed.

Thankfully Alice was so looking forward to return-ing to live with her dear nana and grandpa that she didn't dwell on not being able to see us regularly, which was good. Kitty then thanked me for all I'd done and said she hoped to work with me again in the future. I thanked her for all she'd done. Then Alice helped Kitty and me load Kitty's car with the boxes of toys Adrian had brought down from the landing. We had soon filled the boot, and just managed to squeeze Alice's bike on to the back seat. 'The rest should go in Grandpa's car tomorrow,' Kitty said. 'If not I'll pop back for it next week.'

Kitty then asked if she could say goodbye to Adrian, Lucy and Paula, which was thoughtful. I called them and they appeared from their bedrooms and the front room.

'Bye, kids,' Kitty said. 'Thanks for looking after Alice so well. Might see you again one day. And Lucy, good luck with your application. I hope you get what you want.' News travels fast, I thought, for I'd only spoken to Lucy's social worker about her adoption that morn-ing. 'You couldn't do much better for a mother,' Kitty added, smiling at me.

'Thank you very much,' I said.

I tried to keep our last evening together as normal as possible and followed Alice's usual routine of play-time, television, dinner, bath and bed; I told the children to keep it low key too. I knew Alice must have many conflicting feelings, for although she dearly loved her nana and grandpa and couldn't wait to return to live with them, ten months is a long time in a child's life, and goodbyes are always difficult. Once Alice was tucked in bed I read her a story and then prepared to say goodnight. I saw her face grow serious as she looked around her room, now bare except for the two suitcases and the remaining boxes stacked at one end.

'I'll miss you,' she said, suddenly throwing her arms around me and hugging me tightly.

'I'll miss you too,' I said. 'We all will.'

'I love you, nearly as much as I love my nana, grandpa and mummy,' Alice said.

'We love you too, pet. You're very special.'

I gave Alice a final hug and then called to Adrian, Lucy and Paula to come and say goodnight. They came in and kissed Alice; then Adrian fooled around with Brian the Bear, making him dance and appear to speak, which made Alice laugh. Saying goodnight and 'See you in the morning', we filed out and I closed Alice's bedroom door for her last night with us. Dear Alice: I hoped her mother made a full recovery, for while adoption seemed absolutely right for Lucy, who had no proper family of her own, I couldn't for the life of me

see how it could work for Alice, who loved her nana,
grandpa and mummy more than anyone else in the
world.

Chapter Forty
Finding Home

There was a strange atmosphere in our house that Saturday morning, as excited expectation mingled with the sadness and loss of Alice leaving. We were all up and dressed earlier than usual for the weekend and had had breakfast by 9.30. Alice's suitcases were in the hall with the remaining boxes and bags, and Brian the Bear sat astride one of the suitcases, looking like a jockey under starter's orders. I'd checked all the rooms for any of Alice's possessions that might have gone astray, but all that remained was her coat, scarf and shoes in the hall. We now grouped in the sitting room and gave Alice her leaving gift and card, which I'd hurriedly bought the day before after I'd found out she was going. It was a silver necklace with a pendant in the shape of the letter A – a gift I hoped she'd keep and remember us by.

'Thank you,' Alice said in a small sad voice; then she asked Paula to read the words in the card. Each of us had written something and signed our names and added kisses. Paula had written: 'I loved having you as a younger sister. Take care. Love and best wishes, Paula xxxx'. Lucy had put: 'It's been great having you stay, Alice. Good luck for the future, hugs and kisses, love Lucy, x'. And Adrian had written: 'You're a good kid, Alice. Look after your nana and grandpa, best wishes, Adrian x'. I had purposely kept my message light and short: 'Dear Alice, I love and miss you, Cathy xxxx'.

'Thank you,' Alice said in the same small voice when Paula had finished reading. I could see she was close to tears.

'I'll put your present and card in your suitcase,' I said, going over to her, 'then how about we play a game before Nana and Grandpa arrive?' I didn't want Alice having time to mope and then leaving us in tears. I thought a game might provide a distraction.

'Bingo,' Paula suggested. 'It's Alice's favourite.' We'd first played bingo with Alice at Christmas and she'd loved being able to show off all the numbers she knew.

'Yes?' I asked, looking at Alice, and she nodded.

Paula went to the conservatory-cum-playroom, where we kept all the board and boxed games, to find the bingo, while I went down the hall to pack Alice's present. Unzipping the suitcase, I carefully tucked in the necklace box and card; then I returned to the sitting room, where Paula had found the game and was handing out the cards and tiles. Alice said she'd like to be the caller, so Paula gave her the plastic number tiles. 'Eyes down for a full house,' Alice said, once we were settled. Then she began picking up the numbers one at a time, reading them in a nice loud voice: 'Nine, twenty-five, three' and so on.

Alice did very well at recognizing the numbers and needed help with only a few of the higher numbers. Now that she was happily absorbed in the game her face had lost the sadness that had been there since waking.

Twenty minutes later, having covered all the numbers on his card, Adrian shouted 'Bingo'.

'Well done,' I said, and we all clapped. In our house, tradition (and possibly the rules of the game) dictated that whoever won the last game of bingo became the caller for the next, so Alice gave Adrian the numbers and took a card and tiles from the box so she could play.

'I wonder who will win this game?' I said pointedly, glancing at Lucy and Paula.

'I hope it's Alice,' Paula said, nudging Lucy just in case she was in any doubt.

And sure enough, fifteen minutes later Alice was shouting 'Bingo' to rapturous applause. 'Another game,' Alice said. 'I won, so I can be the caller again,' which would have been true had not the door bell rung. Alice continued for a moment – picking up the first tile, ready to call it out – before she realized the significance of the ring. 'Oh,' she said, suddenly becoming still. 'Do I have to go?' Wide eyed, she looked round at us.

'Yes, I think so, love,' I said gently. 'I think that will be your nana and grandpa. Let's go and see.'

Alice clambered down from the sofa and, tucking her little hand in mine, came with me down the hall. I thought how strange it must be for her: walking towards the familiar door, as she'd done so many times before, but now to open it on a completely unfamiliar scene: her nana and grandpa coming to take her home. It was as though her two lives, past and present, were finally coming together, and very soon her life with us would be past as she resumed life with her grandparents.

As I opened the front door a large bouquet of flowers landed in my arms. 'Good morning, Cathy,' Mr Jones said brightly. 'Thanks for everything,' Bending down, he scooped up Alice and gave her a big kiss. 'Hello, my lovely.' Alice grinned.

'You shouldn't have bought these,' I said. 'They're beautiful. Thank you so much.' I kissed their cheeks. 'Come in.'

'It's nothing,' Mrs Jones said. 'We can't thank you enough for all you've done.'

Alice was clinging like a koala bear to her grandpa, with her arms and legs tightly wrapped around him and her head snuggled into his shoulder. I closed the front door and suggested we went through to the sitting room. 'Would you like a tea or coffee?'

I saw Mr and Mrs Jones exchange a glance and look a little uncomfortable. 'Would you mind awfully if we didn't stay?' Mrs Jones said, touching my arm. 'Don't think we're ungrateful, but we'd really like to get Alice home and get her settled. We've waited so long for this moment. I hope you understand.'

'Yes, of course,' I said. 'But at least say hello to the rest of the family. They'd like to meet you.' Adrian, Lucy and Paula had come out of the sitting room and were now hovering at the far end of the hall. They came over and I introduced them: 'This is my son, Adrian.' He shook hands. 'And my daughters, Paula and Lucy.' They shook hands with Mr Jones and kissed Mrs Jones's cheek.

'What a fine family you have,' Mr Jones said. 'Alice has told us so much about you. Cathy is right to be proud of you all.'

'Thank you,' I said. I saw Adrian blush.

'You've made Alice's stay such a happy one,' Mrs Jones added, looking at Adrian, Lucy and Paula. 'She's played so many games she hasn't had time to be upset.' Then her gaze fell to the suitcases in the hall and she let out a little gasp. 'Oh, my! I'd completely forgotten those were here. That dreadful day when I had to pack all Alice's things …' Her face clouded and I saw her bottom lip tremble as she thought back and remembered.

'And there's Brian the Bear!' Mr Jones exclaimed jovially, lightening the mood and nodding to where Brian perched on the suitcase. 'Has he won any good matches?' He set Alice down and she picked up Brian and tucked him under her arm.

'No, he hasn't,' I said. 'Hopefully this afternoon's match will be better than last week's. They should never have missed that penalty.'

'Agreed!' Mr Jones said, while Adrian, Lucy and Paula looked at me oddly, wondering when I had become such an authority on football.

'Shall I give you a hand loading the car?' Adrian asked Mr Jones.

'I'd appreciate that. Alice's social worker brought over a carful last night. Just as well or we'd never get it all in.'

While Adrian helped Mr Jones load his car with Alice's luggage, I lay my flowers on the hall table and helped Alice into her coat, scarf and shoes, as clearly they wanted to leave as soon as possible. Lucy and Paula were now standing very quietly watching Alice, their faces glum. I knew they were struggling to keep a lid on their emotions, now that the moment of Alice leaving had finally come. It's always difficult saying goodbye to the children we look after, even when you know, as in Alice's case, they are going to a loving home and it's the right decision. Alice had been part of our lives for nearly a year and, perhaps because she was so young and vulnerable, or because of the journey we'd travelled together, or simply because she was such a joy to look after, we'd loved her from the start.

Mr Jones and Adrian finished packing the car and returned to the hall. All that remained now was for us to say goodbye to Alice. We stood for a moment in awkward silence, looking at Alice, who was ready to go in her shoes, coat and scarf, with Brian the Bear tucked under her arm.

'OK,' I said, bravely taking the initiative. 'Let me give you a big hug.' I knelt down and, drawing Alice to me, held her close. I felt her arms around my neck and her warm cheek press against mine. I smelt the child's shampoo I'd used on her freshly washed hair and knew I would never smell it exactly the same again. Her little arms, so dainty, almost fragile, now felt strong as she hugged me hard. I kissed her cheek, then drew slightly away and looked into her eyes. 'Goodbye, love,' I said. 'Take care. You're very special.' She blinked and her eyes misted. With a final hug, I straightened and moved away.

Adrian stepped forward; he seemed so large beside little Alice. He bent down and ruffled her hair. 'Bye, little 'un,' he said. 'You're all right for a girl. Give me five.'

Alice grinned and slapped his outstretched palm. 'Bye, Adrian. You're all right for a boy.' We all managed a laugh.

Paula now took Adrian's place and hugged and kissed Alice but didn't say anything. As Paula moved away I saw tears on her cheek, and she turned from Alice so she wouldn't see how upset she was. I took Paula's hand as Lucy now said goodbye. She knelt to hug her, as I had done, and gave Alice a big kiss on her cheek. 'Bye Alice,' she said. 'You'll be fine. You've got a good family and they'll look after you now.'

Mrs Jones thanked us all again for looking after Alice and then, taking Alice's hand, followed Mr Jones out of the door. We too went down the path and on to the pavement, where we waited as they got in. Mrs Jones and Alice sat in the back of the car as Mr Jones climbed into the driving seat. Although it was cold they wound down their windows so they could wave goodbye.

'You'll phone us in two weeks,' Mr Jones confirmed, before he started the engine. 'Then we'll arrange for you to visit.'

'Yes, please,' I said.

The engine started and Mr Jones began waving vigorously from the front window and Mrs Jones from the rear window. Alice sat passively beside her nana, head down and clutching Brian the Bear. The car began to pull away, and then slowly down the road, with only Mr and Mrs Jones waving from their respective windows. Then, just before the car turned left and disappeared from view, a little arm appeared out of the rear window, beside that of Mrs Jones. Not a child's arm, not Alice's: this one was brown and furry. Then a little furry head and shoulders appeared and Brian the Bear was dancing up and down and waving his paw.

'Don't forget to watch the football,' I called after them as the car turned left and disappeared from view.

Lucy, who was standing beside me, left out a heartfelt sigh. 'I'm so pleased I won't ever have to leave,' she said. 'I wouldn't cope with another move.'

I turned to her and smiled. 'No, but then Alice is going home. You *are* home now. It took us a while to find you, but now you're home for good.'

Chapter Forty-One
Moving On

When a child leaves us, especially a child who has become very close as Alice had, there is a sense of bereavement: a loss, a sadness, a gap in the family — emotionally and physically. The child's chair is spare at the dinner table; their bedroom, once crammed full of their personal belongings, is now empty; their shoes no longer line up with ours in the hall; their laughter is missing from the house and the air is unnaturally quiet and still.

So it was with Alice, and it would take time to adjust. On that Saturday afternoon I automatically went into the sitting room to switch on the television for the football, before I caught myself and remembered. I wasn't the only one to forget Alice was no longer with us, for an hour later, when it would have been half-time, Adrian, as he had done every Saturday during Alice's stay, poked his head round the sitting-room door to ask what the half-time score was, before he realized. 'Oh,' he said, embarrassed. 'Of course.' A little while later Lucy admitted she'd gone in search of Alice to ask her if she wanted her hair plaited, while Paula said she'd looked in Alice's bedroom to ask if she wanted to play.

And although I could and should have been doing other things, I found myself in the sitting room that Saturday afternoon with the television off, the unread newspaper open on my lap and the imaginary cheers of the football crowd ringing in my ears. I could picture Brian the Bear dancing up and down as a goal was scored or hiding his head under his paws in shame as a goal was missed. I considered switching on the television and watching a match, but I didn't particularly like football and it wouldn't have been the same without Alice. I'd willingly watched the football every Saturday and enjoyed it, for Alice's sake, but my interest and enjoyment had left with her.

At 6.00 p.m., when Alice would have normally phoned her grandparents, I caught myself about to call her to the phone, before I remembered. Dear Alice and her phone calls: all those kisses she'd sent down the phone to her dear nana and grandpa, the kisses that had carried so much love and had had to see them through until they saw each other again. One hour every two weeks – how had they coped? I thought of Alice sitting beside me on the sofa, leaning forward with her arms outstretched and her little hands cupped open, ready to catch the kiss from her nana and grandpa. Now, of course, they could kiss each other goodnight in person; our loss was their gain.

Yes, we were a sad bunch the weekend Alice left us, as we mooched around the 'empty' house, which now seemed far too big and quiet. Then on Monday our school routine began and, while our loss didn't just go, we gradually began to adjust, although I shut Alice's bedroom against the constant reminder that her room was empty.

On Monday afternoon Jill phoned to ask how Alice's move had gone and I told her it had gone 'well'. Knowing Alice would be greatly missed she made a point of asking how we all were and I said, not very convincingly, 'OK.'

'Sure you are,' she said, disbelievingly. 'I'll phone Kitty later in the week, when she's had a chance to see Alice, and find out how she's doing.'

'Thanks.'

But on Wednesday Kitty beat Jill to it and phoned us, having visited Alice after school the previous day. Kitty said Alice was happy and settling in very well, although she missed us and sent her love.

'We miss her too,' I said, 'but I'm pleased she's happy and everything is working out.'

'Let's hope it continues that way,' Kitty said.

Jill phoned again on Thursday and asked if I could look after a nine-year-old boy who would be coming into care later that day, and I said, 'No. I'm sorry, I'm going to have a short break and take two weeks off from fostering.' Jill said she understood and that she had thought that might be the case; she would ask another carer to look after the boy. The two weeks I was taking off wasn't a figure I'd plucked from the air: it was the time I knew I needed to let go of Alice, so that I could dedicate myself to the next child. Two weeks

would also see us past the phone call we were allowed
to make to Alice, which I hoped would bring some
closure. Some foster carers deal with a child leaving by
taking the next child straightaway, but I'd found having
a short break helped, and also gave my family a chance
to re-group.

When we phoned Alice two weeks later Mrs Jones
answered. It was strange hearing her voice without
Alice sitting beside me on the sofa, ready to speak to her
nana. Adrian, Lucy and Paula were also in the sitting
room, waiting for their turn to speak to Alice. Mrs Jones
told me Alice talked a lot about us and her happy memories of her time with us. I was pleased she had so many
positive memories from what must have been a very
anxious period for her. Mrs Jones said the Life Story
book I had given to her was invaluable, as it allowed her
and her husband to share Alice's memories of what she
called the 'missing year' – the time Alice had lived with
us. When Alice came to the phone and I heard her little
voice, a lump immediately rose in my throat.

'Hello, Aunty Cathy,' she said. 'How are you?'

'We're fine, love. It's good to hear you again. How are
you?'

'I'm fine too,' she said.

I asked her what she'd been doing, and she chatted
happily, telling me all her news. She told me how her
grandpa took her to school in his car, which had a
strange rattle under the bonnet; of her school friends
and school dinners; that she had seen her mummy at
the family centre but not her dad; and how Nana had

taken her to the park to ride her bike. Alice finished by saying, 'I love my nana and grandpa so much,' and then, lowering her voice, added: 'but it's very quiet here.' I smiled and thought it would be, with just her and her grandparents, after all the comings and goings in my house.

When I passed the phone to Adrian, Alice repeated much of the news she'd told me. Then Adrian joked, 'Give me five, little 'un,' and Alice laughed and clapped her hands at the other end of the phone.

When it was Lucy's turn, Alice asked her if she could show her nana how she plaited her hair, as her nana couldn't do it properly. Lucy said she would when we visited and I wondered what she was letting Mrs Jones in for – I'd never mastered a successful French plait, despite Lucy showing me many times.

When Lucy passed the phone to Paula, the first thing Alice said was that she missed playing with Paula, which I'd suspected she might. Paula, closest in age to Alice, had spent hours and hours playing with Alice, getting down to her level – more so than the rest of us. Paula said she would play with Alice when we visited and told her to think of what game she wanted to play.

When Paula had finished speaking she returned the phone to me and I spoke to Mrs Jones to arrange our visit: 1.00 p.m., a week on Sunday – a month after Alice had left us and nearly a year since she'd first arrived. I then put the phone on 'speaker' so that we could all call our goodbyes.

'See you soon,' Mrs Jones said, which Alice echoed.

'Brian the Bear is waving goodbye,' Alice added.

'We're waving back,' I called.

The following Tuesday we began fostering a twelve-year-old boy, Simon, who fortunately spent every Sunday with his mother. I say 'fortunately' because it wouldn't have been appropriate for us to take him with us when we visited Alice, and I would have had to leave him with other carers for the duration of our visit. As it was, I was able to drop him off at his mother's at 10.00 a.m. before we left at 12.30 p.m. to arrive at Alice's for 1.00.

Mr and Mrs Jones greeted us at their door, and then showed us through to a neat sitting room, where Alice was waiting, seated on the sofa, hands in lap and looking a little shy.

'Hello, love,' I said. 'Good to see you.'

She grinned sheepishly, then came over and hugged and kissed us all.

Mr Jones told us to make ourselves at home while Mrs Jones offered us a drink and a slice of her home-made cake, which we readily accepted. While she went into the kitchen we sat with Mr Jones and Alice and chatted – politely and a little formally – about Alice's school and the weather. When Mrs Jones returned with the cake and drinks everyone seemed to thaw out a little and conversation became a bit easier.

But while Mr and Mrs Jones made us very welcome I was acutely aware of the conflicting emotions seeing us again would arouse, not only for Alice but also for her grandparents. Our presence was a stark reminder of the circumstances that had brought Alice into care: the family's agonizing separation and, of course, that for nearly a year we had been Alice's family, and I had effectively been Alice's mother. Although Mrs Jones was far too pleasant and polite to show any sign of resentment, I could guess what she must be feeling and I was very careful not to fall back into my role of foster carer/mother towards Alice – scooping her up and smothering her with kisses as I used to, and which would have been very easy to do. It was early days yet and the bond Alice had with her grand-parents, which would have suffered from their sepa-ration, would still be repairing and strengthening. I could see poor Alice was confused – hesitant as to which of the adults she should go to, what she should be saying and to whom; she didn't know if she should be sitting on her nana's lap or mine. It was easier for her to relate to Adrian, Lucy and Paula, for there were no siblings in her grandparents' house to con-fuse her.

Paula played Barbie dolls with Alice and then some board games – Snakes and Ladders and Spot the Difference – while Lucy plaited her hair. Alice didn't ask Lucy to show her nana how to do a French plait so Lucy, diplomatically, didn't draw attention to it by offering, although Mrs Jones did say how nice Alice's hair looked when Lucy had finished.

As we ate the cake and drank our tea I asked Mrs Jones how Leah was, and she said she was very well and still making good progress. She said Leah was going to marry her partner, Mike, in the summer and I asked her to pass on my congratulations. Mrs Jones then added that Alice hadn't seen her father, Chris, since the court case where the judge had decided to return Alice to them; Chris had sent various excuses through his solicitor to the social worker. It didn't surprise me that Chris was no longer seeing Alice, for Sharon had always been the guiding force in wanting Alice to live with them and be a family. With her now gone I thought it was unlikely Chris would show the same commitment. Mrs Jones said that Kitty had told them that if Chris didn't resume contact soon she would apply to the court to have the contact order revoked, as it wasn't fair on Alice to keep having contact cancelled at the last minute.

An hour is generally the accepted time for a post-leaving visit (as ours was deemed to be): time to show the child he or she hasn't been forgotten but not long enough to be intrusive and undo the bonds reforming in the child's family. While Adrian, Lucy and Paula played with and amused Alice I continued chatting to Mr and Mrs Jones and an hour passed easily. I knew I should then make a move for us to leave.

'Well, it's been lovely seeing you all again,' I said, placing my cup and saucer on the tray. 'But I think it's time we left you to get on now.'

Mrs and Mrs Jones smiled and nodded, while Alice looked up from where she sat playing on the floor between Paula and Lucy, surprised.

I stood up from the sofa. 'Thanks for the cake – it was fantastic,' I said to Mrs Jones; then to Alice: 'I bet you have lots of lovely home-made cakes now.'

Alice smiled and nodded. 'Yes, lots.'

'Thank you for coming,' Mr Jones said, also standing. 'And thanks for everything. You're a nice family – doing all you did for Alice. We won't forget your kindness.'

At the front door Lucy, Paula and I kissed Alice goodbye and Adrian extended his hand, which Alice slapped. 'Give me five!' she said, laughing.

We shook hands with Mr and Mrs Jones and then the three of them waited on the doorstep while we got into our car. We wound down our windows to wave.

'Bye!' we called.

'Bye! Safe journey!'

I pulled away, and as I did we caught our final glimpse of Alice – standing between her nana and grandpa on the doorstep of her home.

It was quiet in the car as they disappeared from view and I knew Adrian, Lucy and Paula were feeling, as I was, that while it had been great seeing Alice again, now she had returned to her own family we were quickly being consigned to being the 'nice family' who had been kind enough to look after her. We would send birthday and Christmas cards to Alice but whether Mr and Mrs Jones stayed in touch with us or not would be up to them. Some of the children we had looked after were still in touch years later, while others simply wanted to move on and forget the difficult time of being in care. I had the feeling that Mr and Mrs Jones might fall into the second group, and ultimately whether we ever saw Alice again depended on Leah, if Alice returned to live with her. It would be sad if we never saw Alice again, but that is something families who foster just have to accept.

Epilogue

As I thought might happen, Mr and Mrs Jones didn't keep in touch, and although we appreciated why, we were sad at not seeing Alice. Having had Alice returned to them, Mrs and Mrs Jones just wanted to get on with their lives and didn't want the constant reminder of the past that our presence would have evoked. We wrote to Alice, sent her birthday and Christmas cards but didn't hear anything back. It wasn't for me to phone the social worker and ask about Alice: now Alice had left me I was no longer 'involved' in her case, so I didn't have the right to know, although it would have been nice.

Ten months after Alice had left, however, Jill bumped into Kitty in the social services' offices. They were both in a hurry, on their way to meetings, but Jill managed to ask after Alice. Kitty said she was very well and happy, and was still with her grandparents. She thanked me for our letter and cards, which Alice had shown to her.

Then six months later (sixteen months after Alice had left us) I was shopping in a department store in a neighbouring town when I spotted Mr and Mrs Jones in the glass and china section. They didn't see me. I watched them from a distance for a while, uncertain if I should approach them, and of the reception I might receive. I watched them for a bit longer; then, throwing caution to the wind, went over and said: 'Hello. Do you remember me?'

They looked up from the display stand of cut-glass ornaments, surprised and clearly taken aback. Recovering first, Mr Jones shook my hand, as Mrs Jones returned the ornament she'd been examining to the display.

'Of course, Cathy,' Mr Jones said. 'How are you?'

'I'm very well, thank you. And yourselves?'

'We're fine, thank you,' Mrs Jones said, now shaking my hand.

'You're certainly looking very well,' I said.

'So are you.'

There was an awkward silence before Mrs Jones said, 'Alice is very well too.'

'Good,' I said. 'Is she still living with you?'

'Oh no,' Mr Jones said, surprised. 'Didn't you know?'

'No,' I shook my head. 'Once a child leaves me I'm not kept informed unless the relatives keep in touch.' I hadn't intended it as a criticism, just a statement of fact, but Mr and Mrs Jones looked guilty and apologized.

'I'm sorry,' Mrs Jones said. 'I thought someone would have told you. Alice went to live with her mother and Mike three months ago. Leah and Mike got married last August and I'm happy to say Alice will have baby brother or sister in eight weeks' time.'

'That's fantastic news,' I said. 'I'm so pleased. Please pass on my congratulations and best wishes to them all.'

'Yes, we're very happy,' Mrs Jones said. 'And also that Mike is going to adopt Alice.'

'Really?' I said.

She nodded. 'They're going through the process now. It takes a long time, but Kitty has said there shouldn't be a problem. Chris didn't see Alice again after she left you, and he's not objecting to the adoption. In fact Kitty said he seemed pretty relieved.'

'Probably because he won't have to pay child maintenance,' Mr Jones put in.

'Well, whatever the reason,' Mrs Jones said kindly, 'it's good news for Alice.'

'Absolutely,' I agreed. 'Adrian, Lucy and Paula will be delighted when I tell them.'

'How are your family?' Mr Jones asked.

'They're very well, thank you.'

There was another awkward silence before I said, 'Well, I'd best be getting on then. It was nice bumping into you, and I'm so pleased everything is working out. Please give Alice our love.'

'Yes, we will.' They nodded. 'And thanks again for all you did,' Mrs Jones said. 'We did appreciate it.'

We shook hands and I moved away, leaving Mr and Mrs Jones to the display of glass. Whether or not they would tell Alice they'd seen me I wasn't sure, but I was very pleased and relieved to hear that things were working out for Alice and her family.

Later that afternoon when Adrian, Lucy and Paula arrived home from school, I told them I'd bumped into

Alice's grandparents and gave them the news. They too were pleased for Alice, although they said it was a pity they couldn't see her from time to time, or even speak to her on the phone.

That evening when I said goodnight to Lucy she suddenly threw her arms around my neck, hugging and kissing me for all she was worth. 'I hope Alice knows just how lucky she is being adopted,' Lucy said. 'I know how lucky I am to have you.'

I smiled. Two weeks previously – a year after starting the process – I had finally been allowed to adopt Lucy. 'I'm sure she does,' I said. 'And I know how lucky I am to have you – very, very lucky indeed.'

Cathy Glass

———

One remarkable woman, more
than **70** foster children cared for.

Learn more about the many
lives Cathy has touched.

Another Forgotten Child

Eight-year-old Aimee was on the child protection register at birth

Cathy is determined to give her the happy home she deserves.

Too late to help? A shocking true story of abuse and neglect.

Another Forgotten Child
Cathy Glass
THE MILLION COPY BESTSELLING AUTHOR

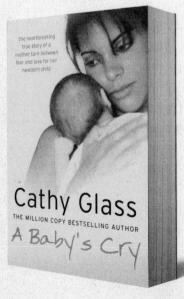

The heartbreaking true story of a mother torn between fear and love for her newborn child

Cathy Glass
THE MILLION COPY BESTSELLING AUTHOR
A Baby's Cry

A Baby's Cry

A newborn, only hours old, taken into care

Cathy protects tiny Harrison from the potentially fatal secrets that surround his existence.

The Night the Angels Came

A little boy on the brink of bereavement

Cathy and her family make sure Michael is never alone.

The heartbreaking true story of a young boy's loss

Cathy Glass
THE MILLION COPY BESTSELLING AUTHOR
The Night the Angels Came

Mummy Told Me Not to Tell

A troubled boy sworn to secrecy

After his dark past has been revealed, Cathy helps Reece to rebuild his life.

The true story of a troubled boy with a dark secret

Cathy Glass
THE MILLION COPY BESTSELLING AUTHOR
Mummy Told Me Not to Tell

The Saddest Girl in the World

**A haunted child
who refuses to speak**

Do Donna's scars run
too deep for Cathy
to help?

Cathy Glass
THE MILLION COPY BESTSELLING AUTHOR

The Saddest Girl in the World

The true story
of a neglected and
isolated little girl
who just wanted
to be loved

Cathy Glass
THE MILLION COPY BESTSELLING AUTHOR

Cut

The true story
of an abandoned,
abused little girl
who was desperate
to be part of
a family

Cut

**Dawn is desperate
to be loved**

Abused and abandoned,
this vulnerable child pushes
Cathy and her family to
their limits.

Hidden

The boy with no past

Can Cathy help Tayo to feel like he belongs again?

Damaged

A forgotten child

Cathy is Jodie's last hope. For the first time, this abused young girl has found someone she can trust.

Inspired by Cathy's own experiences...

Run, Mummy, Run

The gripping story of a
woman caught in a horrific
cycle of abuse, and the
desperate measures she
must take to escape.

Cathy Glass

THE MILLION COPY BESTSELLING AUTHOR

Run, Mummy, Run

A novel inspired by a true story

My Dad's a Policeman

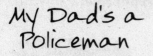

The dramatic short story about a young boy's desperate bid to keep his family together.

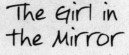

The Girl in the Mirror

Trying to piece together her past, Mandy uncovers a dreadful family secret that has been blanked from her memory for years.

Sharing her expertise...

Happy Kids

A clear and concise guide to raising confident, well-behaved and happy children.

Happy Adults

A practical guide to achieving lasting happiness, contentment and success. The essential manual for getting the best out of life.

Happy Mealtimes For Kids

A guide to healthy eating with simple recipes that children love.

Be amazed
Be moved
Be inspired

———